BEFORE THE MACHINE

D1027905

Before the Machine

Published by Clerisy Press
Printed in the United States of America
Distributed by Publishers Group West
First edition, first printing

For further information, contact the publisher at:
Clerisy Press
PO Box 8874
Cincinnati, OH 45208-08074
www.clerisypress.com

Library of Congress Cataloging-in-Publication Data
Schmetzer, Mark J.
Before the machine : the story of the 1961 pennant-winning
Cincinnati Reds / Mark J. Schmetzer.
p. cm.
Includes bibliographical references.
ISBN-13: 978-1-57860-463-0
ISBN-10: 1-57860-463-X
1. Cincinnati Reds (Baseball team)--History. 2. World Series
(Baseball) I. Title.

GV875.C656S36 2011
796.357'640977178--dc22

2011007056

Edited by Jack Heffron
Cover designed by Stephen Sullivan
Text designed by Annie Long
All photos in this book, including the cover photos, were taken by
Jack Klumpe. They appear courtesy of the Rhodes/Klumpe Reds
Hall of Fame and Museum Collection.

BEFORE THE MACHINE

The Story of the
1961 Pennant-Winning Cincinnati Reds

MARK J. SCHMETZER

CLERISY PRESS

To Dad:

I still feel now the anticipation I felt then when seeing in the distance the lights of Crosley Field when you took us to games. Thanks for getting me started in sports–and for knowing the usher who could upgrade our seats.

For my wife, Sharon,

whose 1960 Pirates gave the Reds hope, and for our daughter, Kalli, who still dreams of a championship team all her own.

table of contents

foreword

Fifty years have passed, and I still remember where I was September 26, 1961–in the driveway of our house in Richmond, Indiana, in our 1955 Buick, leaning on the horn with full force. The Cincinnati Reds had just clinched the 1961 National League pennant.

Up and down our usually quiet suburban street, the neighbors were out celebrating this most unexpected triumph. My sister stood in our front yard and banged pan lids together. Other car horns joined in the serenade.

Maybe our little celebration was out of the ordinary, but I doubt it. I suspect such jubilation was repeated throughout Reds country–Ohio, Indiana, Kentucky, West Virginia, and nowhere more enthusiastically than in the heart of Cincinnati itself, at Fountain Square, the symbolic center of the city. Thousands of fans spontaneously descended on the Square, where they nearly mobbed the team bus carrying the Reds, who had just returned from winning an afternoon game in Chicago.

The Cincinnati victory, combined with the Los Angeles loss in Pittsburgh around 9 p.m. that evening, made it official: the Reds had won the pennant and would go to the World Series for the first time in twenty-one years.

You'll find all the details from that evening, as well as the rest of that season in this long-overdue tribute to that 1961 team. And more. Mark Schmetzer has captured the mood of the city and Reds fans in this most unlikely of seasons, bring the city of the early 1960s to life. He evokes the experiences we fans recall so well—Waite Hoyt's play-by-play, Ed Kennedy and Frank McCormick on the TV broadcasts, the irrepressible Ruth Lyons, the diva of Cincinnati TV in 1961, as she celebrated and promoted the Reds throughout the season.

I have known Mark for many years, but didn't realize until he told me about this book that we shared such fondness for those "Ragamuffin" Reds. Robinson, Pinson, Coleman, Jay, O'Toole, Purkey, and, of course, Hutch. The names come flooding back. The memories are still fresh.

Mark traces the arc of the season, the ups and downs of the early months, followed by a push to the lead in early June. But the Dodgers kept it close, and every Reds-Dodgers game seemed pivotal. And those night games from the West Coast? Reds fans lost a lot of sleep that season, and many parents found a transistor radio tucked beneath their kids' pillows the morning after those games.

In *Before the Machine,* we also get a look at the front office and the work of Bill DeWitt, who had just assumed control of the Reds after the death of long-time owner Powel Crosley Jr. in March 1961. The series of moves DeWitt made prior to and during the 1961 season—trading for Joey Jay, Gene Freese, and Don Blasingame, installing Gordy Coleman at first base, and calling up Johnny Edwards and journeyman pitcher Ken Johnson—all worked beyond anyone's expectations. The 1961 Reds improved twenty-six games over the 1960 squad, a remarkable turn-around in the era before free agency.

Cincinnati fans will forever condemn Bill DeWitt for the 1965 trade of Frank Robinson, but this book will help balance out the scales. The Reds don't win the 1961 pennant without Bill DeWitt in the general manager's chair. And the foundation he built in his tenure in Cincinnati from 1960 to 1966 ended a dismal sixteen-year stretch in the 1940s and '50s, when the Reds only managed two winning seasons. DeWitt put the Reds on a winning track for four decades. Between 1961 and 2000 the Reds were the winningest team in the National League.

You'll find all this and much more in Mark Schmetzer's wonderfully crafted tribute to the 1961 Reds. The ragamuffins deserve it. Rally 'round the Reds, boys!

Greg Rhodes
Team Historian
Cincinnati Reds

introduction

At first glance, the 1961 National League schedule only looks like it was put together by somebody who had no idea of how to do it.

As it turned out, the league couldn't have done a better job, especially giving the Reds two days off in the middle of the last week of the season. The team—the town, for that matter—needed every one of the forty-eight hours consumed by September 27 and 28 to recover from its biggest party since V-J Day marked the end of World War II sixteen years earlier.

Everybody in Cincinnati had much to celebrate on September 26, 1961, and they had plenty of time to prepare. The pressure to let off the steam had been building like beer in a shaken-up keg. One day earlier, on September 25, the Reds had flown to Chicago to play one game against the Cubs. Cincinnati, picked by most observers before the season to finish sixth in the National League in 1961, owned a four-game lead over the second-place Los Angeles Dodgers with four games left to play. The Dodgers, though, still had six games to play and remained mathematically alive. If they swept their last six games and the Reds lost their last four, Los Angeles would win the pennant. On the other hand, one more Reds' win and one more Dodgers' loss would complete what many in

1

Cincinnati and around baseball would consider to be nothing short of a miracle.

It took only the next day the two teams played. The Reds beat the Cubs, 6–3, at Wrigley Field on Frank Robinson's two-run homer to tie the game in the seventh inning and Jerry Lynch's two-run homer to give Cincinnati a 5–3 lead in the eighth. Besides coming out of the bullpen to allow one hit with four strikeouts over the final three innings to get the win, relief pitcher Jim Brosnan drove in Robinson with an insurance run in the ninth, and the Reds immediately flew back to Cincinnati.

Meanwhile, the Dodgers had won the first game of a doubleheader in Pittsburgh, 5–3. The second game still was being played as the Reds plane landed at the airport in Northern Kentucky, where Cincinnati mayor Walt Bachrach and a group of fans greeted the returning heroes. More fans lined both sides of much of the bus route to downtown Cincinnati, creating a parade feeling, and an estimated 30,000 gathered at Fountain Square, making it nearly impossible for the team bus to move more than a few inches at a time.

"I'll never forget that," said pitcher Jim O'Toole, a Chicago native who had left his wife and their newborn son with family in Chicago. "That was the biggest thrill of my life, to leave the airport and parade down I-75 all the way to Fountain Square. People were rocking the bus—on top of the bus. We were all so excited."

Everybody was monitoring the second game of the Dodgers-Pirates doubleheader, some with transistor radios. When Los Angeles left fielder Jim Gilliam flied out to Pittsburgh left fielder Bob Skinner at Forbes Field to wrap up an 8–0 Pirates win, the party was officially on. While giddy fans created

G.M. Bill DeWitt proudly displays a team photo.

pandemonium on Fountain Square, the Reds gathered for their own celebration in a room located by manager Fred Hutchinson at the Netherland Hilton hotel.

"Hutch was up there singing some Frank Sinatra songs," O'Toole recalled. "The players were having a great time."

Earl Lawson, who covered the Reds for the *Cincinnati Post & Times-Star*, remembered the party as a "wing-ding" in his book *Cincinnati Seasons—My 34 Years with the Reds*.

" 'Earl, how in the hell did we do it,'" Lawson recalled being asked by third baseman Gene Freese upon arrival. " 'We've got the worst infield in baseball.' "

"It was a good question. His comment had considerable merit. Freese was a guy who could poke fun at himself.

"Freese stood on the bandstand that night and bellowed,

'Hutch, I may have bobbled some groundballs, but I never let one get through me.' Teammates howled as Freese opened his sport coat, revealing a plastic baseball which he had attached to his shirt front."

Freese was a major reason the Reds were able to rise from the team that finished sixth in 1960 to a champion. The veteran journeyman and second-year first baseman Gordy Coleman turned in virtually identical seasons, each hitting twenty-six home runs and driving in eighty-seven—production that kept opposing teams from pitching around Frank Robinson, helping the outfielder turn in a season that led to him being named the NL's Most Valuable Player.

Freese was one of several key players acquired in a series of shrewd moves made by first-year general manager William O. DeWitt, who could do almost nothing wrong that year. Virtually every move made by DeWitt, the living, breathing definition of a lifelong baseball man, paid off that year—and for many years down the road.

DeWitt didn't exactly save the franchise for the city with that season. To say that would be, at best, a stretch. To say, however, that the season put back on track a franchise that had been foundering would be, at worst, defensible. To say that seeing the team confound the so-called experts by winning the championship summed up the times would be an underestimation.

The National League—indeed, Major League Baseball in general—was in a state of upheaval at that time. From that point of view, Cincinnati winning the pennant was almost to be expected.

More unexpected was the impact that season had on the franchise. Starting with that season, which ended with a 93–61 record and .604 winning percentage, the Reds were one of only two teams in Major League Baseball to finish over .500 at least nineteen times in the next twenty-one years. Starting in 1961 and going through 1981, Cincinnati finished below .500 only twice—in 1966 and 1971. Only the Baltimore Orioles match that run. The Orioles also finished under .500 twice—1962 and 1967. The Los Angeles Dodgers come the closest to sustaining that level of consistent excellence, but they finished under .500 four times in that span of time.

Not only was Cincinnati's franchise back on healthy ground, but the seeds were being planted that would lead to the phenomenally successful 1970s. Infielders Pete Rose, Tony Perez, and Tommy Helms already were in the organization. First baseman Lee May would be signed out of high school that year. Outfielder Bernie Carbo and catcher Johnny Bench would be the team's top two picks in the first amateur draft in 1965. Right-handed pitcher Gary Nolan would be the last number one pick of the DeWitt era, in 1966.

They all would play roles in making the Reds a dynasty in the 1970s that reminded veteran fans of earlier times—when teams were built for the long haul.

By the end of World War II, no sport at any level could match the popularity of Major League Baseball, a title that was so safe that its proprietors felt no need to slap a trademark on it, so it didn't need to be capitalized. College football was popular, but there were so many colleges that the fan base was splintered, and the turnover in players was too frequent to allow fans to hold on to any specific star for long-term adoration. Pro football still was more than ten years away from the epic playoff game between the Baltimore Colts and New York Giants that would allow it to grab a share of the national spotlight. Pro basketball didn't even have a league until 1946 and only became the National Basketball Association when two leagues merged in 1949.

One reason for baseball's popularity was its easy familiarity. Baseball was in its fifth decade of virtually no changes in its basic framework. As far as at least two generations of Americans were concerned, there always had been two major leagues, American and National, each containing eight teams. The teams always had played in the same cities. Four cities—Boston, Philadelphia, Chicago, and St. Louis—each had two teams, one in each league. New York, of course, had three—two in the National League. Five had to settle for serving as the home of just one team: Cincinnati and Pittsburgh in the National League, the so-called Senior Circuit because it was older than the American League, home of teams in Washington, D.C., Cleveland, and Detroit. All of the teams were located in the northeast quadrant of the country, none of them farther west than the Central Time Zone.

The scarcity of teams made following them easy. Listening to the games on the radio and reading about your team and others in the local newspapers and *The Sporting News*—the weekly "Bible of Baseball"—gave you a level of information that would make even an Internet junkie jealous.

One man, Maxwell H. Lapides, put it quite well in a comment he made to Roger Angell, the long-time fiction editor for *The New Yorker* magazine who dabbled in writing about baseball. Angell quoted Lapides in a story about three devoted Detroit Tigers fans called "Three for the Tigers," which ran in the magazine as well as in a collection of his columns published in 1978 entitled *Five Seasons*.

"You have to try to remember how much easier it was to keep up with all of the baseball news back then," Lapides told Angell. "For us, there were just the Tigers and the seven other teams in the American League, so we knew them by heart. All the games were played in the afternoon, and none of the teams was in a time zone more than an hour away from Detroit, so you got just about all the scores when the late-afternoon papers came. You could talk about that at supper, and then there were the stories in the morning papers to read and think about the next day. Why, in those days we knew more about the farms than I know about some of the West Coast teams right now. By the time a Hoot Evers or a Fred Hutchinson was ready to come up from Beaumont, we knew all about him."

There also was a certain level of comfort in following a particular player. The reserve clause still was in affect, restricting player movement to the whims of owners and general managers or to retirement. Fans who wanted to follow, say, Joe DiMaggio or Ted Williams or Pee Wee Reese could feel much more secure in the knowledge that their favorite player would be with the same team for the bulk—if not all—of his career. Heck, one guy—Cornelius Alexander McGillicuddy, better known as Connie Mack—managed the Philadelphia Athletics for exactly fifty years, from 1901 through 1950.

The continuity was downright impressive, especially when compared to the current state of the game, which can be traced in part to Lou Perini's decision to move his National League franchise from Boston to Milwaukee for the 1953 season. That opened the floodgates. Franchises started following the post-war migration of the United States population to the west and south. The St. Louis Browns, forever the second team in the Gateway City behind the beloved Cardinals, bucked the trend by moving east to Baltimore after the 1953 season, but the Orioles still thrived. The Athletics left Philadelphia for Kansas City the next year.

The seismic shift came after the 1957 season, when both New York National League teams, the Giants and the Brooklyn Dodgers, made the transcontinental leap to the West Coast. The Dodgers ended up in Los Angeles, while the Giants landed in San Francisco.

Suddenly, almost nothing could be counted on. Fans in other cities had to be wondering which team would be the next to seek greener pastures. Among the more nervous were the fans in Cincinnati.

The Reds by then already had a proud history. They invented the all-professional team back in 1869 and were among the original National League teams in 1876. Their track record wasn't as glowing as, say, the Giants or Dodgers or Cardinals, but they'd had stretches during which they were regular contenders and could boast of three league championships and two World Series titles.

By the late 1950s, though, the legs of this franchise were shakier than others. The team had enjoyed a sensational season in 1956, cracking home runs at a near-record pace and attracting one million fans to the ballpark for the first time in franchise history. The Reds hit 221 homers, tying what was at the time the major league record. Slugging first baseman Ted Kluszewski and his biceps—so bulging that the sleeves of his uniform jersey constricted them, forcing him to play bare-armed and eventually prompting the Reds to adopt vest-type jerseys—were fan favorites. Frank Robinson, at twenty-one years old, tied a league record for rookies with thirty-eight home runs. Cincinnati contended for the pennant for much of the season before settling for third place with ninety-one wins, snapping at eleven the team's streak of consecutive losing seasons.

Unfortunately, they couldn't build on that improvement. Cincinnati slipped to fourth place in 1957, fourth place again and under .500 in 1958–costing manager Birdie Tebbetts his job–and fifth place in 1959, which included the dismissal of Mayo Smith as manager after just a half-season. Picked to replace Smith was Fred Hutchinson, the former Detroit pitcher who'd previously managed the Tigers and Cardinals with no notable success. Hutchinson was thirty-nine years old when he took over the Reds.

"The franchise had been under .500 seemingly forever, except for 1956 and 1957," recalled Jim Ferguson, who helped cover the Reds for the *Dayton Daily News* from 1959 through 1972 before becoming the team's publicity director. "They were a pure power team, but they had terrible pitching. They couldn't score enough runs to win. They hadn't had any success, with the exception of those two seasons, for a couple of decades."

The managerial changes did little to calm the nerves of Reds fans. Cincinnati's home ballpark, Crosley Field, was the smallest in the league in terms of seating and offered little room for parking, a growing problem in a society that was spending more and more time behind the wheel. Folks didn't take trains or buses or trolleys to ballgames any more. They drove, and they were more inclined to visit places where they figured they could safely leave their cars.

The Reds needed only to look over their right field fence to see the future. A stretch of Interstate 75–part of the United

States Interstate Highway System, the country's version of Germany's Autobahn—was being built almost within arm's reach of Crosley Field.

Options to aging, tiny Crosley Field had been discussed in Greater Cincinnati since the late 1940s, but nothing had come of those talks. Meanwhile, New York had a vacancy that was screaming to be filled. Cities such as Atlanta, Houston, Dallas, and Denver—growing in population and vibrancy—also were hoping to get a piece of the major league action. A Denver sports leader named Bob Howsam participated in efforts to start a new "major league"—the Continental League, the brainchild of New Yorker William Shea.

Major League Baseball moved quickly to nip that in the bud. The American League allowed its Washington franchise to be moved to Minneapolis-St. Paul and awarded new franchises to Washington, D.C. and Los Angeles. The AL expanded to ten teams and a 162-game schedule in 1961. The disparity in the number of games played by each league and the desire to see the seasons start and end at the same time meant that the NL teams would get more days off—leading to situations such as the Reds getting back-to-back days off in the middle of the last week of the season.

The National League awarded new franchises to New York and Houston but decided to wait an extra year before putting them in play. They would start in 1962 in a 162-game schedule.

While those moves calmed fears of any imminent departure of the Reds from Cincinnati, they did nothing to improve the ballclub. The 1960 Reds finished sixth, their worst since the 1953 team also finished sixth, and their .435 winning percentage (67–87) was the lowest since the 1950 team went 66–87

(.431) while also finishing sixth. They limped home with seven losses in their last eight games, including being swept in three games at Philadelphia in the final series of the season, and nine losses in their last eleven games, going 0–3 against Pittsburgh, 1–5 against the Phillies, and 1–1 against Milwaukee.

Just as bad, if not worse, they drew just 663,486 fans to Crosley Field, the lowest in the majors that season and the franchise's worst single-season attendance figure since the 1953 team attracted 548,086.

"Nobody expected much out of them," Ferguson said. "They were really a team with no stars."

Clearly, something had to be done.

ONE

Makeover

By the end of the 1960 season, the only person who'd been involved with the Cincinnati franchise longer than Gabe Paul was the owner, Powel Crosley Jr., but only by a couple of years.

Crosley had purchased the Reds in 1934 at the urging of flamboyant general manager Larry MacPhail. When MacPhail left in 1936 to take over the Brooklyn Dodgers, Crosley replaced him with Warren C. Giles, business manager of the Rochester Red Wings of the Triple-A International League. Giles brought Paul with him from New York.

Paul was only in his mid-twenties, but he already had a

decade's worth of education in how to run a baseball team. He started as a Red Wings batboy at the age of ten. Six years later, he was helping cover the team for a Rochester newspaper as well as for *The Sporting News,* already highly regarded as "The Bible of Baseball." Paul was eighteen years old in 1928 when Giles named him the team's publicity director and twenty-four in 1934 when he was promoted to road secretary.

Paul took over as Cincinnati's publicity director when he and Giles moved from Rochester. After serving in the Army during World War II, he returned to his familiar role and remained in it until 1951, when Giles became National League president and Paul was promoted to general manager.

The Reds were unable to win a championship during Paul's ten years as general manager. In fact, they managed just two winning seasons—1956, when they finished third with a 91–63 record and 1957, when they went 80–74 and finished fourth.

Paul was named Major League Executive of the Year in 1956, the season in which the Reds reached seven figures in attendance for the first time in franchise history, but his record in trades as general manager was mixed. His best acquisition was outfielder Gus Bell from the Pittsburgh Pirates for three toss-away players shortly after the 1952 season. Bell became one of Cincinnati's most consistent and popular players throughout the decade.

Paul also traded for pitchers Bob Purkey and Jim Brosnan and infielder Eddie Kasko, all solid performers through the late 1950s, and the club signed prospects such as outfielders Frank Robinson and Vada Pinson and pitchers Jim O'Toole, Jim Maloney, and Ken Hunt. Purkey won seventeen games in two of his first three seasons with the Reds, 1958 and 1960, while Kasko was named the team's Most

Valuable Player in 1960 and Brosnan established himself as a dependable relief pitcher.

Robinson burst onto the scene in 1956, tying what was the National League record for home runs by a rookie with thirty-eight while turning twenty-one years old during the season. Pinson, who was three years behind Robinson at McClymonds High School in Oakland, California, showed signs of stardom after being called up for good in 1959, but the pitching prospects still were developing as the 1960s approached.

Paul, after going through seven managers in his first eight and a half seasons, finally found his man in Fred Hutchinson, who replaced Mayo Smith during the All-Star break in 1959.

Other Paul deals didn't work out as well. He traded power-hitting outfielder Wally Post, another player popular with fans, to the Philadelphia Phillies for left-handed pitcher Harvey Haddix after the 1957 season. Haddix spent just one season with the Reds, going 8–7, before being dealt to Pittsburgh with catcher and pinch-hitting specialist Smokey Burgess and fiery power-hitting third baseman Don Hoak for pitcher Whammy Douglas, utility player Jim Pendleton, and outfielders John Powers and Frank Thomas. None of the new Reds spent more than a year with the team, and Douglas didn't even play a game for Cincinnati, while Haddix, Hoak, and Burgess all contributed to the Pirates' 1960 World Series–championship season.

Thomas's biggest contribution to the Reds was being part of the package sent to the Chicago Cubs on December 6, 1959, in a trade that brought left-handed relief pitcher Bill Henry to Cincinnati.

Paul's contributions to the 1961 Reds are undeniable, but they had yet to yield anything by the end of the 1960 season, when he was pondering his own change of scenery. The owners of the fledgling Houston franchise, which was scheduled to start play in 1962, were looking for an experienced baseball man to run their operation. Paul, with his experience in several different areas, was an attractive candidate, and when the Colt 45s—later to be called the Astros—approached him during the 1960 season, he was more than intrigued. He announced his decision to leave Cincinnati for Texas on Monday, October 25.

"I met with the Houston people one week ago today, and I had no intention of taking the job," Paul told reporters. "As the day wore on, I changed my mind."

Paul made his decision while the aging Crosley, who turned seventy-four on September 18, was hospitalized in Savannah, Georgia. Giles, who had moved the National League offices to Cincinnati's Carew Tower after taking over as president in 1951, helped with the search for a new general manager. It quickly led to Detroit, where another lifelong baseball man named Bill DeWitt was looking for a way out of his job as president and general manager of the Tigers.

William Orville DeWitt Sr.'s baseball roots ran even deeper than Gabe Paul's. He started in 1916, at the age of thirteen, selling soda at St. Louis ballgames before becoming an office boy in the front office of the American League Browns, where he started learning the business from Branch Rickey.

Rickey, who is to baseball what Paul Brown is to football, practically invented many aspects of the game now taken for granted, everything from the framework of the farm system to batting helmets. He is most famous, of course, for tearing down baseball's color barrier with the signing of Jackie Robinson.

When Rickey moved from the Browns to the Cardinals in 1917, DeWitt followed. While working for the Cardinals, he went to night school to study shorthand and typing, which led to being named Rickey's secretary. DeWitt would go on to fill several jobs in the organization—ticket seller, ticket taker, scoreboard operator, concessionaire—and he handled the tickets for St. Louis's first appearance in the World Series in 1926. At the same time, he was attending St. Louis University, Washington University, and St. Louis University Law School, all at night, and he eventually passed the Missouri bar examination in June 1931.

DeWitt eventually rose to the role of team treasurer before being named in 1936 an assistant vice president specializing in procuring players for the major- and minor-league teams, which allowed him to indulge his eye for talent. He spent less than a year in that job before returning to the perennially woebegone Browns as vice president and general manager in 1936, and in 1944 he put together the only team to win an American League championship while the franchise was located in St. Louis. The Browns lost to the Cardinals in a six-game World Series, but *The Sporting News* recognized DeWitt's accomplishment by naming him Major League Executive of the Year.

The Browns couldn't maintain the momentum of the mid-1940s and struggled in the shadow of the more successful Cardinals, who appeared in nine World Series and won six in the twenty-one-year span from 1926 through 1946 while sharing Sportsman's Park with their American League counterparts. DeWitt displayed his taste for dramatic deals in November 1947 when he traded outfielder Vern Stephens and pitcher Jack Kramer to the Boston Red Sox for nine players and $310,000. The deal couldn't lift the Browns out of the second division, which didn't keep DeWitt and his brother, Charlie, who was working as the team's traveling secretary, from scraping together enough money to purchase controlling interest in the Browns in 1949. The DeWitts sold the franchise in 1951 to a group led by the flamboyant Bill Veeck, but Bill DeWitt stayed in the front office until Veeck was forced to sell the team, which was moved to Baltimore and became the Orioles for the 1954 season.

DeWitt landed in New York as assistant general manager of the Yankees for two years before taking over administration of a fund designed to help needy minor league teams in 1956. He spent four years in that job, but he never lost the urge to run a ballclub and put together a contender, so when a group of investors who admittedly knew little about baseball bought the Detroit Tigers, they turned operation of the franchise over to DeWitt.

He wasted little time indulging his own flair for flamboyance while trying to improve a team that finished two games under .500 and in fourth place in the AL. Early in the 1960 season, he pried first baseman Norm Cash from the Chicago White Sox for little-used infielder Steve Demeter. Cash would win the 1961 AL batting championship and spend fifteen years with the Tigers, playing a key role in their 1968 World Series championship.

Five days after acquiring Cash, DeWitt and the even more flamboyant Frank Lane, general manager of the Cleveland Indians, hatched an eye-popping trade in which 1959 batting champion Harvey Kuenn went to the Indians for 1959 home run champion Rocky Colavito. Lane and DeWitt later collaborated in August on the only trade of managers in major league history, with Detroit skipper Jimmy Dykes taking over for Joe Gordon in Cleveland.

The deals made headlines, but did little to improve the teams. DeWitt's Detroit team lost five more games in 1960 than it had in 1959, and his employment circumstances had gone similarly downhill, recalled his son, William O. DeWitt Jr.

"He was in Detroit, and he'd gone up there as president, general manager, chief executive officer," said DeWitt, who followed his father into baseball and retraced the family's roots back to St. Louis as chairman of the board and general partner of the Cardinals. "A group had bought the team, and they didn't have any baseball background. They wanted a baseball man. They said, 'You'll have ultimate authority to run the business.' Then, after the first year, John Fetzer bought the other guys out and became the controlling partner. He said to my father, 'I still want you to be the GM, but I'm going to run the team and oversee everything.' My father said, 'I understand, but if I get another opportunity, I'm going to take it, because that's what I signed up for.'"

The younger DeWitt, who turned twenty in the summer of 1961, was a student at Yale University at the time. He recalls his father being approached by Cincinnati banker Tom Conroy, who was secretary and treasurer of the Reds.

"He knew my father," DeWitt Jr. said. "I can't tell you the background, but when Gabe Paul left, I think he suggested to Powel Crosley that my father could be available and if so, that he should be the guy who should come and replace Gabe Paul."

Giles, who had known DeWitt since the two first met in Rickey's office in St. Louis in 1920, had the same recommendation. At least two other men were rumored to be interested in the job—Cedric Tallis, general manager of the minor league team in Seattle, and Dewey Soriano, president of the Pacific Coast League in which Seattle played—and Giles and Crosley spent two days discussing the situation. In the end, Crosley liked DeWitt's extensive major league experience.

"We discussed the job," Crosley told reporters on November 2. "I didn't make up my mind until this morning. I feel that DeWitt is the most qualified man for the job."

Despite his long career in baseball and his accomplishments, the DeWitt name wasn't well-known, at least in Cincinnati.

"I had no clue who DeWitt was," said pitcher Jim O'Toole, who made his off-season home in Cincinnati. "I didn't realize he was hanging around with Bill Veeck. He'd been around forever, but he was a very intelligent financial genius."

How shrewd was DeWitt? While he was getting paid by the Reds to be the team's general manager, he was still getting paid by the Tigers to not work for them.

"None of the owners knew anything about baseball," DeWitt said at the time. "Fetzer wanted to be president, which he now is, and he used me against Harvey Hansen, who was president. That didn't help me a lot with Hansen. Making things worse was the fact that the Detroit farm system hadn't produced anyone worthwhile in seven years. When Fetzer moved in as president, he wanted to put me in cold storage for two years as his assistant, but I had a contract as president rendering me $100,000 in three years. When the call came from Cincinnati last October 25, I settled the remainder of my Detroit contract for 50 percent, so I will be paid $16,666 a year by the Detroit club until November 1, 1962."

DeWitt stepped into a situation desperate for stability.

Crosley's illness had allowed questions regarding the franchise's future in Cincinnati to linger. The latest example was a newspaper report a week earlier that Harry Wismer, a flamboyant New York broadcasting entrepreneur who already owned the American Football League New York Titans, was trying to form a syndicate to buy the Reds.

"If we get the club, I'll keep it in Cincinnati," Wismer said. "We have learned there is a chance the Reds may be for sale, and we have been working on this for a couple of weeks. I think if Powel Crosley gives us an even break in negotiations, we will wind up with the franchise."

Wismer dangled the possibility of Cincinnati getting an AFL franchise as a sweetener. Paul had approached Wismer on Crosley's behalf about Cincinnati getting an AFL franchise.

"Things were pretty well set for the football franchise, but Powel backed out at the last minute," said Wismer, who knew his promises about keeping the baseball team in Cincinnati would do little to comfort local fans. They easily recalled that New York was supporting two National League teams as few as four years earlier and might like the Reds at least as much as the Mets, who were due to start playing in 1962.

"Why would we want to move out of Cincinnati?" Wismer said. "Cincinnati is a wonderful, rich, aggressive baseball town. All it needs is for some management to put money into the operation, and it will really go places."

That man, however, was not Wismer. He didn't have enough money to operate the Titans. The situation grew so dire that making payrolls grew iffy. The other AFL owners, realizing the league needed a successful team in New York, arranged for Wismer to sell the team to a more financially stable owner. The team was renamed the Jets.

Rumors about the impending departure of the Reds to another city were common, according to Jim Ferguson, who shared coverage of the Reds for the *Dayton Daily News* with sports editor Si Burick. Ferguson even wrote some of the stories based on those rumors.

"It was very much a fear, whether it could really happen or not," Ferguson said. "The fear was losing a team to New York. Baseball wanted an NL team in New York, and the Reds obviously weren't a team drawing a lot of people. They weren't drawing any people, so there were all these rumors. It wasn't every day, but stories would pop up that somebody in New York wanted to buy the team.

"There were lots of stories in 1959 and 1960–especially 1960–about the Continental League. They were going to form the Continental League, and one of the strongest guys was Bill Shea in New York. That forced expansion, and when the Mets were awarded a franchise, that definitely eased off the situation with the Reds.

"Another factor against the Reds leaving was that Powel Crosley was the owner. Crosley, as a local guy, wasn't going to let this team leave Cincinnati."

DeWitt had to put possible changes in ownership on the back burner in favor of working on turning around the fortunes of the team on the field. His first step was to talk with Hutchinson.

"I'm going to call Hutch," he told reporters. "I want him to come to Cincinnati next week. We'll sit down and discuss who the club needs to strengthen itself for next year."

That comment immediately snuffed out any suspicion that DeWitt would bring in another manager–somebody with whom he was more familiar, maybe somebody he'd worked with in the past. That was a practice common among general managers. DeWitt might have been tempted to bring in Luke Sewell, his pennant-winning manager in 1944 with the Browns, but Sewell had already failed in just short of three seasons in Cincinnati. He led the Reds to back-to-back sixth-place finishes in 1950 and 1951 before being fired by Paul with the 1952 team 40–61 and headed for another sixth-place finish.

"It was different in those days," Ferguson said. "It wasn't an automatic thing, when you had a new general manager, that you had to have a new manager and farm director. There was less of that in those days. Hutch was pretty well established at that point. He was a very solid baseball guy and a very strong person. That team didn't have a lot of leaders on the field."

DeWitt Jr. wasn't surprised that his father stuck with Hutchinson.

"He had heard good things about Hutch," DeWitt Jr. said. "I think he wanted to get the lay of the land here, and I know that his view was that Hutch was a good manager and that was one of the good things he'd inherited when he came here. They developed quite a good relationship."

DeWitt didn't feel the same way about the players. The previous season's sixth-place finish made it clear that the combination on hand wasn't working, especially the pitching, which posted the league's second-worst team ERA at 4.00. Only seventh-place Chicago's 4.35 was worse.

Hutchinson, a pitcher in his playing days, believed that the Reds had a core of talented young pitchers who simply needed experience. They included left-handed O'Toole and right-handers Jay Hook, Ken Hunt, and Jim Maloney. O'Toole was twenty-three and had just three seasons of professional experience, two in the majors. Maloney was twenty and had

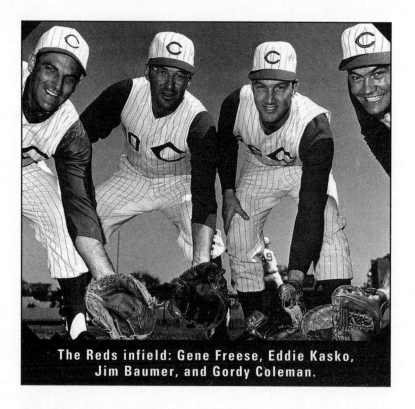

**The Reds infield: Gene Freese, Eddie Kasko,
Jim Baumer, and Gordy Coleman.**

two years of professional experience, including eleven major-league games. Hook was twenty-four and had only one full major-league season and parts of two others under his belt. Hunt was twenty-one and hadn't even tasted major-league life in three professional seasons.

DeWitt and Hutchinson also agreed that the team's middle infield needed shoring up. The six-foot, 180-pound Eddie Kasko had been named by members of the Cincinnati chapter of the Baseball Writers Association of America the team's Most Valuable Player in 1960 while primarily playing third base, but he was a shortstop by trade and didn't have the power most teams look for in third basemen. The bespectacled former Cardinal, who'd been acquired after the 1958 season, also played some games at second base in 1960, but Billy Martin had been the primary second baseman and had hit just .246 at the age of thirty-two. The Reds sold him to the Braves after the season.

The Reds also had a couple of middle-infield prospects in Cuba native Leo Cardenas and Venezuelan Elio Chacon, but Cardenas was just twenty-one, had played just forty-eight games in the majors, and his defense was unproven. Chacon was twenty-three, but similarly inexperienced.

The biggest job was getting the pitching in shape, and DeWitt knew he wasn't going to acquire good pitchers without giving up something of value. He also knew that he had at least two dependable shortstops on his team in Kasko and Roy McMillan, a fielding wizard who'd won the first three Gold Gloves at his position after the award was initiated in 1957. The first year's awards weren't split between the leagues, meaning McMillan was considered to be the best-fielding shortstop in baseball. Gold Gloves were presented in both leagues starting in 1958, and McMillan won the National League's in 1958 and 1959, but he never was a good, consistent hitter, and six seasons of playing 150 or more games in each season seemed to be catching up to him. He played in just seventy-nine games in 1959 and 124 in 1960, while turning thirty-one years old.

Meanwhile, Hutchinson had identified a hulking right-hander named Joey Jay as a pitcher who might fit into the Reds plans. The six-foot-four, 228-pound Jay had broken into the major leagues in 1953 at the age of seventeen as a bonus baby with the Milwaukee Braves, who had given him such a large amount of money to sign that rules of the time made it mandatory that he be on the team's major-league roster—one of that group of players known as "bonus babies." His first career start, in fact, was a three-hit shutout of Cincinnati in Milwaukee on September 20, 1953, but his biggest claim to fame stemmed from being the first product of Little League baseball to reach the major leagues.

Jay also had pitched well enough to be named the National League Player of the Month for July 1958, when he was 5–2 with a 1.39 ERA, five complete games and two shutouts in seven starts, but the true indication of where he stood in Milwaukee's pitching plans came in the World Series. He wasn't even included on the post-season roster.

Jay suffered from joining a staff dominated by accomplished veterans such as left-hander Warren Spahn and right-handers Lew Burdette and Gene Conley, which left few opportunities for a precocious youngster to work. He never made more than nineteen starts in any of his first seven seasons, and he didn't help himself with constant struggles to keep his weight down, which led to slow starts that helped create a reputation for laziness.

"Jay had good potential, but he'd never done a lot for Milwaukee," Ferguson said. "He had a tough time cracking their starting rotation. People thought he could be a good pitcher, but he hadn't done it a lot."

Jay also suffered from a classic tradeoff. Sure, the large signing bonus was great, but experience is priceless. Few managers are willing to give regular work to an eighteen-year-old kid with no experience. Charlie Grimm, Milwaukee's manager when Jay joined the Braves, wasn't any different.

"Charlie Grimm resented me for that reason," Jay recalled. "Nothing against me personally, but I was taking up

Big Joey Jay was a key addition to the Reds.

a roster spot. It cost me a couple of seasons, because by the time I was able to go to the minors, I'd already lost those first two years."

Hutchinson decided to find out for himself. He launched an under-the-radar investigation, talking to several people about which was the true Joey Jay—the guy he'd heard about or the guy who'd gone 6–3 over the last two months of the season, including 4–1 in the last month of the season.

One person he spoke with was Bob Scheffing, a coach with the Braves in 1960 who'd been named manager of the Tigers.

"He's always been a slow starter," Scheffing later told reporters. "If he's physically sound, you don't have to worry about him–and if the Reds don't want him, I'll gladly take him. He'll win more games than any other Reds pitcher. I tried to get Jay myself after I signed with the Tigers, but we needed a center fielder more than a pitcher, and after giving up Frank Bolling for Bill Bruton, we didn't have anything else to offer in a trade."

"I was told that it was true that Jay goofed off the first half of the season," Hutchinson said. "The second half, though, he gave a concentrated effort. They told me he reached maturity. He finally reached the point where he believed he was a major leaguer and was willing to work toward it."

Jay was well aware of his reputation.

"I guess it all dates back to when I was just eighteen," he said. "In those days, I didn't know beans about nothing. I ate up a storm during the winter and reported to the Braves training camp weighing 244 pounds. Once you get the reputation for being lazy, it's hard to shake. During each of the last three springs I spent with Braves, I was told by the manager that I was going to be the fourth starting pitcher, but it never worked out that way. I didn't pitch much with the Braves, but I couldn't see where it was my fault. Last spring, I even made a special effort to get off to a good start. I came to camp at 222 pounds, eight less than my usual reporting weight, but it was almost the end of May before I got a chance to pitch, and sitting around during the first weeks of the season isn't good for any pitcher."

Another source tapped by Hutchinson was, of all people, Braves pitcher Lew Burdette.

"Hutch asked Lew about the Braves' young pitchers, and Lew recommended me," Jay said. "I was very pleased. I knew Cincinnati had a good club—hitters like Frank Robinson and Vada Pinson, pitchers like Purkey, O'Toole, and Brosnan."

Hutchinson's case for Jay was strong enough to convince DeWitt to go after the pitcher. The Braves, concerned about the decline of long-time shortstop Johnny Logan—who would be thirty-four going into the 1961 season, his eleventh in the majors—were so interested in McMillan and so confident in their pitching depth that they also were willing to include left-handed pitching prospect Juan Pizarro with Jay in a trade that was completed on December 15, 1960.

"He's the pitcher I didn't want to give up," Milwaukee manager Chuck Dressen said later, referring to Jay.

"Yeah, I can believe that," Jay responded with a hint of sarcasm. "They even tried to trade me during the season last year."

"I knew Bill DeWitt was serious when he went out and got Joey," O'Toole said. "Joey was a big ox out there. He was so nonchalant, we were trying to figure out where he was coming from. He was only twenty-five when he came over here, and he'd already been in the big leagues for seven seasons with Milwaukee. He could do it all out there on the mound. He'd give you eight or nine innings every time out."

"He's going to get a chance to perform every fourth or fifth day, and he's no dummy," Hutchinson promised. "He knows if he can't pitch for us, he'll have to start thinking about the minor leagues.

"A lot of people think we gave up on Roy McMillan. It

isn't so. Joey Jay and Juan Pizarro are a couple of good, young pitchers. The Braves were willing to give them up only for what they wanted, and that was McMillan."

McMillan, a native of Bonham, Texas, had become so settled in Cincinnati that he purchased a pizza franchise in Hamilton, located about thirty miles north of the city. Still, he wasn't surprised about being traded.

"When you read in the paper every day that you may be going, you're not surprised when you go," he said. "When you hear so many rumors, it's not just general manager's talk. I knew it, but I hoped it wouldn't happen. No baseball player likes to be traded. It's the toughest thing in the game. It's worse than a bad year. You get used to the fellows on the ball club and the town and the way of doing things, but I've been around in baseball long enough, so I wasn't surprised. I knew I was going to be traded.

"I'll tell you something. I didn't like being traded, but I'm glad I'm with a club that has a chance to win it. Third place is the highest we ever finished in Cincinnati. I sure wouldn't mind playing in a World Series this year." He would miss, of course, that opportunity.

Pizarro was only twenty-three, but he also was blocked in Milwaukee's pitching plans. The Puerto Rican made just ninety appearances, including fifty-one starts, in four seasons with the Braves. Those are averages of twenty-three appearances and thirteen starts. He was 23–19 in those appearances, but by going 6–7 with a 4.55 ERA in twenty-one 1960 games he convinced Milwaukee that he wasn't going to pan out.

The presence of O'Toole and Henry and the acquisition of Jay made Pizarro expendable, and DeWitt knew exactly what he wanted to do. He had his sights set on Chicago White

Sox third baseman Gene Freese, an outgoing twenty-six-year-old native of Wheeling, West Virginia, known as much for defensive lapses as he was for the pop in his right-handed bat. The solidly built Freese had just completed his sixth season in the majors, but Chicago was already his fourth team. He'd hit twenty-three home runs and driven in seventy runs with Philadelphia in 1959, prompting the Phillies to trade him to the White Sox for outfielder Johnny Callison. Freese's homer output dropped to seventeen, but he drove in seventy-nine runs while hitting .268.

Freese was listed on official rosters at five feet eleven and 175 pounds, but he admitted that his height was an exaggeration.

"I lied on my bubblegum cards," he said. "I said five-foot-eleven just to make me feel bigger. Other guys lied about their age. I lied about my height."

Despite that, DeWitt saw Freese as the power-hitting third baseman common to most winning teams, and he knew the Reds had enough pitching depth to tempt the White Sox. Just hours after completing the deal with Milwaukee, he sent Pizarro and a thirty-five-year-old right-hander grandly named Calvin Coolidge Julius Caesar Tuskahoma McLish—who'd gone 4–14 with a 4.16 ERA for Cincinnati in 1960—to the White Sox for Freese.

Ironically, McLish had joined the Reds exactly one year earlier when he was traded with Martin and first baseman Gordy Coleman by Cleveland for second baseman Johnny Temple.

"I knew Chicago was going after pitching help, and by the process of elimination, I figured I'd be the one to go," said Freese, who was nicknamed "Augie" but liked to refer to his bat and, occasionally, himself as "The Old Destroyer." "I was the only one they figured they had a replacement for."

He also knew that his defense was the butt of jokes. Sometimes, he made them himself.

"They don't make jokes when I'm swinging 'The Old Destroyer,'" he pointed out.

Though he didn't know it yet, with those two bold, decisive moves, DeWitt had added what would become critical pieces of the team that would win the NL championship. He hadn't answered all of the questions—Hutchinson still had concerns about his second base situation—but DeWitt was confident that he'd shored up the pitching and improved the run production.

Unfortunately for DeWitt—a portly man who wore rimless glasses and whose wide eyes made him look as if he were perpetually startled—the brilliance he displayed in completing

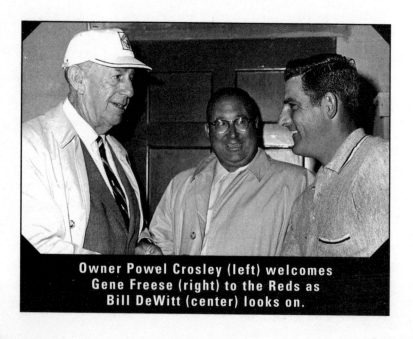

Owner Powel Crosley (left) welcomes
Gene Freese (right) to the Reds as
Bill DeWitt (center) looks on.

the 1961 team will forever be overshadowed by his headline-making trade of Robinson to Baltimore after the 1965 season. In one book about Cincinnati's baseball history, the Robinson trade was ranked on the list of the ten worst trades in Reds history. The December 15, 1960, deals didn't make the list of ten best trades, even though it took a lot of courage to trade away a very dependable shortstop who also was one of the team's most popular players in exchange for two unproven pitchers.

In many ways, the 1960 deals compare favorably with Bob Howsam's headline-making November 29, 1971, trade of first baseman Lee May, second baseman Tommy Helms, and utility specialist Jimmy Stewart to Houston for second baseman Joe Morgan, pitcher Jack Billingham, outfielders Cesar Geronimo and Ed Armbrister and third baseman Denis Menke—the historic deal that turned the Big Red Machine into eventual World Series champions.

"One thing about him was he did what he thought was right and made the deals that he thought would be successful and didn't think too much about 'gosh this guy was a fixture' and what was the media going to say," Bill DeWitt Jr. said of his father.

Even a pitcher such as O'Toole didn't flinch at seeing an accomplished defender traded away.

"DeWitt made some tremendous trades," O'Toole said. "McMillan was near the end of his career. He was still a great shortstop, but we had some guys in the background that could fill in that spot, and you can never replace good pitching. I wasn't really that concerned, because there are a lot of guys around who can catch the ball. Eddie Kasko was a perfect example, and we had Cardenas backing him up, so we were fortunate in that regard."

Maloney, watching developments from his off-season home in Fresno, California, didn't know what to think.

"I didn't know too much about Gene Freese," Maloney recalled. "I'd heard of Joey Jay, and I knew that he was the first Little League player to go to the big leagues. McMillan had been with the Reds quite some time. When I signed with the Reds, he was one of the older guys who sort of took me under his wing—him and Gus Bell. When they traded McMillan, I was sorry to see him go. To me, he was 'Mr. Shortstop.' He was a nice guy, but I was just getting my feet wet. I didn't know a lot about how teams operate. I was just keeping my mouth shut and my eyes open and taking direction."

In what turned out to be an off-season of quality over quantity, DeWitt would make just a couple more deals before spring training. He sold Martin's contract to Milwaukee on December 3 and traded left-handed pitcher Joe Nuxhall to the Kansas City Athletics for twenty-seven-year-old right-hander John Briggs and twenty-four-year-old right-hander John Tsitouris.

Nuxhall, a Hamilton native, was best known for being the youngest person to play in a major-league baseball game when he took the Crosley Field mound for the Reds against the Cardinals at the tender age of fifteen on June 10, 1944. He'd made the National League All-Star team in 1955 and 1956, but by the time he turned thirty-two in 1960, he couldn't stick his head out of the dugout without being greeted by a torrent of boos. Going 1–8 with a 4.42 ERA and letting his explosive temper get the best of him at times didn't help.

"I asked for it," Nuxhall recalled. "That particular year, nothing went right. It was a horrible year. I could pitch six shutout innings, and all of a sudden, something would happen.

The fans were on me, and I just felt, 'Well, I want to get out of here. I'll see if they'll trade me.'"

A more stable and effective Nuxhall would be back with the Reds in time to go 5–0 with a 2.45 ERA in twelve games, including nine starts, in 1962, and he would go on to finish his career as a player before becoming a much-beloved broadcaster. He would never say he was haunted by the irony that he spent fifteen of his sixteen big-league seasons with the Reds and that they won a championship in the only season he missed, but his disappointment was understandable.

"You don't know if we would have won if I'd been here," said Nuxhall, who died in November 2007. "Those things you don't know. In fact, it was a miracle year, from whatever people tell me about it. They weren't that great of a ballclub, but everything popped into place, which is really what has to happen in a lot of cases. It just happened to fall that way, and they won the pennant.

"Sure, hell, I would've loved to have been here. That's the dream of any professional athlete–to play for the world's championship. Like I told some people at a banquet, I don't care what you're doing in sports as a team, your ultimate goal is to be in a championship, whether it's Little League, municipal league, whatever. You say, 'Well, I'm just playing for fun.' Basically, I don't buy that, because you know at the end of the season, somebody has to be the champion, and if you don't have that feeling, then you're wasting your time, in a sense. You might as well go jog or something."

Perhaps DeWitt's best move of the off-season was one he didn't make–out of bed in the wee hours of the morning of February 10, 1961. DeWitt was called at his home by

Earl Lawson, the Reds beat writer for the *Cincinnati Post and Times-Star* who'd been tipped off that Frank Robinson had been arrested and charged with carrying a concealed weapon. Lawson told DeWitt that Robinson could be released at 8 a.m. if someone would post $1,000 bail, and the reporter admitted being "a little startled" when DeWitt said, "Well, I guess one of his friends will bail him out."

Robinson had been arrested following the second of two altercations that night at a Cincinnati diner. He and two friends had stopped for hamburgers after a night of bowling and basketball and gotten into an argument with three youths. The cook called for help from two police officers who were eating in their cruiser. They came in and, while trying to calm the situation, referred to Robinson and his two African-American friends as "boys," prompting one of Robinson's friends to grow irate enough that the officers arrested him for disturbing the peace.

After he was bailed out, the three went back to the restaurant to retrieve their food—as did the two police officers. The officers left the restaurant and went back to their car while Robinson and his friends decided to stay and eat at the restaurant. At some point, Robinson looked into the kitchen and saw the cook looking at him and making throat-slitting gestures. That was the last straw for Robinson, who challenged the cook, as he described in his 1968 autobiography, *My Life Is Baseball,* co-authored with Al Silverman.

"He started toward me, with a butcher's knife in his right hand," Robinson recalled, adding that the restaurant layout prevented other diners from seeing the knife. "I saw him all right. He was coming at me with that butcher's knife poised in his right hand."

Robinson pulled a .25 Beretta–a small, Italian-made pistol–from his jacket pocket and held it in the palm of his left
hand. He'd purchased the gun during spring training a year
earlier, primarily because he often carried large amounts of
cash and had to walk fifty yards in a dark area from where he
parked his car to his Cincinnati apartment.

The cook stopped and yelled, "Hey, that guy's got a gun,"
bringing the officers back inside. Robinson slipped the pistol
back into his pocket and lied when asked by one of the officers
if he had a gun. They found it after frisking him and arrested
him.

Robinson was as surprised as he was disappointed that
DeWitt did nothing. Gabe Paul and Birdie Tebbetts had personally rescued Robinson after he became involved in a police matter during spring training in 1958. No charges against
Robinson were filed after that incident, and Robinson understandably expected similar help from DeWitt after the later
problem–even though the accepted practice at the vast majority of businesses is to leave employees to handle their own
personal legal issues. That's what adults do, and that's what
DeWitt made the twenty-five-year-old Robinson do.

That wasn't the first time in their short relationship that
Robinson had problems with DeWitt. They didn't personally
meet after DeWitt was hired until bumping into each other in
the team's downtown Cincinnati offices.

"When Mr. DeWitt took over the club, I just thought
the right thing for him to do would be to at least call up the
players, especially the ones who lived in town, and intro-
duce himself, say hello, maybe talk a little with them," Robinson wrote in his book. "But nothing. I met him by accident
one day when I was in the office talking to the switchboard

operator. He happened to come out of his office and saw me and introduced himself, the official greeting."

Relations grew frostier during contract negotiations. De-Witt was a notoriously soft touch for sob stories and down-on-their-luck ex-players, and he gave everybody in the Cincinnati front office a 10 percent raise immediately upon taking over and gave them another one ten months later. But he wanted Robinson to take a pay cut before the 1961 season, while Robinson wanted to be paid at least as much as he earned in 1960.

"He said, 'I hear you don't hustle all the time,'" Robinson wrote. "I blew up. I said, 'Have you ever seen me play?' He said, 'No, no not really, not over a full season.'

"Well, until you do, don't tell me that I don't always put out on the field. I do."

DeWitt pointed out that Robinson seemed to play better when he was angry, and that DeWitt planned to keep Robinson angry throughout the upcoming season.

"He was going to keep poking me, keep me at the boiling point, he implied, to get the best performance out of me," Robinson explained. "I left Mr. Bill DeWitt feeling that I had struck bottom in my career, and that there was only one way to go—up. I was wrong."

No, that low point was the long night Robinson spent sprawled on the hard bench of a Cincinnati jail cell, with just his jacket for a pillow.

"The most disturbing thought of all, the one that haunted me all night long, was what the kids would think of me," he wrote. "So many kids idolize big-league ballplayers. So many of them mold their whole lives around their heroes. What were they going to think? How were they going to react?

"And then it began to dawn on me that I had a responsibility to the game of baseball. Baseball had been good to me, and I had taken a lot out of it, but what had I given back? I felt a deep responsibility to baseball, especially to the young kids who look up to the players. I felt that I had let them down.

"For the first time, I began to realize that I wasn't a kid any more, and that I had better stop acting like one. I knew that I had been wrong, dead wrong, all the way. But looking back, it may have been the best thing that ever happened to me. It matured me, it made me a better man. No, not a better man—a man. Let me put it that way because I don't think I was a real man before."

Robinson's problems that night had started when the police officers called him a boy while he thought he was a man. By the end of the night, he was acting like one.

Not that his troubles were over. As he expected, he heard a great deal in spring training early and often about the incident. It started when he reported to camp and found a water pistol in his locker, left there by teammate Ed Bailey.

"Thanks, Ed, but I can't use it," Robinson said, playing along while handing the toy back to Bailey. "I'm on parole."

When the Reds traveled to Bradenton, Florida, for an exhibition game against Milwaukee, Hank Aaron and Felix Mantilla serenaded Robinson from the Braves' dugout, singing, "Lay that pistol down, babe, lay that pistol down." Milwaukee pitcher Lew Burdette snuck up on Robinson and frisked him, reporting to Braves third baseman Eddie Mathews, "It's all right, Eddie. He's clean."

Mathews, who'd gotten into a fight with Robinson the previous season, responded with, "Hey, Robby, I'm not fooling around with you this year."

St. Louis Cardinals first baseman Bill White called him "John Dillinger."

"He'll probably get a lot of that this year," one Reds player said.

The roster wasn't the only aspect of Reds baseball that underwent something of a makeover between the 1960 and 1961 seasons. The ballpark itself was brightened up with a paint job, the old green being covered up with a couple of coats of white, while additional space had been found on the massive scoreboard in left-center field for the two new American League teams.

More glaring was the change in the area around Crosley Field, which showed unmistakable signs of the ever-growing dominance of the automobile. For decades, space for parking cars around Crosley had been an afterthought. Most of the fans arrived for games in buses or trolleys or on trains that pulled in a few blocks south of the ballpark at Union Terminal. Most fans could walk back and forth easily, while most of those who drove to the games had to settle for finding parking spots on the narrow, neighborhood streets around the ballpark.

The unexpected success of the 1956 team, and the relative explosion in attendance, forced Reds management to face the fact that more and more fans were going to be driving cars to games and would need safe places to park. The one, 400-spot lot one block south of the ballpark on Dalton Street wasn't nearly enough. Powel Crosley started talking with city officials about finding a way to add 5,000 spots around the area, and he wasn't shy about holding the future of the franchise over the city's head.

"There are so many other cities ready to offer a stadium, adequate parking space, and everything of that sort, practically for nothing," Crosley said. "In this competitive situation, we are entitled to ask for some additional parking space."

The Reds, located in one of the smallest markets in major league baseball, always had been a regional team. As the 1950s turned into the 1960s and the development of the interstate highway system made it less time-consuming to drive long distances, license plates from Indiana, Kentucky, and West Virginia became more common sights in parking lots at Reds games.

Eventually, on April 28, 1958, the Reds and the city signed an agreement under which the city agreed to build parking lots and Crosley guaranteed that the franchise would remain in Cincinnati for at least five years.

Beginning in 1959, the city was able to start working out deals with surrounding property owners and clearing lots for parking spaces. Before the 1961 season, one major landmark fell victim to the needs. The Superior Laundry building, located across York Street beyond the left field wall, was demolished. The demolition also meant the loss of the Siebler Suit advertising sign, which guaranteed a new suit for any player who hit the sign with a home run. Reds slugger Wally Post had picked up more than ten Siebler suits through the years, while Willie Mays of the New York/San Francisco Giants had led visiting players with seven.

The team's official 1961 yearbook includes a page featuring an aerial view of Crosley Field from the south. The word "parking" is stamped over eleven different lots around the ballpark, adding spaces for a total of 6,000 cars, up from 3,500 available in 1960. The city spent just less than $1,200,000 to buy the properties, clear them, and build the lots.

"The city-owned parking lots will all be surfaced and have

guard rails of some sort around each lot," the article reports, adding, "New roads, such as the Dayton Expressway, are making it much easier for Reds fans to get to Crosley Field."

As added evidence of the automobile's growing dominance, fans could see, just beyond the center- and right-field walls, the pathway for what eventually would become the Mill Creek Expressway portion of Interstate 75. This was the latest link in the chain of a Hamilton County highway that had been started in 1941 as a four-mile stretch from Hartwell Avenue north to Glendale-Milford Road, which helped make it easier for workers to get to the Wright Aeronautical Plant–later a General Electric facility–in Sharonville, where engines for World War II bombers were being built.

The stop-and-start nature of the interstate system at that time made getting to Reds games much different than it is today. Ferguson recalled the challenges of getting to Crosley from Dayton.

"There were three or four ways to come," he said. "You could come straight down U.S. 25 right through Miamisburg, or you could take a couple of side roads over to (state route) 741 that ran parallel to 25, east of there. Another way we took was going partway down 25, then swinging west past Middletown over to 747. Eventually, that would hit Spring Grove Avenue when it went way on out."

By the late 1950s, according to a history of Interstate 75 written by Jake Mecklenborg for "Cincinnati-transit.net," the highway had advanced south to the Ludlow Viaduct, getting closer to linking up with the Kenton County expressway in Northern Kentucky. The last link was the four-mile stretch from the Ludlow Viaduct to the Ohio River, including

The city cleared out the buildings
on York Street, behind Crosley Field,
to create additional parking spaces.

construction of the Brent Spence Bridge. Space for the stretch
through Cincinnati's West End and Queensgate neighbor-
hoods still was being cleared in 1961. Eventually, as many
as 20,000 people from close to 5,000 families, as well as 551
businesses, would be displaced.

Before construction prevented it, the Reds were able to
use the cleared area beyond the outfield walls for—you guessed
it—parking.

TWO

Taking Aim

Considering the concealed weapon charge Frank Robinson still was dealing with when he arrived in Tampa, Florida, for spring training in 1961, some people might have found it a bit ironic that the sound of gunfire was common around the Cincinnati camp.

Nobody was particularly alarmed, however, for two reasons—it was expected, and the guns shot only BBs.

They were part of an exercise designed by a Columbus, Georgia, company known as Unlimited Enterprises to improve the players' focus. A brainstorm of ever-innovative owner Powel Crosley Jr., the idea was for the players to shoot

**Reds players shoot at the sky
during spring training.**

BBs at targets tossed into the air. The targets got progressively smaller and smaller, from baseballs to discs to pennies, all the way down to BBs, which meant the shooter was trying to hit a BB with a BB. The instructors–Lucky McDaniel, Mike Jennings, and John Hughes–eventually would tell shooters to "look at the shiny side of the BB."

Outfielder Wally Post hit six consecutive discs in one stretch before knocking out a wad of paper stuffed into the middle of the disc on his seventh shot.

"It was eye-hand coordination stuff," pitcher Jim O'Toole said.

"The object of all this is for the boys to correlate their attempts to hit my targets with their attempts to hit baseballs," Hughes said. "I'm trying to get the players to concentrate on their target, whether it's a baseball or disc. I have the boys shoot with both eyes open, and I teach them that they should think of the gun or bat as merely a working member of their body."

Shooting BBs at BBs actually had been implemented by Crosley a couple of years earlier.

"My best year was 1959, and that was the year we had a week of this shooting in spring training," outfielder Vada Pinson recalled. "Last year I bought a little gun and worked out myself, but that's not as good as when you have someone helping you. These drills teach you to concentrate, and they help you to pick up the ball faster. Learning to do those things isn't going to hurt any batter."

Pitcher Bob Purkey was convinced the drills also helped the mound staff.

"Sometimes a pitcher gets out there and just throws without concentrating completely on his target," Purkey admitted. "I've done it. These drills help me concentrate. You can't hit the spots if you aren't concentrating. That's the difference between a thrower and a pitcher—concentration."

"They got us down to where he would throw a BB in the air and we could hit it," young pitcher Jim Maloney said. "We'd started with big washers, bigger than a silver dollar, ten feet in front of you. Within two to three weeks, we were doing that every day. It broke up the monotony of just standing around shagging balls.

"We went from hitting a washer to hitting a piece of

paper inside of a washer. Then we got it down to three feet in front you."

Shooting at BBs was just one of several unusual methods tried by the Reds in their efforts to get the franchise turned around. When the pitchers and catchers reported on February 22 to Plant Field at Tampa for the team's twenty-eighth spring training in the city, most of them—if not all—had little idea of what was waiting for them.

One new person on hand to greet them was Otis Douglas, a coach described as a physical conditioning consultant. The fifty-year-old Douglas was a fascinating character, sort of a Renaissance man of sports.

The Reedville, Virginia, native, who owned with his wife, Eleanor, a 3,300-acre pheasant preserve in Hague, Virginia, lettered and served as team captain in football and track while earning Bachelor of Science, Master of Arts, and Doctorate of Education degrees at the College of William and Mary in Williamsburg, Virginia. He taught physical education, directed intramural athletics, worked as an assistant football and track coach and as head swimming coach while also serving as head athletic trainer for all of the Indian teams before moving on to the University of Akron in 1939 as assistant and then head football coach.

Besides teaching physical education Douglas also coached wrestling, swimming, track, gymnastics, and freshman basketball and again served as athletic trainer before being named Akron's athletic director in 1941.

Douglas served as an officer in the Naval Aviation Physical Fitness Program from 1943 to 1945 and was player-coach with the Jacksonville, Florida, Naval Air Station football team in 1945. After the war, he embarked on a professional football career as a player and trainer with the Philadelphia Eagles while coaching football at Drexel Tech at the same time before landing the job as head coach at the University of Arkansas, which he gave up for a job as an assistant with the Baltimore Colts. From there, he spent a year as an assistant at Villanova and another on the staff of the NFL Chicago Cardinals before going north to be head coach of the Calgary Stampeders of the Canadian Football League.

After a year of scouting talent for the Minnesota Vikings in 1960, Douglas joined the Reds.

"He put the Reds through a sprightly course of calisthenics designed to stretch shoulder-girdle muscles, loosen hamstrings and strengthen ankle and knee joints," *Sports Illustrated* reported. "The Reds, a bit wary of all this exercise, finally were won over by the diffident but appealing personality of Mr.–or Dr.–Douglas and went into the regular season as well-conditioned a baseball team as there was in either league."

Frank Robinson, who'd had problems with his throwing arm since 1954, overcame them with Douglas's help. Robinson's arm was so bad that he spent most of the 1959 and 1960 seasons at first base, though he was an outfielder by trade.

"Douglas had been hired by the Reds to get the ballclub in condition, and he did just that, though he nearly killed us in the process," Robinson recalled in his autobiography. "He had us doing pushups and situps and all sorts of impossible exercises that baseball players are never supposed to do. He had us out there until our tongues were hanging out and we were screaming for mercy. But then he would come around and work on my arm, and that made up for all his tortures. He had real strong hands and he was able to massage my arm and dig down deep and break up the knots that always formed in the arm, and he got it in good shape."

Not right away, though. Robinson missed some time in spring training because of his arm, exasperating manager Fred Hutchinson, who had no room for Robinson at first base with Gordy Coleman ready to take over.

"He's had enough trouble with that arm to know by now how to take care of it," Hutchinson growled to reporters, pointing out that Robinson consistently unleashed long throws from the outfield instead of hitting cutoff men and, in the view of the manager, didn't warm up properly. "Damn it, I want his arm ready to go for the season. If Robinson isn't ready to play the outfield, he'll sit on the bench until he is–and he'll take a [pay] cut."

Douglas, who also possessed a commercial pilot's license, was one of three newcomers to Hutchinson's coaching staff. Antioch, Tennessee, native Jim Turner, who'd pitched on Cincinnati's 1940 World Series-championship team and spent eleven seasons as pitching coach for the Yankees, returned to the majors as the Reds pitching coach after spending the 1960 season as general manager and manager of the Class A minor league team at Nashville. Turner, known as "The Colonel," replaced Cot Deal as the Reds' pitching coach.

Another newcomer was hitting coach Dick Sisler, an outfielder in his playing days who was most famous for the tenth-inning home run he hit off of Brooklyn's Don Newcombe in the last regular-season game of the 1950 season to help the Philadelphia Phillies–the "Whiz Kids"–clinch their first National League championship since 1915 and their last until 1980. Sisler had spent three seasons as Nashville's manager before taking Hutchinson's old job as manager at Seattle in 1960. Sisler replaced Wally Moses as the Reds hitting coach.

Also missing from the previous season's staff was Whitey Lockman. The only holdover coach was Cuba native Reggie Otero, who was helpful in communicating with Latin American players such as infielders Elio Chacon and Leo Cardenas.

Visa problems, which hamper players and coaches trying to get to baseball training camps from outside of the country, teamed up with airline labor issues to keep Otero and several players from reporting on time, but the other coaches had no problems getting there and gleefully participating in Hutchinson's ambitious workout schedule. The schedule for February 28, the first day the entire squad was due, called for the players to workout from 10 a.m. to 3 p.m., with a half-hour lunch break.

"Fred Hutchinson had his Redlegs sweating this spring," *Sports Illustrated* observed. "They ran, did push-ups, ran some more, worked on fundamentals, did more running and even went to night school. Hutchinson's reasoning was simple. The Reds last year were a dead team. They finished sixth—comfortably. If they finish sixth again this season, as far as Hutchinson is concerned, they will do it uncomfortably.

"The running that took place at the end of each practice was enough to drop a tough Marine. In spring training running usually consists of a friendly jog of perhaps 50 yards across the outfield, then a leisurely walk back over the same course. Generally, the players are left to themselves: they decide when they have run enough. But at Tampa Jim Turner, the old Yankee pitching coach, stood beside the outfield fence, a counting device in his hand, his cool blue eyes surveying the drooping athletes. When some of them cut the length of the course from, say, 50 yards to 30, old Jim told them to stretch it out again. When one of them insisted that the 20 laps he was supposed to run had been completed, old Jim just smiled and said that his indicator had registered only 17. When the running was finally over and the exhausted athletes walked to the clubhouse 100 yards away, they looked as if they would never make it."

"Yeah, I'd say things are a little different this spring," O'Toole told reporters.

On several days, the work didn't end with the end of the workouts. Fundamentals such as hitting cutoff men also were primary focuses of several night classes convened by Hutchinson in Cincinnati's 1961 spring training. They were mostly closed to the media, except for one newspaper photo showing

Fred Hutchinson puts his players through rigorous exercise during spring training.

the skipper operating a film projector. He also diagrammed on a blackboard the proper ways to execute rundowns and pickoff plays and which players should be backing up which bases in different situations.

The camp looked more like one Vince Lombardi might have run for the NFL Green Bay Packers than a baseball camp. The only things missing were helmets, shoulder pads, footballs, and tackling dummies.

"Hutch was a good teacher," O'Toole recalled. "The night classes were game situation fundamentals—don't miss the cut-off man—that could lose a ballgame. Actually, it seemed like there was always some innovation."

If nothing else, the innovative approaches and increased focus on conditioning and fundamentals broke up the usual monotony and stirred some excitement in the Cincinnati camp. The off-season deals had left many of the players unsure about what to expect when they showed up at aging Plant Field, which had been built by Henry B. Plant in 1899 as an area to provide activities for guests staying at his Tampa Bay Hotel. The Reds worked out at Plant Field before moving to Al Lopez Field for Grapefruit League exhibition games, clearing the way for Cincinnati's minor league teams to start their camps.

"For a minute, I thought I had the wrong camp," outfielder Gus Bell said shortly after arriving for spring training. "There sure are a whole lot of fellows here I don't know."

"When we went to spring training, you would wait to see who's coming through the door," Maloney said.

Several players expected the faces to change as camp progressed. Going into camp, general manager Bill DeWitt believed Hutchinson's biggest challenge would be developing a second base combination out of the mix of Cardenas, Chacon, Eddie Kasko, and Jim Baumer. Cardenas, twenty-two by then, was generally regarded as an outstanding defensive shortstop, but he'd hit just .232 in forty-eight games with the Reds in 1960 after being called up from Jersey City of the International League on July 24. Cardenas replaced Chacon, twenty-four, who'd made the Reds out of spring training in 1960, but he hit just .181 in forty-nine games before being sent to Jersey City.

The twenty-eight-year-old Kasko had been named the Reds Most Valuable Player in 1960 after hitting .292 while playing mostly third base, which automatically became Gene Freese's spot after DeWitt acquired him from the Chicago White Sox in a December trade.

Kasko, who played with Freese for St. Louis in 1958, also was a possibility at second base, though the favorite going into camp was Baumer, a former prospect who'd broken into the major leagues at the age of eighteen with the White Sox in 1949. He appeared in eight games with Chicago that year and then didn't return to the majors until 1961 at the age of thirty.

Baumer had been picked by the Reds out of the Pittsburgh system in the 1960 Rule 5 draft after hitting .293 at Salt Lake City the previous season. Salt Lake City general manager Eddie Leishman was on record as believing the right-handed-hitting Oklahoman could hit .260 and drive in runs at the major league level.

"I think I can do better than that," Baumer said.

"He'll have to play his way off this ballclub," DeWitt said.

Catcher Hal Bevan, who played for Seattle against Baumer in the Pacific Coast League in 1960, also respected Baumer's potential.

"He's one of the most consistent players I've ever seen," said Bevan, a PCL All-Star in 1960. "He does a good job every day."

Others were less impressed. Rumors of trades swirled around camp the entire spring. One had relief pitcher Jim Brosnan being dealt to San Francisco for his former Cardinals teammate, second baseman Don Blasingame. Well-traveled relief pitcher Bill Henry fully expected to not open the season with Cincinnati.

"I thought sure I would be traded during the winter," said Henry, who believed he'd fallen behind left-hander Marshall Bridges in the bullpen pecking order. "In fact, I began getting the feeling last summer. If you'll remember, I wasn't used much after the All-Star Game. I was going badly, and the other fellow got a chance and made good."

Bridges, a drawling Mississippian from Jackson known as "Fox" and "Sheriff," had gone 4–0 with a 1.07 ERA in fourteen games after being picked by the Reds from St. Louis on waivers in August, but Henry still possessed a crackling fastball that made him too valuable to give up—at least, for the time being.

Bevan was among a corps of inexperienced candidates to back up incumbent Ed Bailey behind the plate. Though thirty years old, he had a total of twenty-one games of major-league experience, none since appearing in three games for Kansas City in 1955.

The other choices were John Edwards, a Columbus, Ohio, native and Ohio State University student, and twenty-six-year-old Jerry Zimmerman, a former Boston prospect who'd been signed by the Reds as a free agent in September

1959. Neither player had appeared in a major league game. Edwards, a chemical engineering student, reported late because he was finishing the semester.

The rest of the regulars seemed to be fairly settled. Coleman, who won the Southern Association Triple Crown with Mobile in 1959, looked ready for full-time duty at first base after hitting .324 in ninety-three games with Seattle and .271 with six home runs and thirty-two RBI in sixty-six games with the Reds in 1960. He might've opened the 1960 season with the Reds if he hadn't struggled through a miserable spring training.

"There's sure a big difference in him this spring," Hutchinson said about Coleman. "He's relaxed—not all tensed up."

Dick Sisler, who managed Coleman at Seattle in 1960, believed that the raves from winning the Triple Crown undermined the big, affable first baseman.

"He tried to justify all of the publicity he got, and the pressure got to him," Sisler said.

Pinson and Robinson were destined to hold down two of the three outfield spots, with Bell and Post battling for right field after combining to hit thirty-one home runs in 1960.

Also in the outfield mix was Jerry Lynch, though it was more likely that he would resume the role of primary pinch-hitter for which he'd already become famous. The left-handed batter, known for his aggressive approach, set the National League's single-season record for pinch-hit appearances with seventy-six in 1960—beating the record of seventy-five set by Sam "Sambo" Leslie for the New York Giants in 1932—and turned in nineteen hits, three short of Leslie's record. Lynch also drew eight walks.

Other than the middle infield situation, Hutchinson

focused on the pitching, especially the rotation. Purkey, invariably described by sportswriters as "the handsome changeup artist," had led the team with seventeen wins and a .607 winning percentage in 1960 despite possessing less-than-overpowering stuff. The Pittsburgh native had good size and could occasionally uncork a fastball with some speed on it, but he depended more on style than on substance. He also liked to mix in knuckleballs, which would make his fastball look even more imposing.

O'Toole was coming off a 12–12 season in just his second year in the majors and third in professional baseball. He had won six of his last ten decisions after getting married on July 2, still making his scheduled start on July 3 at Chicago, which he lost, falling to 6–8.

The newly acquired Jay, because of his potential and what the Reds gave up to get him, was penciled in for a third starting slot, but after him, the competition was wide open.

One frontrunner was the immensely talented Maloney, who wouldn't turn twenty-one until June 2. Maloney had been called up to the Reds during a massive reshuffling toward the end of July in 1960. He made the jump from Double-A Nashville, where he'd gone 14–5 and been picked to play in the all-star game, an appearance he couldn't make because, by then, he was with the Reds.

Almost simultaneously, Coleman was brought in from Triple-A Seattle, where he'd put together an all-star half-season, and Cardenas was called up from Triple-A Jersey City.

Maloney suffered through the expected growing pains, going 2–6 with a 4.64 ERA in eleven games, ten of them starts. Still, he showed signs of the dominant pitcher everybody expected him to become. One was his 5–0 complete-game win over Philadelphia on September 24.

"Altogether, six guys got called up to get their feet wet in the middle of the 1960 season," Maloney recalled. "I just knew that I'd gotten a taste of the big leagues and had a chance to stay on the team going to spring training."

Maloney may have been the most famous of the youngsters. He'd been a hotly pursued prospect after an outstanding career at Fresno High School, where he hit .310, .340, and .500 in his last three seasons and .485 in an American Legion tournament, in which he was named the outstanding player, while playing for Fresno Post No. 4 in 1957. There were as many teams that wanted him to play shortstop as wanted him to pitch, even after he put together a stretch of nineteen consecutive no-hit innings for Fresno City College.

Maloney often has been described as a "bonus baby," but he wasn't one in the traditional sense—a group that includes Joey Jay and Dodgers left-hander Sandy Koufax. Teams that signed these prospects for significant bonus money were forced to keep them on their major-league rosters for at least two seasons. The idea was to prevent teams with higher economic resources from throwing tons of money at all of the best prospects and then burying them in the minor leagues while keeping teams with less money from getting a chance to acquire them.

"I signed for a bonus," Maloney said. "When Koufax signed, if you got more than a certain amount, you had to be on a major-league roster for two years. They did away with that by the time I signed. A bunch of teams were after me to sign. The Reds worked me out in 1958 at Seals Stadium (the first home of the Giants when they moved from New York to San Francisco).

"The night I graduated from high school, I could've signed with several teams for anywhere from $30,000 to $60,000.

The team had high hopes for talented young Jim Maloney.

I also had a scholarship to [the University of] California. My dad, Earl, was sort of my agent.

"Baltimore flew me out to Kansas City. Paul Richards was the general manger. I could've signed as an infielder or a pitcher. Baltimore offered $30,000, but it broke in the papers that they offered $150,000, and my dad didn't like that. The Reds flew me from Kansas City to Crosley Field for a workout.

"We didn't have much money, so we were asking $75,000 to $100,000. We didn't get it, so I went back to school at Fresno City College, but I didn't like it. There was all kinds of ruckus in the fraternity house, and I felt like a fish out of water. One day, we got a phone call from Gabe Paul and [scout] Bobby Mattick, trying to sign me. They offered me a major league contract. There was a minimum salary of $7,000, but they were going to guarantee me $10,000 for three years and a $50,000 bonus, so that was $80,000 guaranteed. I signed on April Fool's Day [1959], flew all the way to Tampa and finished up spring training there."

Maloney was assigned to Topeka, Kansas, of the Class B Three-I League, where the manager was Johnny Vander Meer—who, of course, had authored a memorable string of consecutive no-hit innings of his own back in 1938, when he pitched no-hitters in back-to-back starts for the Reds. Maloney moved up to Nashville the next year, where he came under the tutelage of Jim Turner.

"I got things turned around there—got off to a fast start and never looked back," Maloney recalled. "After I got called up to the Reds, I started to feel like I could play at that level, so I felt pretty good when I went home for that winter."

"Maloney doesn't necessarily have the inside track, but you'd like to see a kid like him win it," was the manager's assessment at the time. "I'll be satisfied if Jim wins ten or twelve for us. Sure, he has a lot of ability, but the major leagues are tough, and there's no substitute for experience. Jimmy will make it big eventually, I'm sure, but he has a lot to learn."

While Maloney was a frontrunner for a starting job, by no means was he a lock. Left-hander Claude Osteen, a local favorite from the small town of Reading, Ohio, located just north of Cincinnati, also was one of those 1960 late-July callups. Osteen was only seventeen when he made his major league debut with the Reds on July 6, 1957, but he made just three appearances that season and two in 1959 before going 0–1 with a 5.03 ERA in twenty games, including three starts, in 1960.

Also in the mix was right-hander Jay Hook, for whom time was running out. Baseball had been waiting for years as Hook decided which course he wanted his life to take. Pitching was one option, especially after the Waukegan, Illinois, native signed on August 17, 1957, for one of the largest bonuses ever paid to a pitcher. Hook, in fact, was among the traditional bonus babies from that era. He joined the Reds on September 2 and made his second big league start on September 29 and pitched five hitless innings in Milwaukee against a Braves team that would go on to win the World Series.

Hook teased the Reds with occasional performances of that caliber over the next three seasons, just enough to keep the franchise hopeful of seeing its investment pay off, but he also seemed distracted by his other option. A very intelligent man out of Northwestern University, Hook graduated in 1959 with a Bachelor's degree in mechanical engineering. He would earn a Master's degree in thermodynamics in 1964, prompting him to retire from baseball and take a job with Chrysler.

Hook's career conflict didn't go unnoticed by his teammates.

"What do you think of the academic quality of the Engineering School at the University of Cincinnati?" he asked relief pitcher Jim Brosnan, a conversation recounted in *Pennant Race*, Brosnan's diary of the 1961 season. Hook and Brosnan were aboard the team bus in St. Louis on their way to Hook's first start of the season.

"I no more knew the answer to that question than a girl hop-scotch player would know how to handle Warren Spahn's curve, so I paused, pseudo-sagely, and said, 'One of the best in the country.'

"Hook nodded, saying, 'I've got to start a lab project somewhere. My whole summer is just about wasted, don't you see? Research-wise, that is.'

"'Sorry baseball's interfering with your career,' I mumbled.

"'How about researching twenty-seven hitters for tonight's game,' I thought to ask, but held my tongue, foregoing such mundane matters. Maybe Hook relaxes before a game by planning his future."

Barely on the Reds' radar going into spring training was Ken Hunt, a big right-hander from Ogden, Utah, who had struck out twenty-one batters in one game, averaging two per inning, and thrown two no-hitters in high school. He also was an all-state basketball player and attended Brigham Young University before signing with the Reds in 1958. He went a combined 5–16 in his first two seasons before finding the key in 1960 with Columbia, South Carolina, of the Class A South Atlantic League, also known as the Sally League. Hunt helped Columbia to the regular-season championship while leading the league with sixteen wins, a .727 winning percentage, and 221 strikeouts. He was the only unanimous pick for the league's post-season all-star team and was named by the National Association of Baseball Writers as the pitcher on the all-star team for all Class A-level leagues. That performance earned an invitation as a non-roster player to Cincinnati's spring training camp.

One of the reasons Hutchinson and Turner imposed workouts more strenuous than normal on the team—especially the pitchers—early in the spring training was they wanted to make sure they did everything they could to get the team ready for the regular season.

"We'll hit that running hard," Hutchinson promised. "We'll run and run and run. That's what spring training is for— to get the body in shape. I want to be sure they're ready when the season starts. After Opening Day, we go to St. Louis and then to the [West Coast] for games with San Francisco and Los Angeles, so we don't figure to have any postponements."

Instead, it was Hunt who got the early jump in the competition for the opening in the rotation, starting with an overpowering performance against the Chicago White Sox early in the Grapefruit League schedule. He impressed White Sox broadcaster Ralph Kiner, who led the National League in home runs for seven consecutive seasons from 1946 through 1952.

"The kid sure looked good, and what impressed me the most was the way he changed speeds," Kiner said. "Usually, a youngster like that will go out and just blow the ball in, but this Hunt, while he can really fire the ball, pitched with the poise of a veteran and depends greatly on changing speeds."

"Eyes blinked in disbelief when Hunt, displaying all of the poise and pitching savvy of a veteran, mowed down the Chicago White Sox with ridiculous ease," reported Earl Lawson of the *Cincinnati Post and Times-Star.* "By Opening Day, he had convinced manager Fred Hutchinson that his initial performance was no fluke and he was signed to a Reds contract. He could throw the heck out of the ball."

Hunt actually was one of the few bright spots for the Reds that spring. Despite the extra-long workouts and night classes, the team was consistently hampered by physical and mental errors throughout the twenty-three-game Grapefruit League schedule. They won just eight games before leaving Tampa— and looked bad doing it.

"Do these guys play this way in the summer?" DeWitt wondered aloud late in March. "I was misled, signing these players before I saw them play."

Hutchinson's frustration grew as the team blundered its way through the exhibition schedule.

"I don't like losing, but I'm not real concerned, because we have been getting good performances from the pitchers we expect to use," the manager said after the Reds fell to 1–5. "Our biggest trouble is we're giving away two or three runs per game."

Al Lopez Field—where the Reds
readied for their season.

His patience, though, was already wearing thin, which became apparent just three days later, when he threatened to start fining players for mistakes.

"If it takes a fine to get them to remember things they've been practicing since spring training began, then that's what they'll get," he told writers.

His observation one day later, after yet another humiliating performance?

"I rant and rave and it seems as if they just don't give a damn."

From an anonymous player the writers learned that a come-from-behind win over Milwaukee on March 19 saved the Reds from an extra workout.

"I understand that, if we had lost that game to the Braves on Sunday, Hutch was going to make us stay and work out after it was over," the player was quoted as saying, a harbinger of a disciplinary tool Hutchinson didn't entirely forget and eventually would put to use.

Progress was further hampered by the usual assortment of training camp aches and pains, including sore arms that sidelined Maloney and Baumer, as well as Frank Robinson. None of the ailments was serious, as Jerry Lynch observed about Maloney.

"His arm's feeling a little better every time Hunt pitches," Lynch joked to reporters.

All of that took a back seat on March 28, when the team learned of the death of Powel Crosley at his home in Cincinnati. In the days before e-mails and cellphones, news didn't travel quite as quickly.

"On spring break, I went to Florida," remembered Bill DeWitt Jr., son of the new general manager. "The Reds were going to play in Miami against Baltimore. I had some buddies. I called and said leave us some tickets. We drove there and went to the game. They said the game was cancelled. We said, 'Why?' It was a beautiful day. How could that be? It turned out Powel Crosley had died. That's how I found out. He had died and they cancelled the game."

Crosley was buried two days later at Spring Grove Cemetery in Cincinnati. National League president Warren Giles, brought to Cincinnati by Crosley as the Reds general manager in 1937, and DeWitt were on hand. The franchise was among Crosley's assets that were transferred to a charitable organization he'd set up known as the Crosley Foundation.

The team honored Crosley's memory by wearing black armbands on their jersey sleeves for the entire 1961 season—which wasn't easy, since the team wore vest-type, sleeveless jerseys. The late owner's memory was honored with a black stripe that encircled the edge of the left shoulder.

Losing 1–0 to the Yankees on April 2 left the Reds with a 7–14 spring record. They had cut their roster to twenty-seven players, one under the twenty-eight with which teams were allowed to play the first month of the season at the time. They split the next two games, with Jay throwing seven strong innings in a win over the Phillies in Cincinnati's Florida finale—an indication of things to come for the new Reds pitcher.

"The biggest disappointment I've had this spring?" Hutchinson echoed a question. "I guess it's the fact that we haven't done better in the won and loss column. I'll have to agree that we're playing lousy ball. We haven't been making any sensational plays, and we've been lousing up some of the routine ones. I've tried a lot of things, but so far, I haven't hit upon the right remedy. Sure, the guys may be a little tired, but they should be able to knuckle down to the job three hours a day. Hell, spring training should even be fun for the younger fellows."

Most vexing was the lack of a clear-cut answer at second base. Hutchinson had decided a few days earlier that he would open the season with Kasko at shortstop and Baumer at second base, though he was by no means convinced that he'd hit upon the final solution. Baumer finished the spring with a .214 batting average and three home runs.

"Some players take a long time to come around in the spring, but we've been in training six weeks now," Hutchinson said. "How long can it take? Baumer plays a couple of good games, then he lets you down."

The concern was so prevalent that the Reds were rumored to be continuing talks with the Giants and willing to settle for Joe Amalfitano or Jose Pagan.

The Reds left Tampa, but spring training wasn't over. They were scheduled to barnstorm north with the Braves, playing a series of exhibition games along the way.

The trip served as a shakedown cruise for the next step in the career of Avery Robbins, who'd joined the team as traveling secretary shortly before Grapefruit League play got under way. Robbins replaced John Murdough, who'd been promoted to business manager.

Robbins was a native of Upper Arlington, Ohio, a suburb of Columbus, who saw his first major league game when his father took him to Crosley Field. Robbins played baseball, football, and basketball in high school, helping his baseball team reach the state semifinals, where they met a team that included a first baseman named Glenn "Bo" Schembechler, who later became a legendary football coach at Miami (Ohio) University and the University of Michigan.

Robbins started his college career at Miami (Ohio), where he played freshman football and basketball and renewed acquaintances with Schembechler. He later transferred to Ohio State, graduating with a degree in business administration.

Robbins got into baseball with the Columbus minor league team, affiliated at the time with the Pittsburgh Pirates. After four years in Columbus, he spent four years as general manager of the Tampa Tarpons, where Johnny Vander Meer was the manager.

The job of a major league traveling secretary at that time involved, of course, making travel arrangements with airlines, bus companies, and hotels, as well as working with the home team on getting accurate turnstile counts and taking care of the checks that represented the visiting team's share of the gate receipts. Travel arrangements included the writers who covered the Reds and usually traveled with the team.

Unlike today, when equipment managers and media relations directors travel with their teams, the traveling secretary also was usually responsible for making sure the equipment got from city to city and dealt with the media on the road.

"We were pretty much responsible for other situations that might come up," added Robbins.

Traveling secretaries were responsible then—and are now—for handling players' tickets. Each player receives a certain number of free tickets for each game, and it's the traveling secretary's job to make sure the tickets get to the right people, who usually pick them up at a will call window. That part of the job has its own problems.

"It can be challenging," Robbins said. "It has a tendency to be. As you travel, you frequently come into the home

territory of various guys on the clubs. I remember Jim O'Toole
had quite a clan indeed in Chicago."

Robbins's first exposure to the Reds was being introduced
around by Murdough.

"He walked me over to the clubhouse an introduced me
to various guys," Robbins said. "Murdough introduced me to
Hutch and the coaches. I remember meeting Wally Post. That
aspect was kind of interesting. I was kind of the same age as guys
like Post and Gus Bell—around thirty-one or thirty-two years
old. They were famous people when I got to know them."

Planning ahead is imperative to making the traveling
secretary's job work, and Robbins was relieved to learn that
Murdough already had taken care of many of the details of
that season's trips, but he still found himself scrambling many
times to handle emergencies—almost from his first day on the
job. His first plane flight with the team couldn't get to Tampa
because of fog and had to return to Miami.

As the team prepared to leave on its trip north, the chartered bus scheduled to take them from the Floridian Hotel, the
spring training headquarters, to the train depot didn't show up.
After the Reds arrived in Jacksonville, the bus from the train depot lost its brakes, and the team had to wait for a replacement.

"It was a matter of learning in a hurry," he said. "We
always had that kind of stuff, and it would be my fault. You
had things like that happen. You have a bus driver get lost.
You kind of had to roll with the punches. We had 99 percent
good guys."

In Charlotte, North Carolina, as was often the case during
spring training and the trip north, the players changed into
their uniforms at their hotel and took a bus to the game. The

bus, though, headed for the airport instead of the ballpark, the driver seemingly oblivious to the odd prospect of the players traveling in their uniforms.

"You should see the flashy sports coats we play ball in," Robbins was able to joke.

Robbins also was grateful to be traveling with Donald Davidson, the long-time, near-legendary Braves traveling secretary who hadn't let being a dwarf get in the way of earning tremendous respect around baseball.

"We had not met before, and we had to become buddies in a hurry," Robbins said. "We were on that special train, playing our way north. That was a learning experience. I knew I could go to Hutch or the coaches or the newspaper guys if I needed help handling something I hadn't seen before."

One thing Robbins had learned about during his four years in Tampa was segregation, During spring training, black players weren't allowed to stay at the Floridian. Instead, they were put up in the homes of black families.

"Segregation was one of our biggest speed bumps," Robbins said. "We couldn't have black guys eat with us in the same restaurants. We couldn't stay in the better hotels in Houston [in 1962] because Hutch wouldn't break up the team. The black guys were the victims. That was a hardship. To be in a management capacity, that was tough. We would have a team dinner arranged on the way north, and some guys would go eat in black families' homes. John Murdough had worked with them previously. That was a bad aspect of it, but it was all part of the job."

The first stop for the Reds and Braves was Jacksonville, Florida, where Cincinnati beat Milwaukee 5–4 on April 5, a win tempered by the loss of Baumer for a few days after he was hit on the left wrist by a pitch. The next day, in Columbia, South Carolina, the Reds pulled out another one-run win, 6–5. The teams moved on to Charlotte, North Carolina, where O'Toole tuned up for his Opening Day start by cruising through four one-hit shutout innings, and pitcher Howie Nunn—who grew up a few hours north in Westfield—threw three shutout innings of relief and hit a thirteenth-inning home run off of much-ballyhooed rookie right-hander Tony Cloninger for a 3–2 win. The homer was Nunn's first on any level in eight seasons as a professional.

"Honest, I don't think I've come closer to fainting than I did when I saw that ball go over the fence," Nunn said.

The teams made one last stop, at Louisville, Kentucky, where they were supposed to play two games. They squeezed in the first, on Saturday, April 8, with the Reds sending ten batters to the plate during a six-run third inning against Milwaukee ace right-hander Lew Burdette on their way to a 7–5 win. The teams split up after the Sunday game was rained out, with the Reds making the short journey home to Cincinnati, where a "Meet the Reds" luncheon on April 10 would be followed the next day by the season opener.

Despite the nagging question at second base, Hutchinson was convinced even before the Reds left Florida that his team would improve on its 1960 performance.

"Our club will be better this year because of pitching alone," he said. "Of course, I'm basing that on what I'm expecting of the pitchers, not on what I've seen of them. Our pitching has been below expectations, but it's bound to get better. Our finish in the standings depends on how much better it gets. We can match the power of any club in the league, and we've got more than most of them."

Robinson had slammed eight home runs while hitting .275 during the exhibition games. Post hit .316 with seven homers, while the competitive Bell hit .301 with three homers. Pinson cranked out 33 hits for a .327 average with four homers, and Freese showed signs that his acquisition would pay off by hitting .342 with three homers. Cardenas and Chacon both hit .300 or better, and Coleman was right behind at .286 and three home runs.

Still, the Reds had finished spring training with a league-worst 12–15 record. They could take solace in knowing that the Yankees, the defending American League champions, went 9–19, a .321 winning percentage that was the worst of the spring.

Perhaps the best indication of the prospects most observers had for the Reds was that of *Cincinnati Enquirer* sports editor Lou Smith, who doubled as the lead baseball beat writer. Late in spring training, he observed, "Seven more exhibitions and then there'll be only 154 games to go."

"In the spring, I don't think the ballclub evidenced that it was going to win," Purkey said. "I don't think, realistically, you could look at that ballclub and say it was going to win the pennant."

"I don't think anybody in their right mind would think that, after the year we had in 1960, things were going to be different in 1961," said O'Toole. "Little did I know."

THREE

The Scene

When Jim O'Toole strode to the mound to start against the St. Louis Cardinals on April 11, 1961–Opening Day–professional baseball of one form or another had been played on the near-triangular lot at the northwest corner of Findlay Street and Western Avenue for seventy-seven years.

The current ballpark, Crosley Field, had opened as Redland Field in 1912–the same season Fenway Park opened in Boston. Redland was renamed in 1934 when Powel Crosley Jr. bought the franchise.

Redland Field was built in a hurry, between the 1911 and 1912 seasons at a cost of $400,000, to replace the Palace of the Fans, which occupied the same site for exactly ten years, according to *Cincinnati's Crosley Field*, by Greg Rhodes and John Erardi. Redland's original seating capacity of 20,696 had grown to 30,274 by 1961, primarily by the extension of the upper deck down both lines, and various experiments with the distances to the fences through the years had led to the current configuration: 328 feet down the left field line, 387 to center and 366 to right. Home plate was separated from the grandstand by seventy-eight feet, and looming over left-center field was the massive scoreboard that stood fifty-five feet high and was sixty-five feet wide. The height included the big Longines clock on top, flanked by two advertising signs. One was for Sixty Second Shops, a local chain of fast-food restaurants, and included an offer of $100 for any Reds player who hit the sign with a home run.

That was a nostalgic nod toward the famous Siebler Suit sign, which had been perched on top of the Superior Towel and Linen Service building across narrow York Street—which was really more of an alley—beyond the left field wall before the building was demolished after the 1960 season to make way for a parking lot. As mentioned earlier, players who hit that sign with home runs won free suits. The Sixty Second Shops sign was somewhat ironic, since it was in one of those restaurants that Frank Robinson had his infamous altercation just two months earlier.

Fans had become used to the size of the massive score-board, which was built in 1957, but the below-capacity crowd of 28,713 that showed up for Opening Day in 1961 was greet-ed by a new addition—a huge net, rising thirty feet above the left field wall and stretching forty-one feet from the scoreboard to the light tower built just behind the field-level seats in the

Crosley Field sported a new screen in left field to protect cars parked in the new lot.

extreme left-field corner. The net was another product of the team's push for increased parking at Crosley. Its purpose was to protect the cars parked in the new lot behind the left-field wall, the site previously occupied by the laundry.

Southeast of the scoreboard, overlooking right field, was the famous Sundeck–Moondeck for night games–that contained 4,500 bleacher-type seats. Tickets for Sundeck seats cost seventy-five cents–fifty cents for women on Ladies Days, of which there were nine on the 1961 home schedule. Usually, they were sold on the days of games, but they occasionally would go on sale in advance for special days.

Each of Crosley's 9,834 box seats could be purchased in advance and cost three dollars for adults, two dollars and twenty-five cents for children, and two dollars on Ladies Days. The 15,940 grandstand seats were available in advance for two dollars and twenty-five cents for adults, one dollar and fifty cents for children, and one dollar and twenty-five cents on Ladies Days. Unreserved grandstand seats could be bought on the days of games for one dollar and fifty cents for adults, seventy-five cents for children, and fifty cents on Ladies Days.

Fans in Cincinnati could buy tickets at the team's downtown ticket office, located in what then was the Union Central Building on the southwest corner of the intersection of Vine and Fourth streets. It later became known as the Central Trust Building and now is the PNC Bank Building. The team's offices also were in the Union Central Building, one block south of the Carew Tower, where former Reds general manager Warren Giles had moved the National League offices when he was named the league's president.

Tickets also could be bought at the ballpark starting two hours before the first pitch of that day's or night's game. After the 2:30 p.m. Opening Day game, afternoon single games usually were scheduled to start at 1:30, while night games didn't start until 8:05. Afternoon doubleheaders usually got under way at 1 p.m., and the first pitch for twi-night doubleheaders was scheduled for 6 p.m. The Reds had thirteen doubleheaders on their 1961 schedule, eight of them on the road. They had no twi-night doubleheaders scheduled at home, but there were two on the road, both at Los Angeles.

Fans also could order tickets by mail, paying for them with checks or money orders made out to "Cincinnati Baseball Club Company" and sent to the team's ticket office at 307

Vine Street, or they could go through Western Union. The ticket order would be telegraphed to the team, which would either hold the tickets at Crosley's Window No. 9 or mail them to an address specified by the buyer.

Another option was visiting one of the nineteen out-of-town tickets agencies, which were located anywhere from The Style Shop in Celina, Ohio, to Imfeld's Music Store in Hamilton to American Legion Post No. 39 in Winchester, Indiana, to Humphrey's Southside Pharmacy in Huntington, West Virginia. Fans in Lebanon, Ohio, who wanted to make sure Bashford Sporting Goods was open before leaving home to get tickets could call the store at 31761. The Style Shop's number was even easier to remember—2537.

Even though Crosley Field was most famously located at Findlay and Western, the ballpark's main entrance actually was located in a two-story area farther west on Findlay Street, closer to its intersection with McLean Street. The entrance, which was attached to the ballpark behind the plate and included some offices on the second floor, looked almost like an afterthought, jutting out from the grandstand. What looked from some angles like a chimney sticking out of its roof was actually an elevator providing access to the press box perched on the roof.

Fans could learn all of this information—and much more—by spending fifty cents for a team yearbook. The 1961 edition had an electric blue cover with the smiling Mr. Red icon, sporting a handlebar mustache and old-style white pillbox cap with two red stripes, chasing down a "fly ball" which actually was a white circle with the year inside of it.

Information inside started with photos of the team's administrators—including business manager John Murdough, publicity director Hank Zureick, traveling secretary Avery Robbins, and farm director Phil Seghi—before going on to the meat. That would be detailed information and photos of the team members considered by fans to be most important: vice president and general manager Bill DeWitt, manager Fred Hutchinson, his coaches and players.

The information about the uniformed members of the team included lifetime statistics and biographical details such as ancestry, hair and eye color, marital status, wife's and children's names and birthdates, and home addresses.

Yes, home addresses.

Hutchinson got a deserved full page, dominated by a photo of him with his wife and two of their four children. Many of the players' and coaches' entries included family photos, shot at the previous season's Family Night.

Hutchinson married the former Patricia Finley on April 24, 1943. Two of their four children were included in the photo: Patty, twelve at the start of the 1961 season, and six-year-old Joe. Hutchinson's ancestry was Scotch-Irish. He had brown hair and eyes. Golf was his hobby. His winter address was Bradenton Beach, Florida.

Frank Robinson? Born Aug. 31, 1935, at Beaumont, Texas. Ancestry—Negro. Marital status—Single. Winter address—3549 Alaska Ave., Cincinnati.

That was the kind of information dreamed of by kids such as Dave Parker and Bruce Johnston, but they probably couldn't afford the yearbook. If they had enough money to buy any type of guide, it probably was limited to the less expensive scorecard for that day's game.

Parker, who would be named 1978 National League Most Valuable Player as the Pittsburgh Pirates right fielder and be named to the 1985 and 1986 NL All-Star teams as the Reds right fielder, turned ten years old in 1961 while living virtually in the shadow of Crosley Field with his family—father, Richard, mother, Dorothy, sister, Bessie, and younger brother, Jimmy—on the first floor of a six-family, three-story apartment building on Poplar Street.

"We lived on the first floor, thank goodness," Parker recalls. "There was a toilet on each level, and that was unusual. Now that I think about it, all the luxuries they have today, and we're sharing a toilet with another family. We had three stories—two families on each floor.

"People would sit out on their steps listening to the games. It was one of those things where the village raised the child. I knew, if I did something wrong, I'd get spanked by them, and then they'd tell my mother, and I'd get spanked again. It was one of those kinds of communities that you wish you had today with all the tragedy.

"It was nice for a young kid to grow up down on Poplar. We played stickball against the Crosley Field wall."

Roger Kahn, the author of several baseball-oriented books, including the masterful *The Boys of Summer*, describes growing up in Brooklyn and listening to Dodger games on the radio. When radio announcer Red Barber—who broke into broadcasting major league baseball games with the Reds in 1934—would describe a Dodger home run, Kahn would run to his apartment window in time to hear the cheers from Ebbets Field. It was like stereo.

Parker's neighborhood, known as the West End, was similar. The family settled there after moving to Cincinnati from Mississippi when he was four years old. He remembers the impact of the Mill Creek Expressway.

"Construction made it hard to get around," he recalls. "Most of the people were employed by the post office down there—not like now. They worked in the neighborhood. It didn't have a major effect on the whole neighborhood. It made it better for us kids."

The post office Parker refers to is the bulk mail facility on Dalton Street, one block south of Crosley Field. The imposing building takes up the entire block.

Bruce Johnston couldn't see Crosley from where he and his family—mother, Joyce, older brother, David, and younger sister, Teresa—were living that summer, on the first floor of a three-story, eighteen-unit apartment building on Ravine Street in Clifton Heights, about a football field south of McMillan Avenue. If he walked a couple of blocks west to Fairview Park, he was treated to a panoramic view of the entire Mill Creek Valley, including Crosley Field. It looked close enough to touch.

"My father died when we were very young," said Johnston, now a senior scientist for Procter & Gamble, Cincinnati's household products giant. "I was seven, so basically, it was my mother, my brother, and I. I had a younger sister, three years old. My mother wasn't interested in sports. My brother was two years older, and he and I were the sports nuts in our family.

"I was nine years old in 1961. My brother was eleven. Both he and I played baseball at that age. We played Knothole for the Carson Masonic Lodge. I played second base and then catcher."

Knothole was, and is, the Greater Cincinnati version of Little League.

"We got our first baseball gloves with Top Value stamps," he recalled. Top Value and S&H Green stamps were issued by retailers to shoppers. The more merchandise the shoppers bought, the more stamps they received. The stamps were pasted into books, which could be redeemed for items such as baseball gloves.

"When we were nine to eleven years old, we went to the ballgame ourselves," Johnston continued. "We would take the old Cincinnati Transit buses, the old yellow and brown buses, down there. We used to always try to get doubleheaders. They played a lot more of them. We could see twice as much baseball for the money, and then we'd get the program, keep the box score.

"We were very excited about going to the games. This was something we would plan. After my father passed away, we were, well, to say poor would be putting it mildly. We didn't have much in spendable assets, so when we got to go, it was a really big deal for us. My mother was good at managing the budget, and occasionally she would treat us. We never had much extra. I don't want to make it sound like we had a poor childhood. We didn't. We had a very rich childhood, although meager in terms of finances. We'd do little odd jobs, like kids back in those days, to earn money—maybe wash cars for somebody, help clean out a garage, work in the yard.

"It was a twenty-minute bus ride. You figure the stops we were making, it wasn't exactly a direct route. They didn't have direct routes. We'd take the bus down to Government Square and then transfer.

"You had the characters around the stadium that you had to keep your eyes out for, the hangers-on on the outside. We were told not to talk to strangers—all the standard things—but at the same time, because my father died when we were very young, both my brother and I were much more mature than other kids our age. It was a different situation.

"It would be an all-day affair. We'd get down there very early—usually well in advance of batting practice. Back in those days, we always ha either grandstand or Moon Deck-Sun Deck tickets because those were the least expensive, but even with those inexpensive tickets, unlike today, you could mingle anywhere in the stadium before it started. We'd go down and get autographs from the players around the dugout. Back then, most of them were very free in giving you their autographs, unlike today. Of course, they didn't make as much money.

"We always had to buy a program. I think it was only ten or fifteen cents. We always went there in hopes of getting a ball, like all kids do. The balls we would buy were these old sawdust-filled things. You hit them a couple of times and they were lopsided, so if you got a ball down at Crosley Field, we'd wear that out playing with it. That was a big deal, getting the real McCoy.

"We'd have the typical food—hot dog and soft drink, popcorn. I wasn't a Cracker Jack fan."

Among the snacks available at Crosley Field was popcorn in a four-sided cardboard container meant to be used as a megaphone. Wax paper fastened with a rubberband kept the popcorn contained until it was ready to be eaten. One of the side panels was left blank for autographs—kind of the Swiss Army knife of snack packages.

"We were avid sports fans, just sitting there taking in the game, keeping track of all the box scores and hoping like heck the Reds would win," Johnston said. "I can remember Frank Robinson hitting some late-in-the-game home runs over the scoreboard.

"I still remember the smell of the place. You didn't have any responsibilities—just get there and get back safe."

The Johnston boys didn't only follow baseball, though the Reds certainly were their top interest. Cincinnati sports in the early 1960s were dominated by the Reds and the University of Cincinnati basketball team, which won the first of back-to-back NCAA championships in 1961. Xavier University also was enjoying a successful run. The Musketeers reached the NCAA Tournament in 1961, the second of back-to-back seventeen-win seasons.

The only other professional team in town at the time was the National Basketball Association Cincinnati Royals, led by star rookie and UC product Oscar Robertson, who'd graduated as college basketball's career scoring leader.

Autumn, especially with the Reds not having reached the World Series since 1940 and pro football still eight years away, was left to the college football played by UC, Xavier, and Miami (Ohio).

"We always got the newspaper at home," Bruce Johnston said. "My brother and I would go through the sports sections." The Johnston boys followed the Reds closely enough to know that the time between the end of the 1960 season and the start of the 1961 campaign wasn't a typical off-season. Bruce actually recognized the name of the team's new general manager.

"I knew that was a great baseball name who'd been involved in several franchises," he recalled. He also knew that trading McMillan was a big deal. "I knew that McMillan was one of the best shortstops of his day," he said. "That left us with Leo Cardenas, who always reminded me of a grasshopper—such a slight figure, very thin."

Dave Parker didn't get to go to many games, at least until they started letting fans in free, usually around the seventh inning, or when he could sneak into the ballpark. He swears it wasn't his idea. He was just following his older brother.

"They had the Sun Deck and an entry for trucks and a wrought iron gate for fans," he recalled. "That was the place. The gate would only go so far down, and that was the place to roll under. That was the time when I was a follower."

He was inventive enough to realize he didn't have to work in the ballpark, as he did when he grew older, to make Reds games pay off.

"It was great for me," he said. "I used to do the hustles. I would go over and collect the balls they hit out of the stadium and sell them when the crowds started coming. It was a great hustle for kids my age–a way to make money for candy bars and chips and pop. I loved it.

"Guys parked their cars a street over, two streets over, and we'd tell them, 'I'll watch your car for a dollar,' and the guy would think about the investment of having his car watched or come back with the windshield busted. We were good kids. We just sold our services. We never did anything like that. We would really watch the cars."

Remember, the village was raising the children.

"When I became a teenager, I worked at Crosley Field, and whenever my favorite players would come up to hit, whatever I was selling came to a stop," Parker went on. "I used to like to see Willie McCovey hit and Willie Stargell–the big, powerful left-handers."

Parker matured into a six-foot-five, 230-pound, big, powerful left-hander who hit 339 home runs in a nineteen-year career. As a youngster, his favorite Reds were, of course, outfielders–Frank Robinson and Vada Pinson. He liked their style off the field as much as their talent on the field.

"Vada and Frank would come to the ballpark, and they both had white Thunderbirds with porthole windows and red interiors," he recalled. "I think I made up my mind then that this is what I wanted to do, watching them on a day-in and day-out basis.

"I used to love to see Vada. Vada would run, but he would shuffle his feet. He didn't have a big leg kick, but he'd be flat-out flying."

Parker wasn't content to wait for batters to hit foul balls into the stands or hit them out of the park, where he would have to fight other entrepreneurs for the commodity.

"When I made the big leagues, I tried to make Frank Robinson remember," he said, smiling at the memory. "All the kids were around Frank getting autographs. Well, I'm looking in his car and I see gloves and balls, and I said, 'Give me something I can play with,' and Frank gave me a glove. I tried to make him remember. I tried so hard, but he couldn't remember me. Vada Pinson said, 'I remember you. You were the bad green-eyed boy.'"

Robinson and Pinson also were two of Johnston's favorites.

"Of course, Frank Robinson was a Hall of Famer, but I always thought Vada Pinson should have been," he said. "He was one of my favorite players. He was really fast–a very good outfielder with a good arm, batted for average with good speed on the basepaths, kind of a Willie Mays-type player, but not with that much pop in the bat. Of course, Willie Mays is probably the greatest ballplayer I ever saw in my lifetime–a complete ballplayer in every respect."

Johnston appreciated multi-talented players.

"One of my favorite players was Jim Maloney," he said.

"Not only was he was one of our better pitchers, but he was also a pitcher who could hit—hit for power, something very few pitchers today can do."

Maloney hit .379 with a home run and four runs batted in during the 1961 season.

Johnston and Parker were two of several of the Crosley Field regulars of the era, but they were just two of thousands of fans—faces in the crowd. More noticeable were some of the faces and voices that became as much a part of the experience as the sound of cracks of bats smacking baseballs and the smell of bratwursts cooking in the concession stands.

One sound that couldn't be missed was the voice of Paul Sommerkamp, who was starting his second decade as the team's public-address announcer. Sommerkamp, a memorable figure with a distinctive baritone voice who smoked cigarettes with a holder, like Franklin Delano Roosevelt, worked from a seat on the field next to the visitors' dugout on the first base side of the diamond. He'd already become known for his style of announcing the teams' starting lineups. He would announce each player's name, pause a couple of seconds, and then repeat the last name.

"I started doing that in 1954, when Ted Kluszewski, with his home run power, became so popular," Sommerkamp recalled years later. "When I got to the number four spot and announced his name, the roar was so loud and long that the next hitter, whether it was Jim Greengrass or Wally Post, was drowned out. So I came up with the idea of pausing a second or two after the name, then repeating it so the fans would get the idea that was enough, then go to the next guy. It worked, so I stuck with it."

Long-time Reds public address
announcer Paul Sommerkamp

A few younger fans had fun with Sommerkamp's novel
approach. After he announced the name the first time, they
would respond, "Who?" After the repeat, they'd come back
with "Oh."

Other sights and sounds were experienced by fans without easily putting faces to them. One was the Crosley Field
organ, which had a new man at the keyboard for the 1961
season. Webb Bond had replaced Ronnie Dale.

Another was the lush green grass of the manicured field,
a welcome sight after walking through the narrow portals that
led from the dark concourse to the grandstand. The "field"

in Crosley Field and, later, the entire facility had been the domain of the Schwab family almost since the founding of the franchise. Mathias C. "Matty" Schwab started working for his father in 1894, eventually taking over as park superintendent. Lenny Schwab, Matty's brother, was Crosley's head grounds-keeper. Matty's grandson, Mike Dolan, was being groomed to continue the family trade when Matty retired at the age of eighty-three in 1963.

A man with a name just as recognizable—whose face was probably as unknown as Schwab's—was long-time Reds equipment manager Ray "Chesty" Evans, who was outfitting the team in uniforms with a look that was slightly different from the preceding three seasons. The home uniforms still were white with vest-type jerseys and red pinstripes. The home caps remained white with a red bill and red pinstripes on the crown—looking like a baseball version of a train engineer's cap and, perhaps, the ugliest caps in baseball history. The road uniforms still were, essentially, identical to the home except with solid gray replacing the white-and-red-pinstripes from cap to socks.

The differences were a red wishbone "C" trimmed in white and enclosing the word "REDS" in red letters outlined in white—all on a navy blue background—had replaced the simple red wishbone "C" on the left side of the chest. The player's number remained on the right side of the chest.

The road jerseys had eliminated the wishbone "C" completely, substituting "Cincinnati" in red letters arched across the chest. The player's number was moved from the right side of the chest to the lower left section of the jersey.

There were no names on the backs of the uniforms.

Fans watching on television also were going to get the chance that season to put a face with a voice that had become familiar around the area. Ed Kennedy already had more than ten years under his belt as a Cincinnati radio sports broadcaster, including two as the play-by-play announcer for the Royals, when he was named to replace George Bryson and join Frank McCormick as the broadcast team for the fifty-three Reds games–twenty-three in color–that were to be televised by WLWT.

Kennedy, forty-three at the time he joined the Reds television broadcasts, graduated from Covington Catholic High School. He reportedly played college basketball at Xavier, though he never lettered, and played semi-pro baseball. He also earned a Bachelor's degree from the University of Cincinnati, a Master's from the University of Chicago and a Doctorate in Education from Columbia University in New York, which he put to use working for ten years in the Cincinnati Public Schools and as a principal in the suburban Madeira school district.

The married father of six worked part-time at WCPO radio for four years and WKRC for twelve, including seven as program director. He hosted the station's "Sports Vue" program for ten years as well as occasionally filling in on radio broadcasts of Reds games, carried at the time on WKRC.

"I'm going to have to feel my way along at first until I get used to the difference between radio and TV," Kennedy said about adjusting to working before cameras. "I'm not going to try to fool the audience. People who care enough to watch the game know what they're seeing."

Kennedy's broadcast partner was about as popular in Cincinnati as beer. McCormick had played first base on the Reds teams that won the National League championship in 1939 and World Series in 1940, when he was named the NL's

Most Valuable Player. The New York City native and nine-time All-Star hit .301 in his ten-year career with Cincinnati, and he already had three years of Reds television experience when joined by Kennedy. They would spend eight years together, the longest Cincinnati baseball television tandem until George Grande and Chris Welsh spent eighteen seasons together, ending that partnership after the 2009 season.

The primary sponsors for televised games were Hudepohl beer, Sohio gasoline, and Colgate toothpaste. One of Hudepohl's rival local breweries, Burger beer, was the naming sponsor of the Reds radio broadcasts, which remained in the capable hands of Waite Hoyt, the immensely popular play-by-play man and raconteur who might've been the most popular aspect of Reds baseball at the time. If Paul Sommerkamp was the voice of Crosley Field, then Waite Hoyt was the voice of the Reds. The 1961 season would be Hoyt's

Legendary Reds broadcaster Waite Hoyt is flanked by Ken Hunt (left) and Gene Freese (right).

twentieth on Reds' radio, all of them with Burger as the primary sponsor. The network was advertised as the Burger Beer Radio Network.

"We used to love listening to Waite Hoyt, especially during rain delays," Bruce Johnston recalled fondly.

Much of Hoyt's popularity was due to his ability to keep listeners tuned in during rain delays with stories from his playing days with the New York Yankees, when he ran with hard-living Babe Ruth and kept up with the larger-than-life slugger. Hoyt, a Brooklyn native, actually followed Ruth's footsteps to the Yankees. Ruth was traded by the Boston Red Sox to the Yankees after the 1919 season. Hoyt, a right-handed pitcher, was traded by the Red Sox to the Yankees after the 1920 season and ended up going 157–98 in ten seasons with New York. He also was 6–4 with a 1.83 ERA in twelve World Series games, including eleven starts, over six Yankee appearances in the Fall Classic during the Roaring '20s.

Hoyt pitched for six teams in twenty-one seasons, going 237–182—a record good enough to earn induction into the Baseball Hall of Fame after being voted in by the Veterans Committee in 1969. His record was even more remarkable considering his partying ways. Hoyt became an alcoholic, to the point that he disappeared for several days during the 1945 season, when he was broadcasting for the Reds. He eventually turned up and admitted his affliction, which led to him join Alcoholics Anonymous, and he stayed sober for the rest of his life—making his long-time association with a brewery even more interesting.

Hoyt's sobriety didn't keep him from looking at life with a sparkle in his eye, all the way up to his death in 1984. Hoyt was in his seventies when he had a chance meeting with O'Toole, his wife, Betty, and a couple of their children around the batting cage at Riverfront Stadium one day. One of O'Toole's children, upon learning that Hoyt had been a pitcher, asked what was his best pitch.

"My best pitch?" Hoyt responded. "My best pitch?" He turned to Betty O'Toole and asked, smiling, "What are you doing tonight, honey?"

When Hoyt started broadcasting for the Reds in 1942, the games were carried on three stations with three different announcers. That was cut to two during the next two seasons before becoming the exclusive property of WCPO in 1945. Hoyt worked alone while the games were on WCPO, but when WSAI bought the rights in 1955, Jack Moran joined Hoyt to handle the live pre- and post-game shows. They remained a team when WKRC took over the broadcasts in 1957 and stayed together through the 1961 season. Moran would go on to deliver sports reports on WCPO-TV, where he became known for his loud sports coats and for hosting the weekly *King of TV Bowling* show.

The broadcasters worked with other media members in the rooftop press box, which wasn't added until 1938. *Dayton Daily News* sportswriter Jim Ferguson remembers the Crosley press box as being unusual because half of it was open and the other half was air-conditioned.

"There was always a big difference of opinion on whether you wanted to be inside or outside," said Ferguson, who went on to serve as the team's media relations director from 1972 through 1990, watching thousands of games from the totally glassed-in press box at Riverfront Stadium. "Literally half of the press box was opened and half was air-conditioned. The broadcasts booths were on either end."

Ferguson started covering the Reds in 1959 and shared the duties with *Daily News* sports editor Si Burick. Other regulars were *Cincinnati Enquirer* sports editor Lou Smith and writer Bill Ford, *Cincinnati Post and Times-Star* beat writer Earl Lawson, *Hamilton Journal* sports editor Bill Moeller, *Middletown Journal* sports editor Jerry Nardiello, *Dayton Journal* sports editor Ritter Collett, and Claude Wolff of the Associated Press.

Lawson spent thirty-four years covering the Reds and was inducted into the Baseball Hall of Fame in 1986 as that year's recipient of the J.G. Taylor Spink Award, which is given annually to reward meritorious service to baseball writing. Burick had previously been honored in 1982, and Collett would receive a Spink Award in 1991.

"The *Daily News* started covering the Reds on a full-time basis in '56, when that team took off," Ferguson said. "We started covering them like a local team."

That coverage included following the team on most of the road trips.

Writers of the era still depended mostly on Western Union telegraph operators to transmit copy back to the office, especially those who worked for morning newspapers. *The Enquirer* had one operator whose first priority was that paper's copy. That operator then would move on to an afternoon paper after transmitting the *Enquirer's* copy.

"One guy was the Western Union chief," Ferguson recalled. "He'd been there for years."

Writers working for the *Dayton Daily News*, an afternoon paper at the time, had the luxury of driving back to the office and dropping off their copy.

Half of the press box wasn't the only part of Crosley Field that was air-conditioned. The 1961 yearbook touts Crosley as "the only air-cooled park in the major leagues," referring to "jet air fans" located in the rear of both the upper and lower decks. "These fans have the patented Westinghouse air injector rings and air jet straighteners built into them," the yearbook explains. "The air injector rings increases [sic] air-delivery forty per cent by incorporating side air as well as air coming in from the rear.

"The jet straighteners give the Jet fan high velocity; thus air penetration is approximately ninety feet.

"Each fan has air movement of 10,000 cubic feet of air per minute."

That level of turbulence might've wreaked havoc with popups, especially those sailing into the stands, increasing the level of difficulty for fans trying to collect a souvenir. Those who made particularly noteworthy efforts were to be rewarded under a new program started by DeWitt. Any fan who caught a foul ball on the fly would receive an "honorary" contract with the Reds, signed by DeWitt. The language:

"Whereas (name of fan) caught a fly ball at Crosley Field, Cincinnati, on (date), and whereas this performance clearly indicates an extraordinary degree of proficiency, agility and skill as an off-field outfielder.

"Therefore, (fan) is hereby tendered this honorary contract with the Cincinnati Reds. This honorary contract includes a guarantee that at no time will the holder's loyalty to the Cincinnati Reds be traded to any other major league baseball club. The Cincinnati Reds hope that our present mutually satisfactory relationship will be a permanent one."

In many cases, that would depend on the team.

FOUR

Fits and Starts

The United States flag hung at half-staff on
the center field flag pole at Crosley Field as the Reds and the
Chicago Cubs met on Opening Day of the 1961 season. The
home team was honoring the memory of owner Powel Crosley Jr., who'd passed away exactly two weeks earlier, but the
flag's position just as easily could have been symbolizing Cincinnati's chances of capturing the National League championship—as least when considered by the so-called experts.

Earl Lawson, who covered the team for the *Cincinnati
Post and Times-Star*, picked the Reds to finish sixth in the NL—
exactly where they'd finished the previous season. Lou Smith,

sports editor of the *Cincinnati Enquirer* and the morning paper's lead baseball writer, concurred. So did a group of baseball writers from around the nation in a poll.

Picking a team to finish where it had the previous season wasn't exactly going out on a limb, but on the other hand, the Reds hadn't given anybody much of a reason for thinking they were capable of improving on that finish. Though they ended their spring training exhibition schedule with a flourish by sweeping the perennially contending Milwaukee Braves in a four-game barnstorming trip north from Florida, they still compiled the Grapefruit League's worst record at 12–15. Sure, first-year general manager Bill DeWitt had made a couple of significant trades, but the general feeling was the deals could do as much harm as good. Trading a dependable, veteran shortstop such as Roy McMillan for a young, unproven pitcher in Joey Jay was rightfully seen as questionable, and nobody was sure whether third baseman Gene Freese–DeWitt's other noteworthy off-season acquisition–would finally produce more runs with his bat than he allowed with his glove and scatter arm.

By the end of April, the writers' projections were looking downright optimistic. After getting off to a promising start, the Reds stumbled through an eight-game losing streak that left them in last place in the league.

All of that was still in the future as the Reds enjoyed a couple of days off between their last exhibition game, a win over Milwaukee in Louisville, and the opener. Manager Fred Hutchinson, who was frustrated at times while watching his team in spring training, knew the Reds were capable of playing better baseball.

"Throw our Grapefruit League out the window," he told writers. "If we get the breaks and our pitching proves to be as good as I think it will be, we're going to surprise the experts, but I also believe our league is stronger, particularly the second-division clubs, so we'd have to have everything go right to be a pennant contender. I think our young pitchers, particularly (Jay) Hook, (Jim) O'Toole and (Jim) Maloney, will be considerably better than they were last season. There's nothing like experience, you know, especially for a pitcher.

"We've also added some power. In fact, we're going to score a lot of runs. (Frank) Robinson and (Vada) Pinson both are hitting with more power than they did last spring, and I'm counting on Freese to hit 20–25 homers, and don't overlook Wally (Post). He's been the most pleasant surprise, next to young Hunt, in our camp. He's really been stinging the horsehide.

"I'll put it this way. Any manager would be nuts to go into a pennant race admitting that he didn't have a chance. I think we're an improved club, although our exhibition record doesn't indicate so. However, we're conceding nothing to any club. First place is the only place that counts, and that's the spot we're shooting for. If Jay Hook and O'Toole improve this year as they did from 1959 to 1960, we'll be in good shape, and I'm sure (Joey) Jay is going to win for us. I always liked the big guy and thought he had good stuff. He didn't get much of a chance to pitch in Milwaukee, but I'm counting on him as one of my regular starters.

"I don't care about anyone's pick. We've got a club that can go a long way. The young pitchers hold the key to our success. Man-for-man at the other positions, there's no club in the league better than we are."

One pitcher Hutchinson didn't mention was right-hander Bob Purkey, Cincinnati's top winner with 17 victories in 1960.

"What is my observation of the club?" he responded, echoing a reporter's question. "It depends on our young pitching—well, all the pitchers, but really, our young ones. They're good with great potential, and they've looked exceptionally good this spring, but there's a world of difference pitching spring exhibitions and pitching when the bell rings. It's one thing to stand outside a major league ballpark and another to go inside and pitch. Nobody forgets the first time. You get scared—not scared, exactly. Nervous. It's a distinct feeling, but getting back to pitching, once the bell rings and everything counts and bread-and-butter is depending on it, it's different. It's pressure. All athletes react under pressure. Some can't take it."

O'Toole edged Purkey in spring training competition for the coveted job of starting the season opener, which in Cincinnati had been treated for decades like a holiday. The Reds, in recognition of their status as baseball's first all-professional team, traditionally are accorded the honor of opening every season at home. Festivities include the Findlay Market Parade, which started when trolleys were a popular form of transportation and the Reds and their Opening Day opponents would be escorted from the market, which fills the block bordered by Findlay, Race, Elm, and Elder streets, west along Findlay to the ballpark. The parade would end on the field, which would lead to various ceremonies and presentations, followed by the introduction of the teams and, in what had become a tradition in this era, the singing of the National Anthem by soprano Marian Spelman, who also was a regular on live, daily WLWT television shows such as *The Paul Dixon Show* in the morning and Ruth Lyons's *Fifty-Fifty Club* around lunchtime.

The 1961 opener also featured an appearance by ninety-eight-year-old Williams Ellsworth Hoy, known better by his

nickname–"Dummy." Hoy was deaf, an affliction he overcame to put together a fourteen-year major league career from
1888 through 1902, including five seasons with the Reds–1894
through 1897 and 1902. Hoy, an outfielder, is generally considered to be the reason umpires started clarifying their calls with
hand signals–right thumb up for strike and out, extending arms
in a sweeping gesture outward for safe–which gave him the information he needed to stay on top of game situations.

Hoy, who finished his career with a .297 batting average,
threw the ceremonial first pitch from a front-row box seat at
the plate end of the home team's dugout on the third-base side
of the field.

The game was sold out in advance, but cloudy skies, tem-
peratures in the mid-fifties and a generally gloomy season out-
look combined to limit actual attendance to 28,713, the first
Opening Day crowd under 30,000 since 1952.

Lou Smith, the official scorer of the 1960 opener, originally had awarded the win in that game to O'Toole, who turned
in six innings of two-hit, shutout relief in Cincinnati's 9–4 victory over Philadelphia. Starting pitcher Jim Brosnan gave up
four runs in less than two innings of work before giving way
to relief pitcher Brooks Lawrence, who finished the second,
setting the stage for the Reds to score five runs in the bottom
of the inning, taking the lead for good. Months later, NL President Warren Giles overruled Smith and awarded the win to
Lawrence, because he'd been the pitcher of record when the
Reds took the lead.

O'Toole wasn't going to let Giles take another Opening
Day win away. The twenty-four-year-old left-hander, making
the first of three career Opening Day starts, threw a complete-
game four-hitter, and Frank Robinson and Wally Post each hit

**Wally Post congratulates Frank Robinson
on his Opening Day home run.**

a home run as the Reds got off to a solid start with a 9–4 win over the Cubs.

Robinson, playing left field and batting third, hit a two-out solo home run in the first inning to give the Reds a 1–0 lead.

"I really would like for this to be my best all-around year—and maybe forty home runs," he'd said before the game. "I think I can do it."

Chicago first baseman Andre Rodgers tied the game with a home run in the third inning, but Post gave Cincinnati the lead for good by christening the new net in left field with a three-run blast. The Reds added three more runs in the fifth, and O'Toole, who contributed two singles to Cincinnati's fourteen-hit attack, threw first-pitch strikes to twenty-one of the thirty batters he faces and retired the last ten Cubs. Part of the credit, he said, had to go to pitching coach Jim Turner, who'd helped O'Toole adjust his curve.

"It isn't exactly new, but Jim Turner suggested that I hold the ball tighter and give it more spin," said O'Toole, who was pitching in front of his parents, his wife's parents, two brothers, and a sister-in-law.

"I'd like to see Giles or anyone else take it away," he added with a laugh.

"All he has to do now is work on his baserunning," Hutchinson said, referring to O'Toole being thrown out at third base by twenty feet while trying to advance from first on a single to center.

"He pitched two better games last season, but I'll tell you this—he has the guts of a burglar," catcher Ed Bailey said. "His confidence—whew. He'll dare anybody."

The effort even included a pleasantly surprising airtight defense, featuring a diving catch of a sinking line drive by third baseman Gene Freese, who wasn't expected to contribute much with his glove. He also started a double play.

"Pitching makes a difference," shortstop Eddie Kasko pointed out. "When a pitcher is out there on the mound throwing a batter strikes and making them hit the ball, you're on your toes. When he's not, you'll find yourself unconsciously falling back on your heels."

The only Reds player who went hitless in the game was second baseman Jim Baumer, but at least for the first day, the combination of young pitching and power on which Hutchinson was counting paid off. It might've made the front pages of the local newspapers if the Soviet Union hadn't picked 2 a.m. Cincinnati time the next day to launch the first man into space. Astronaut Yuri Gagarin's successful orbit and reentry to a safe landing drew the banner headlines appropriate to the "enemy" gaining an edge in the Cold War.

The teams took Wednesday off and resumed Cincinnati's brief season-opening homestand on Thursday, April 13. The Cubs took a 2–0 lead against Purkey, but first baseman Gordy Coleman followed Freese's leadoff single with a game-tying two-run home run in the fourth, and left-handed-hitting Jerry Lynch came off the bench in the eighth inning to bat for Baumer with two runners on base. The Cubs brought in left-hander Jim Brewer to face Lynch, who still smacked the first pitch for a three-run homer to give Purkey and the Reds a 5–2 win.

"I just swing and hope," said Lynch while listening to Freese call him "Mr. Wonderful" and Kasko describe him as the "indispensable, irreplaceable Mr. Lynch."

Purkey turned in Cincinnati's second consecutive complete game, but only 1,216 fans showed up on a damp, chilly day to see it.

"The Reds look like a solid ballclub," Cubs coach Bobby Adams said. "They're going to surprise a lot of the experts who picked them for a second-division berth."

The only bad news was the loss to injury of backup catcher Hal Bevan, who'd been converted from third base. Bevan had suffered a broken middle finger on his right hand trying to catch a foul tip in an exhibition game against the Phillies on March 17. He tried to play through it before finally going on the disabled list.

So much for easing their way into the season. After opening with two games at home, the Reds faced a grueling twelve-game, two-week road trip, starting with a three-game series at Busch Stadium—previously known as Sportsman's Park—in St. Louis. The former Cardinals among the Reds—Hutchinson, coach Dick Sisler, Kasko, Freese, and relief pitchers Brosnan and Howie Nunn—were quite familiar with the city and the ballpark. Brosnan, in fact, was with the Cardinals for the first half of the 1959 season, which he chronicled in a diary that was published as a book titled *The Long Season.*

The Cardinals, who had opened the season by splitting two games at Milwaukee, celebrated their home opener in a manner somewhat different from Cincinnati's. Oh, St. Louis had a parade—sort of, anyway. The franchise staged kind of a beauty pageant, showing off its six candidates for the title of Miss Red Bird. They were introduced by, of all people, fifty-year-old stripper-actress Gypsy Rose Lee, who, like Hutchinson, was a native of Seattle.

"Not a princess in the bunch," was Brosnan's assessment in *Pennant Race*, his diary of the season.

The Reds again fell behind as the Cardinals piled up five hits, two walks, and three runs in four innings against right-hander Jay Hook. His struggles brought the Cincinnati bullpen into play for the first time in 1961, and it performed as promised. Right-hander Jim Maloney faced the minimum six batters in two innings, and left-hander Bill Henry allowed two hits and walk while striking out three in two more frames before Brosnan pitched a perfect ninth.

The bullpen's work opened the door for another power-propelled Reds comeback, capped by a five-run ninth inning in which the Reds pieced together five hits, including a pinch-hit RBI single by Gus Bell, Kasko's run-scoring single, Pinson's RBI double, and Robinson's run-producing single.

But what left everybody buzzing was the blast that started the comeback. Post followed Pinson's one-out walk in the sixth inning with a tremendous two-run homer to straightaway left field off of left-hander Curt Simmons that made folks wonder how far it would have sailed if it hadn't hit the eagle that was part of the Anheuser-Busch logo perched on top of the scoreboard.

The blow put Hook, the brilliant mechanical engineering student, to work trying to figure out how far the ball would have traveled if it hadn't hit the scoreboard. He settled on an estimate of 569 feet, four farther than what generally was considered to be the record at the time, a blow by the New York Yankees' Mickey Mantle in 1953 at Washington's Griffith Stadium that landed an estimated 565 feet from the plate.

Hook explained that he employed one of Isaac Newton's laws and other mathematics to come up with his estimate.

"I may be off a little, since this was the first problem of this nature I've worked in five years," he said. "I theorized that Simmons threw the ball at eighty miles per hour and that Wally swung the bat at a rate of between 110 and 120 an hour. I'd say closer to 120. At point of impact, I calculated that the ball was traveling at a velocity of 150 feet per second. Now, as I say, I could be slightly mistaken on speed rates. Next was the distance from the plate to the spot the ball struck. It's 410 feet from the plate, or so I was told, to the base of the left field stands in the approximate at which the ball traveled. The ball hit high off the sign, some ninety feet above the ground. Those were the figures I worked with and came up with a distance of 569 feet."

Other interested observers had less sophisticated reactions.

"It is the longest homer to left field I've ever seen in this park, and I've been here since it was rebuilt," said Cardinals public relations director Jim Toomey. "All you can do is estimate how far it might have carried if the scoreboard was not in the way, but I know it would have been well over 500 feet."

"It's the longest homer I've ever seen," said St. Louis star Stan Musial, who was starting his twenty-first season in the major leagues and had hit his first homer of the year earlier in the game. "The homer Post hit made the one I hit in the fourth look like a bunt. It was like a man in orbit."

"Post's ball still had some juice in it when it hit the sign," Hutchinson pointed out. "There was no doubt about where it was going--just a question as to how far."

"I only wish a sequence camera had recorded the swing so I could study what I did right," Post said.

Despite a persistent drizzle, the teams reluctantly straggled back into Sportsman's Park early the next day for the NBC Game of the Week. The Cardinals handled it better, reaching Joey Jay for two runs in the first inning and Nunn for two more in the fifth, building a 4–0 lead that turned into a win when the umpires finally called the game after a forty-seven-minute rain delay with two outs in the top of the sixth inning.

Hutchinson filed an official protest of the game, claiming it should have been called earlier, before it became official. National League President Warren Giles denied the protest days later, clinching Cincinnati's first loss of the season.

O'Toole took the loss in the Sunday finale, which started with the temperature hovering at thirty-nine degrees. That left the Reds with a 3–2 record going into a day off before opening a three-game series at another potentially chilly venue– San Francisco's Candlestick Park. Purkey turned in his second complete game in two starts as the Reds won the opener, setting the stage for the major league debut of right-hander Ken Hunt, who'd generated so much attention in spring training.

Hunt picked up in San Francisco right where he left off. Against a Giants team that featured Hall of Fame sluggers such as Willie Mays, Willie McCovey, and Orlando Cepeda hitting in a ballpark where the fences had been shortened twenty-two feet in right-center field, ten in center and a whopping thirty-two feet in left, the rookie survived a rocky first inning to go eight, allowing five hits and one earned run with four walks and three strikeouts to get the decision in Cincinnati's 4–2 win.

Hunt, understandably nervous with his mother, grandmother, and a couple of other relatives having made the trip from Utah to see his debut, allowed the Giants to load the bases with nobody out in the first inning. One run scored on a double play. He set up another Giants run with a wild pick-off throw in the second, but he settled down after that and kept the Giants scoreless the rest of the way. Coleman tied the game with a homer leading off the fourth inning, and Kasko drove in the go-ahead run with a ninth-inning single, setting up Brosnan's first save.

One observer who was impressed by the Reds was Candlestick's press box attendant—and if anybody knew what a winning Cincinnati ballclub looked like, it was Ernie Lombardi. Known as "Schnozz" for his prodigious nose, Lombardi was a lumbering—painfully slow, in fact—catcher capable of hitting vicious line drives who played for the Reds in the late 1930s and early 1940s. He won the NL batting championship in 1938, the year he became the first Reds player to be named the league's Most Valuable Player, and he was a key contributor to the teams that won the 1939 pennant and 1940 World Series.

"Everybody's picking them sixth, but that could be a mistake," said Lombardi, who caught Reds pitching coach Jim Turner when he pitched for Cincinnati in that 1940 World Series season. "They have explosive power and there's a good chance their young pitchers have come of age."

The glow of Hunt's debut and Lombardi's assessment was tarnished when Cincinnati's second base situation became even more questionable with the loss of Elio Chacon, who needed eight stitches to close a cut near his right kneecap, which he sustained while tagging Mays on a stolen-base attempt in the sixth inning. Chacon was sent back to Cincinnati.

The trade rumors involving second baseman Don Blasingame only intensified upon Cincinnati's arrival in San Francisco. Blasingame, a former Cardinal, wasn't playing for the Giants and definitely was available. Lawson had reported earlier that a Henry-for-Blasingame deal would be done by Monday, April 17, even though general manager Bill DeWitt had stayed behind in St. Louis for the birth of a grandchild.

Blasingame had hit just .235 in 1960 and lost his starting job to rookie Chuck Hiller. He hadn't gotten out of the dugout in any of the five games played by the Giants before the Reds showed up in San Francisco.

"I want to play, that's for sure, but all I can do is what I'm told," he said. "What happened last year? Well, I suppose the Candlestick Park wind bothered me, as it did other players, and I tried too hard to pull the ball to right field. It's not smart to make predictions in this business. I still have my confidence. That's one thing a player can't afford to lose.

"I'm convinced that if the Giants make a trade, I'll be in it. I don't want to sit on the bench. It's been three weeks since I've played in a game. I can't help a club coming off the bench."

Hutchinson admitted that a trade was right there, waiting to be made, but he was reluctant to pull the trigger.

"We can make a deal using Bill Henry any time we want to, but it takes a long time to build up a good bullpen, and when you finally get one, you hate to break it up," he said.

There didn't seem to be that much of a hurry. The Reds were in their seventh day of being tied or all alone in first place, six more days than they had spent leading or sharing the lead in 1960. They were tied for first after winning on Opening Day in 1960, but they fell out of the top spot after losing the second game of the season and never got back.

The 1961 season was to change almost as quickly. The Giants salvaged the final game of the three-game series with a 2–1 win, sending the Reds down the West Coast to Los Angeles for the first series of what would become the biggest rivalry of the season. The Dodgers, a year away from the opening of Dodger Stadium, still were playing home games in the cavernous, oval-shaped Los Angeles Memorial Coliseum, where left field was an alleged 251 feet from the plate and dominated by a screen that rose forty feet high and extended 140 feet from the foul line toward center field.

The Coliseum's short left field didn't help the Reds batters, who suddenly had fallen into a collective slump. They collected only six hits, one a Robinson home run, while losing to the Dodgers on Friday, April 21, in the first April win of Sandy Koufax's seven-year career. Veteran left-hander Johnny Podres and reliever Larry Sherry followed with a 1–0 shutout the next day, wasting a four-hit effort by Jay, who also was robbed of a hit in the fifth inning, on a diving catch of his line drive by center fielder Willie Davis.

Right-hander Roger Craig completed the sweep with a complete-game 5–1 win in the Sunday finale, barely breaking a sweat while dispatching the Reds in one hour and forty-five minutes, the shortest game in the Coliseum's brief major league history. The Reds had gone twenty-two consecutive innings without scoring before Lynch's eighth-inning pinch-hit home run.

The quick game left Hutchinson with plenty of time for a drastic step. With the Reds staying in town at their Sheraton West hotel and a day off on Monday before heading to Chicago, the manager decided that, if his team wasn't going to hit during the game, it would hit afterward. He arranged a post-game session of batting practice that lasted two hours.

"Hutch showed his authority," O'Toole recalled. "He had the pitchers who weren't getting much work throw and not tell the batters what was coming."

"We had really bombed out in that series," first baseman Gordy Coleman said years later. "Johnny Podres had just shut us out, and we had really looked bad. We were in the clubhouse getting undressed, and 'Hutch' came in. He was upset with our performance. He said, 'Nobody will untie a shoe. We're going back and play ball.' Well, we went back out on the field and worked out until it was so dark that we couldn't see.

"I think the frustrations of the summer ended right there. We turned it around and won something like eight in a row."

"This is not punishment or disciplinary action," Hutchinson said. "We've been getting real good pitching and doing nothing with it. We've just got to work our way out of the slump."

Hutch had tried other shakeups and contemplated more. In the loss to Podres, he benched Baumer, moving Kasko to second base and giving Leo Cardenas his first start of the season at shortstop. He was thinking about benching Pinson, who hadn't had a hit in seventeen plate appearances until he managed a bunt single in the fourth inning on April 20 at San Francisco.

"Maybe it would be a smart move," Hutchinson said about benching his center fielder and number two hitter. "Instead, I'll drop him into the number six spot in the batting order. He'll swap places with Gordy Coleman. Maybe the change will help both of them. You can't expect to win games with your number two batter hitting .162 and your number three batter at .184–and Freese, our number five batter, hasn't been a ball of fire."

"He's chopping at the ball instead of swinging," first base-hitting coach Dick Sisler said of Pinson. "Gene Freese is chasing too many bad pitches, and Robinson isn't taking his batting, especially during pre-game practice, seriously enough."

Hutchinson also hinted at platooning Robinson and Coleman at first base in an effort to get the hot-hitting Post more at bats while giving Gus Bell a chance to regain the starting job he'd held for eight years.

"I've never been an advocate of the platoon system, but we may have to adopt it, especially at first base, unless Gordy Coleman starts to hit lefthanders more effectively," the skipper warned. "The way we've been hitting, I've got to make changes. If someone had told me before the start of the season that this would happen, I'd never have believed them. I thought pitching, not hitting, was going to be my biggest worry."

Hutch's efforts to turn his team around didn't stop with a couple hours of extra hitting at the Coliseum. That night, even though the Reds were off the next day, he still had imposed a curfew and conducted a rare bed check, calling the players' rooms from the hotel bar, the Zebra Lounge.

"He caught half the team out–more than half the team," O'Toole said. "I made it back by the skin of my teeth. I was having drinks with Slick Leonard, the basketball player, out at the airport. He drove me home."

Leonard was an Indiana native who'd played college basketball at Indiana University and was in his final season with the Los Angeles Lakers. The favor he did for O'Toole also could have been used by Freese, the pitcher recalled.

"Gene Freese got into the lobby about one (a.m.), and he goes right into the Zebra Lounge, which is right there in the lobby and out of bounds," O'Toole said. "You're not supposed to do that. There was Hutch on the phone, calling different rooms. He calls up Gordy Coleman, who was Freese's roommate, and Gordy says, 'Yeah, he's over there. I can hear him snoring,' and there he is at the bar, buying a drink. He tried, God love him."

O'Toole didn't face the same dilemma with his roommate, Bill Henry.

"I don't think he ever was out late in his whole life," O'Toole said. "He didn't drink or anything."

The fallout wasn't long in coming, he added.

"We had a meeting and each one of them was fined one hundred dollars, which was a lot of money back then," O'Toole said.

Maloney, who would miss a few curfews in his day, learned to pay attention to signals that a bedcheck was imminent.

"He'd check on guys periodically," Maloney said. "If the team was going good, he wouldn't be snooping around, but if we were struggling a little bit, the coaches would come over and say, 'Be aware. Be alive. Be in. There may be a check or there may not.' It was a way to keep guys in check.

"I'm sure I missed curfew at times, but he never caught me."

The slumping Reds had to wait an extra day to learn if Hutchinson's tactics would pay off. They arrived in Chicago in time to be rained out on April 25. The next day, with Pinson dropped all the way to seventh in the batting order, they saw their losing streak extended to five games while scoring only two runs in a ten-inning loss to the Cubs, which was decided on a one-out solo home run by Cincinnati native Don Zimmer. Lynch had given the Reds a 2–1 lead with a two-run homer while pinch-hitting in the seventh inning for O'Toole, who had a one-hitter going at the time. Brosnan started the seventh by giving up the lead, allowing back-to-back doubles by Ron Santo and Frank Thomas.

Cincinnati scored only two runs again the next day with Hutchinson, desperately trying to find some offense, making moves such as sending Henry to pinch-hit for Brosnan. Cincinnati ended the game with pitcher Claude Osteen playing left field and Robinson at third base, but it all only led to a sixth straight loss.

The team's frustrations surfaced in the eighth inning when third base coach Reggie Otero and backup third baseman Willie Jones were ejected for protesting a two-and-one pitch from Cubs' right-hander Don Elston to Jones that plate umpire Jocko Conlan called a strike. Osteen replaced Jones at the plate and struck out, leaving three runners on base.

The Reds limped home with a six-game losing streak and a 5–8 overall record, but their arrival at Greater Cincinnati Airport was anything but routine. The Reds landed and learned that the long-rumored, long-awaited trade had finally happened—but it wasn't Henry or Brosnan who was leaving Cincinnati. Instead, DeWitt had worked out a deal in which long-time, popular catcher Ed Bailey went to San Francisco in exchange for Blasingame, catcher Bob Schmidt, and a player to be named later.

"We hated to part with Bailey," DeWitt said. "He's a fine catcher, but we needed a second baseman very badly. When you figure that we were going to get a second baseman who's a frontline player and a catcher who's a frontline player for Bailey—plus a third player—we felt we had a deal.

"We needed the pitchers ourselves. Then, when they came to Bailey, we said we would need more than just Blasingame."

Hutch stands in the dugout with his newest players—second baseman Don Blasingame and catcher Bob Schmidt.

"We needed someone to pull the infield together," Hutchinson said. "Blasingame filled the bill, so we traded Ed Bailey for him and Bob Schmidt."

The Giants never were interested in pitching, general manager Chub Feeney said.

"Negotiations for Bailey began this year, just a couple of days before Opening Day," Feeney said. "We were always closer to making a deal for Bailey than we were in making one for Bill Henry."

Trading Bailey caught everybody by surprise. He had just turned thirty and had been a three-time All-Star with the Reds while hitting a solid .261. Some, such as former Cincinnati second baseman Johnny Temple, thought DeWitt had just traded the pennant to San Francisco.

"The Giants got the top man in the business in Bailey," said Temple, who was with Cleveland. "Many baseball people consider Del Crandall the best catcher in the National League, but I'll take Bailey ahead of anybody in the game. That goes for all the departments—handling pitchers, receiving, throwing, hitting, and hustling.

"Do you know Bailey? Well, the reason I ask is that Ed may have acquired the reputation of taking baseball a bit too lightly. He's a great and entertaining guy to have on a club. He has a lot of hillbilly-type sayings having to do with fat hogs, etc., but allow me to assure you that Bailey is dead serious and smart once the gong rings—and what did the Giants give for Bailey? No one they intended using."

Temple's manager, Jimmy Dykes, didn't disagree.

"Bailey's a whale of a catcher, but Cincinnati was desperately in need of a second baseman and Hutch knew Blasingame, having had success with him in St. Louis," Dykes said. "Blasingame couldn't throw a lick in Arizona this spring. It looked like he had a dead arm. As a second baseman, Blasingame is a good offensive ballplayer, period. Schmidt is a minor league catcher."

Observers closer to the situation also were somewhat mystified by the move, which didn't seem to fit the template of a winning team.

"That team did some strange things from a front office standpoint," said Jim Ferguson, the *Dayton Daily News* reporter. "The trades were the key to it. Shortstop is a key defensive position, and they'd traded away Roy McMillan, the best in the league at the time. Catcher is a key position, and they traded away Ed Bailey and went with two rookie catchers, Johnny Edwards and Jerry Zimmerman. The thinking was you can't win a pennant with rookie catchers. They opened the season with a rookie second baseman, and then very early in the season, they said he can't cut it. Blasingame didn't have a good year, but he was a solid veteran."

DeWitt chafed at the criticism.

"How many championship clubs did Temple play on?" DeWitt smirked. "I didn't make this trade for someone else's approval. You make trades to help your own ballclub. Of course Bailey will help the Giants, but I didn't make this deal to help them. I made it to help us. This is no aspersion on past deals here, but any time you trade one for three, the percentage is in your favor. If the one guy who went for three should flop, then you've got a bonus. If you get two who make good, you're still ahead. Schmidt's record and all of our information shows he is going to help our club. He is a major league catcher, but if everybody in baseball had the same opinion on ballplayers, there would be no changes."

O'Toole almost welcomed the trade.

"We had the opportunity to get Don Blasingame, but we had to give up Ed Bailey," the pitcher said. "Ed was a great hitter, but not necessarily a great tutor of young pitching. We had young pitching."

An unseasonable mid-afternoon snowfall forced the Reds to postpone that night's game at Crosley against the defending World Series-champion Pittsburgh Pirates, giving Blasingame and Schmidt extra time to ease into their new situation.

"I wasn't surprised, but I definitely welcomed it, especially in Cincinnati," Blasingame said. "The Giants management and fans treated me fairly. I'm only sorry I didn't play to expectations for them. I wouldn't say I was in the doghouse, but I couldn't have played less if I had. I told (Giants' manager) Al (Dark) I wanted to play regularly, but it was his business to run the club. I like the Cincinnati park, and I accept and appreciate the chance to play regularly for the Reds, but I'm not taking it for granted that I am playing second base by default. I intend to win it."

"I heard rumors of my impending trade to Cincinnati at spring training in Phoenix," Schmidt said. "When the season opened and I wasn't playing, I expected it, but when the Cincinnati club played at San Francisco, where negotiations might have been logically completed, and nothing happened, I figured it was just another one of those rumors. Don't get me wrong. I'm glad to join the Reds, a club I think has great potential, far better than the standings today show. I must say I have no quarrel with the Giants, who have treated me wonderfully. I'm glad, though, to get away from Candlestick Park."

Even with the new blood, Hutchinson felt his team needed more of a push, especially with Kasko not available to start with a swollen right ankle, the result of getting hit by a Johnny Podres pitch the previous Saturday in Los Angeles. He would be sent to Christ Hospital for X-rays to see if he'd suffered a possible hairline fracture. That left Cincinnati missing its reigning team Most Valuable Player and facing a three-game series against the dangerous Pirates—the Pirates of right fielder Roberto Clemente, shortstop and 1960 National League Most Valuable Player Dick Groat, second baseman and Series hero Bill Mazeroski, Cy Young Award-winning pitcher Vern Law and relief ace Roy Face.

The Pittsburgh lineup still included combative third baseman Don Hoak, the former Marine who'd been traded from the Reds to the Pirates before the 1959 season in one of the worst trades in Cincinnati franchise history. Hoak's aggressive approach to playing baseball made him enormously popular in Cincinnati, and that didn't change when he joined the Pirates. He hit .282 with 16 home runs and 79 RBIs for the Pirates in 1960, and his leadership was so evident that he finished second in the voting by writers for the MVP award.

Hoak also was the subject of one of the more humorous scenes in Billy Crystal's 1991 movie, *City Slickers*. A female character is trying to understand why men consider things such as trivia to be so important.

"I like baseball," she said. "I just don't memorize who played third base for Pittsburgh in 1960."

Three male characters reflexively respond, "Don Hoak."

Hutchinson knew the reeling Reds needed a spark. He had sent the players out for batting practice before the first game of the series was postponed. For the second game, on Saturday, April 29, he made the decision to bench Pinson, moving Robinson to center field and giving Bell the start in

Robinson's normal left-field spot with Post in right field. Pinson had started 324 consecutive games since being called up from Triple-A Seattle in 1958.

"The way the outfielders are hitting, I might just as well put their names in a hat and pick three," Hutchinson said.

Jay, who still was waiting for the Reds to score a run for him, finally got three in his start against the Pirates on April 29, but he gave up five in six innings as the losing streak reached seven games. Pinson returned to the starting lineup, in center field and hitting second, for the first game of the next day's doubleheader, but he went 0-for-3 while the Pirates reached Hook for seven hits and five runs in 4⅔ innings to wipe out a 3–0 Cincinnati lead on their way to a 6–3 win that dropped the Reds into last place. Clemente—probably the greatest defensive right fielder in baseball history and, besides Willie Mays, the only outfielder to win twelve Gold Gloves—even committed an error and the Reds still couldn't win.

Going into the second game of the doubleheader, Cincinnati was 5–10 and 4½ games behind the league-leading Giants, who had rolled over the Braves, 14–4, at Milwaukee. The Reds, for the most part, were getting the pitching they had hoped for, but the offense was unexpectedly dysfunctional. They had scored a total of eleven runs in the last six games, ten of them on home runs.

The only good news for the Reds was the season still had five months to go.

FIVE

On Track

Cincinnati's struggles on the major league level through the 1950s were well documented, and there were plenty of places to pin the blame.

Bobby Mattick wasn't among them.

Mattick was the star of a Reds scouting and farm system that, by 1961, had produced current or budding stars such as outfielders Frank Robinson and Vada Pinson, infielders Leo Cardenas and Elio Chacon, catcher Johnny Edwards, and pitchers Jim O'Toole, Jim Maloney, and Ken Hunt. When Gabe Paul left for the job as Houston's general manager in October of 1960, Pete Rose, Tony Perez, and Tommy Helms were just starting their professional careers in Cincinnati's system.

One of the reasons for Cincinnati's productive scouting department and farm system was Phil Seghi. The gap-toothed graduate of Northwestern University, who favored bow ties and seemingly was never without his pipe, had replaced Bill McKechnie Jr.—son of the manager who led the Reds to the 1939 National League championship and 1940 World Series title—as Cincinnati's farm director in the mid-1950s. He was promoted by Bill DeWitt to assistant general manager in 1963 and stayed with the team until DeWitt sold it after the 1966 season.

Helping Seghi oversee the farm system was Hank Peters, a St. Louis native who would later go on to serve as general manager of Baltimore Orioles teams that won the American League pennant in 1979 and the World Series in

The Reds farm department: Phil Seghi, Hank Peters, and Art Perkins.

1983. Mattick was one of the key providers of raw talent for the system.

Mattick had come to know the West Coast as well as his hometown—especially Oakland and McClymonds High School, out of which he plucked for the Reds not one or two but three All-Star caliber outfielders in the span of just a few years. The one with perhaps the biggest upside coming out of high school was Vada Pinson, a left-handed hitter who didn't possess as much power as fellow McClymonds graduate Frank Robinson, but had more speed and was a better all-around player defensively. While Pinson might have had as much or more overall talent, Robinson's intensity burned hotter.

Baseball wasn't the only sport in which McClymonds cranked out Hall of Fame-caliber athletes. It also was the alma mater of Boston Celtics center Bill Russell, other National Basketball Association stars such as Paul Silas, Joe Ellis, Nate Williams, and Antonio Davis and Olympic gold medal sprinter Jim Hines.

Pinson, a Memphis, Tennessee, native who'd been a couple of years behind Robinson at McClymonds, was only nineteen when he made his major league debut in 1958, but the potential he displayed earlier left Paul confident enough to trade yet another McClymonds product, future All-Star center fielder Curt Flood, to St. Louis in December 1957.

Flood would help rock Major League Baseball in 1969 by challenging the contractual reserve clause, which bound players to one team as long as wanted by that team. Flood chose to sit out a year, a move he claimed revoked the restraints of the reserve clause. The case reached the United States Supreme Court, which found in favor of Major League Baseball. Flood's case failed in the short run, but the owners and the players agreed on a limited form of free agency that started after the 1976 season.

Before all of that, though, Flood played on three National League championship teams and two World Series-winning teams with the Cardinals and was a three-time All-Star while winning seven Gold Gloves. Yet he was the player deemed by the Reds expendable in favor of Pinson, and even though Flood finished his career with more awards, Paul's decision wasn't necessarily wrong. Pinson, probably because he played in a smaller city and made fewer postseason appearances, never earned the accolades he deserved. In 1961 alone, while mostly hitting third in the batting order, ahead of Robinson, he finished second in the NL in hitting and stolen bases and led the league with 208 hits while also winning a Gold Glove after making routine the spectacular play—particularly the diving catch. By that time, he'd already played in All-Star Games in 1959 and 1960.

No less an authority than Stan Musial, winner of seven NL batting championships and a teammate of Flood's in St. Louis, projected Pinson as the league's best hitter in the 1960s.

"There's no reason why he shouldn't hit .325 to .330 every year," the St. Louis star said. "A couple of years ago, I would have said Hank Aaron, but he's become too much of a swinger now. Pinson's a hitter, and he's got that tremendous speed going for him. Anyone who can run as Pinson should never go a couple of days without a hit."

Houston scout Bobby Bragan, a former manager, agreed.

"In my book, Pinson is a better all-around hitter than Willie Mays," Bragan said. "He's going to get better, too. He'll be the one to beat for the league batting championship for the next ten years—maybe more."

Few players in baseball possessed Vada
Pinson's blend of hitting and fielding skills.

That's why Cincinnati manager Fred Hutchinson was so
frustrated as the month of May loomed in 1961. Pinson would
finish April hitting just .143, slumping so badly that Hutch decided to keep him out of the starting lineup on April 29. The
temporary benching didn't seem to work as Pinson went hitless in three at-bats in the first game of the next day's doubleheader against Pittsburgh, so he was on the bench for the start
of the nightcap.

The move at first seemed to be just another of Hutchinson's failed attempts to wake up his team, though the Reds
actually had shown signs of life in the first game. Frank Robinson stole third base while Pirate right-hander Bob Friend was
intentionally walking Gene Freese in the third inning. The

move led to nothing after catcher Bob Schmidt forced Freese at second base with a grounder to Pittsburgh second baseman Bill Mazeroski, but the hustle was appreciated, and the Reds already had scored a run in the inning to take a 3–0 lead that Jay Hook proved unable to hold.

In fact, the entire losing streak looked worse on the surface than it did with just a little digging. The largest margin of defeat in any of the games was four runs, which meant Cincinnati was in every game with a chance to win. After scoring a total of five runs in the first four losses, the hitters were showing signs of breaking out of their collective slump by producing a combined ten runs in the last four games. They still hadn't scored more than three in any one game since their last win back on April 19–and four would turn out to be a decisive number.

Pittsburgh center fielder Bill Virdon greeted Cincinnati starting pitcher Bob Purkey with a line drive off the center-field fence on the first pitch of the second game. Scant minutes later, shortstop and reigning National League Most Valuable Player Dick Groat smartly drove in Virdon with a single to center field, and the Reds looked a lot like a team on their way to a ninth straight loss.

Thanks to a spark provided by shortstop Leo Cardenas, making one of his six 1961 starts in the leadoff slot, the Reds were able to come from behind in the second game for a 4–2 win and snap the losing streak.

Hutchinson, desperately searching for some kind of run-producing combination, moved Cardenas up in the batting order against imposing Pittsburgh left-hander Joe Gibbon, a six-foot-four, two-hundred-pound Mississippi native. The skinny Cuban known as "Spider" responded by going three-for-four and teamed up with Purkey and catcher Jerry Zimmerman on textbook examples of fundamental baseball that yielded two big runs. Zimmerman walked to lead off the third, Purkey sacrificed him to second, and Cardenas singled to left to tie the score at 1–1. The Reds stayed with the book to take a 3–1 lead in the fifth. Gordy Coleman walked and moved to third on Zimmerman's single to right. Zimmerman was thrown out by right fielder Roberto Clemente trying to stretch the hit into a double, but Coleman scored on Purkey's successful squeeze bunt. Purkey moved to third on Cardenas's double to right field and scored on Don Blasingame's sacrifice fly to left field.

The Reds added an insurance run in the seventh on Zimmerman's one-out single to center, Purkey's sacrifice–his third effective bunt of the game–and Cardenas's RBI single to left. Purkey, keeping the Pirate hitters off-balance with his wide-ranging assortment of off-speed pitches, finished the game, and the losing streak was history.

"The only thing impressive about Bob Purkey is the fact that he wins," former Reds manager Birdie Tebbetts had once said of Purkey. "Watch him warm up on the sidelines, and you wouldn't give five cents for him."

"Nah, I'm not offended when they say I throw junk," said Purkey who improved to 3–1, a positive sign since he'd ended up with 17 wins in 1960 after going winless in April. "That is because I know something they don't know. My fastball is my best pitch. I set up the batters with my other pitches, then I jam them with my fastball. I can spot it anywhere I want–inside or outside. The other pitches–knuckler, slider, and sinker–I just throw for strikes. I used to have real good luck using my fastball on Willie Mays. He's wise to me now. Whitey Lockman squealed on me–told Willie how I was going to pitch to him."

Winning the nightcap helped send the Reds into May with a little bit of momentum and, with perennially cellar-dwelling Philadelphia due into Crosley Field for a four-game series, some confidence. Cincinnati and the Phillies hadn't yet played each other in 1961, but the visitors had reason for going into the series with a certain level of confidence, having won thirteen of twenty-two games against the Reds in 1960. The Phillies beat the Reds more than they beat any other team in 1960.

Unfortunately for manager Gene Mauch and the Phillies, 1961 was a new season in more ways than just the calendar, and they were unlucky enough to catch the Reds at the wrong time—when they were ready to get on track and rolling.

The process would start by running over Philadelphia with a four-game sweep, beginning with back-to-back 3–2 wins in which Jim O'Toole pitched a complete game and Hunt threw eight solid innings.

"O'Toole doesn't care about me, you, or anyone else," Hutchinson said. "He just wants to win, and let him smell that victory and he's tough to beat. If you're the batter, O'Toole's not worried about you. He thinks you should worry about him."

Pitching coach Jim Turner, who previously filled the same role with the Yankees, saw resemblances between O'Toole and New York ace left-hander Whitey Ford.

"As competitors, they're very much alike," Turner said. "You wouldn't find either one of them laughing off a loss."

Though brought to the Reds primarily for his bat, Freese contributed with his glove and legs. He made a backhand stab to set up a groundout in the third inning and snapped a 2–2 tie in the fourth by scoring from second base on Don Blasingame's infield single to shortstop Ruben Amaro.

"There is the greatest third baseman in the league," O'Toole said after the game. "Who said he was a poor fielder?"

Freese said he had scored by mistake.

"If I had known Amaro had stopped that ball of Blasingame's, I might not have tried for home," Freese said. "I thought the ball went into left field."

Hunt stranded nine Phillies baserunners in his win, which relief pitcher Jim Brosnan clinched with a perfect ninth.

"He was just wild enough to be effective," Philadelphia coach Bob Lemon said of Hunt. "If he's that wild and gets his curve over, he'll be tougher than hell."

"We've got a great system," general manager Bill DeWitt said. "Let the kids scare the hitters for seven innings and then bring the old-timers out of the bullpen."

"Hunt has a major league arm," Mauch observed. "What goes on inside the kid, I don't know, but it's something you'll find out before the season is over."

"He's not the emotional type," Hutchinson said of the rookie. "Maybe he gets a little nervous inside, but it doesn't show. Unusual for a youngster? Not necessarily so. Some guys are just that way. Others can pitch for twenty years and still be as jumpy as a toad.

"I just hope our good pitching continues, because it's beginning to look as if we're going to have to win without a lot of hits," Hutchinson added. "I don't care who the other club trots out to the mound, we don't hit him. We think we have good hitters. They've done the job in the past, but they didn't do it last year, so maybe they aren't as good as we think. I don't know how else you can put it."

The next night, the Reds erupted for nine runs, setting up the possibility of a sweep that became reality behind one of the most impressive performances by a Cincinnati pitcher short of a no-hitter. Jay–the hard-luck newcomer who'd lost his first three decisions as a Red, the first two by shutouts–dominated the Phillies on May 4 with a one-hit shutout in a 4–0 win that extended Cincinnati's winning streak to five games. Philadelphia's only hit was right fielder Johnny Callison's one-out single through the hole into right field in the first inning. Callison was stranded, and the Phillies' only other baserunner was shortstop Ruben Amaro, who walked to lead off the third and was quickly erased when Philadelphia starting pitcher and Cincinnati native Art Mahaffey grounded into a double play.

Joey Jay earns his first victory as a Red with a one-hit shutout of the Phillies on May 4.

The Reds offense took pressure off of Jay by scoring two runs in the first inning, and he took care of the rest, pushing the Reds back to the .500 level at 10–10. Afterward, Jay startled observers by claiming that the performance wasn't his best.

"I threw a two-hitter against the St. Louis Cardinals back in 1958," he said. "Only one ball went to the outfield."

Jay also showed that the Reds weren't going to let the rest of the league push them around. After Mahaffey hit Frank Robinson with a pitch leading off the eighth inning, Jay sent a message with two pitches behind Amaro's head leading off the ninth inning. Plate umpire Eddie Vargo warned Jay after the second pitch, raising Hutchinson's ire to such a level that the skipper later was fined one hundred dollars.

Cincinnati took a head of steam to Milwaukee for a brief three-game road trip, one of the many oddities of the 1961 NL schedule. The Reds' offense still wasn't as consistent as Hutchinson wanted it to be, but coming back from a three-run deficit with four ninth-inning runs to take a 5–4 lead in the Friday night series opener was a hopeful sign for him.

The first series against the Braves, Jay's former team, set the stage for what would be a contentious season between the two teams. On a chilly night at Milwaukee's County Stadium, the Braves struck for two runs despite seeing Cincinnati starter Bob Purkey knock down Hank Aaron and Joe Adcock. Milwaukee starter Lew Burdette countered by plunking Purkey with a pitch in the top of the second.

Milwaukee took a 4–1 lead into the ninth before little-used infielder Harry Anderson—acquired by the Reds from Philadelphia as part of the June 15, 1960, deal in which outfielder Wally Post was brought back to Cincinnati—started the rally against Burdette with a pinch-hit single to center while batting for Zimmerman. That appearance would be Anderson's last in the major leagues. He was lifted for pinch-runner Elio Chacon, who moved to third on Blasingame's one-out double and scored on Pinson's line-drive single to right. Milwaukee manager Charlie Dressen replaced Burdette with left-hander Seth Morehead, and Hutchinson played the percentages by replacing left-hander Gus Bell with the right-handed-hitting Post, who promptly smacked a three-run, go-ahead homer.

"The hitting in the ninth was the best we've had in any one inning this season," Hutchinson said. "Every ball was hit hard."

Brosnan came in for the save, but his throwing error allowed the tying run to score, pushing the game to twelve innings. Brosnan ended up going 3⅔ innings and got the win after Gene Freese tripled with one out and scored on Cardenas's sacrifice fly, allowing the Reds to move into fourth place—the upper half of the league, the first division. They would never drop out.

Weather postponed the next day's game, setting up another Sunday doubleheader. Left-hander Warren Spahn—who'd practically owned the Reds in a career that started back in 1942, when the Braves still were based in Boston—was scheduled to start the opener. Spahn was 57–21 in his career against the Reds going into that game and was on the verge of making it 58 wins, taking a 4–0 lead into the eighth inning.

Then the power, for which Hutchinson had been nervously waiting, showed up. Robinson hit a two-out, two-run home run, and Post followed with a solo shot to cut Spahn's lead to one run. Cardenas led off the ninth with a game-tying homer, and Gordy Coleman—who, as a left-handed batter still learning plate discipline, was supposed to be particularly vulnerable to the craftiest of crafty veterans—followed with a go-ahead shot that lifted the Reds to a 5–4 win.

Left-hander Jim O'Toole overcame three Cincinnati errors, including one of his own, with a five-hit 4–0 win in the nightcap, giving the Reds the sweep of the road twin bill. All five Milwaukee hits were singles as O'Toole logged his first career win over the Braves after eight losses. Some of the losses were more memorable: 2–1 on an error, 4–3 on a three-run, pinch-hit homer, 2–0 despite pitching a two-hitter, and an eleven-inning, 4–3 loss to Spahn.

"I wasn't beginning to get a complex, but I have to admit that the games I had lost to them were on my mind whenever we faced them," O'Toole said. "The four runs we got were the most I've ever had against them. This time, when I had to make the good pitch, I did. In other games with the Braves, I didn't. That was the big difference."

"If they win like that on the road, I'll stay away from them, and if it'll help any, I'll even go out of town when they're at home," DeWitt joked.

Another hopeful sign for Hutchinson was the resurgence of Pinson, who put behind him his weak April by going a solid eight for thirteen in the three games at Milwaukee.

However, Pinson's slump had been deep enough for Hutchinson to briefly bench him and then place him second in the batting order at Milwaukee in an effort to get Pinson's stroke in shape. The move seemed to be paying off.

"With Vada hitting, it makes a hell of a difference," Hutchinson said. "We'll be even better when Blasingame starts hitting. Right now, he's getting some solid knocks, but they're not finding the holes."

Everybody had their own thoughts on why Pinson struggled so much in April, when he hit just .143.

"He's slapping at the ball instead of taking a good cut," Hutchinson said.

"He's hitting off the front foot and losing his power," was hitting coach Dick Sisler's assessment.

"It's the cold weather," was Pinson's opinion. "You wear so many clothes trying to keep warm that you're not free and loose at the plate. You try not to worry about slumps, but unconsciously, it's there. I knew I would come out of it. The question was when. I felt all right, but obviously I was doing something wrong. Frank and Hutch both detected the fault. I was striding and getting my body through and therefore getting no snap into my swing. How did I shake it? Practice."

The suddenly hot Reds returned to Cincinnati for a two-game series against St. Louis, a very short homestand in the quirky NL schedule—and it became even shorter when the May 9 game was postponed. The winning streak reached nine on May 10 with a 3–2 win. Jay, less effective than in his overpowering start against Philadelphia, lasted seven innings before left-handers Marshall Bridges and Bill Henry each threw a shutout inning of relief.

Even through the losing streak, the bullpen had been living up to Hutchinson's expectations, and he appreciated the effort of his relievers.

"I wouldn't trade (our bullpen) for anybody in the league," Hutchinson said. "If you want to count Jim Maloney and Jay Hook, we've got six good relief pitchers."

"A few years ago, when a starting pitcher left a game with a one-run lead, he did not have much chance of winding up with a victory," Purkey said. "Not so today. We've got the best bullpen in the league."

While the pitchers were stifling opposing offenses, the Reds outscored their opponents 41–20 during the winning streak. One person who wasn't surprised by the turnaround was Robinson, who saw the signs even during the eight-game losing streak.

"I can think of three during that losing streak which could have been won with just one hit," he said. "We had the runners on but couldn't get them in."

Coleman traced the turnaround to the maturation of Cincinnati's young players, which he credited to Hutchinson.

"He gave us young fellows a chance to play, and that has made the difference," the first baseman said. "He was willing to

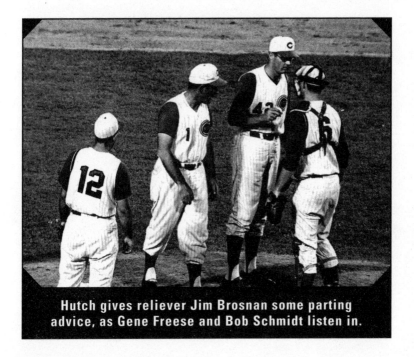

Hutch gives reliever Jim Brosnan some parting advice, as Gene Freese and Bob Schmidt listen in.

take a chance on us after we were brought up last season, and his faith in us gave us the confidence we needed. That goes for Leo Cardenas as well as the young pitchers like Hook, O'Toole, Hunt, and Maloney."

DeWitt also believed Hutchinson and pitching coach Jim Turner were the keys to Cincinnati's surge.

"It takes a lot of people to build a winning ballclub," he said. "However, if one man had to be picked out, I believe the credit for our success must go to Hutch. He didn't lose confidence in his boys, even when they were in the depths of the recent eight-game losing streak. Everyone agrees that pitching is at least seventy-five percent of a ballclub, and he and Jim have done a marvelous job with the young pitching staff.

"Another important phase of managing is handling your men, getting the most out of them and keeping the spirit of the team high, even when it is losing. Certainly, Hutch has done a wonderful job here."

Hutch saw the winning streak as something that was waiting to happen.

"We haven't been out of a game yet," Hutchinson said. "It's not one thing, no one individual. A batter slips into a slump, somebody picks it up, and the pitching has been excellent. In all, we've been playing good ball, and as a matter of fact, we played good baseball even in the eight-game losing streak.

"We've acquired the confidence and winning habit that could take us all the way. Wouldn't that be something if we did?"

Jim Ferguson, the *Dayton Daily News* sportswriter who helped cover the team, recalled that Cincinnati's inexperience would continue to crop up at times during the season.

"One thing that stuck out that whole year was they were

a very, very inconsistent team," Ferguson said. "They had a lot of winning streaks and losing streaks both. They were in first place a good part of season, but they would get four or five games ahead and look like they were going to open up some ground, and then they would lose four or five in a row. It was a frustrating team because it was so inconsistent. They could never build on it. They would play really well, then play poorly. There was never an even flow."

Ferguson paused and chuckled.

"You have to think, 'Hey, nobody thought they had a chance, anyway, so why would you think they can break it open?'"

The players returned to their Crosley clubhouse after beating the Cardinals to learn about the departures of Anderson, left-handed pitcher Claude Osteen, and second baseman Jim Baumer, the Opening Day starter. In those days, major league teams were allowed to keep as many as thirty players on their active roster for the first thirty days of the season before they had to cut to twenty-five.

Baumer, who hadn't played since April 27, ended up hitting .206 in ten games before being traded to Detroit for backup first baseman Dick Gernert, a right-handed batter who gave Hutchinson some flexibility in pinch-hitting for Gordy Coleman. The thirty-year-old Gernert had hit just .200 in six games for the Tigers, who were contending in the American League.

"He can play first base, the outfield, and pinch hit," DeWitt said. "Actually, we got him as insurance, say that something happened to Gordon Coleman. Pray that doesn't occur."

"I didn't mind moving from one hot club to another," Gernert said upon joining the team.

While Baumer was traded out of the organization, Osteen

and Anderson were sent to the Indianapolis Indians of the American Association, which had replaced the Seattle Rainiers as one of Cincinnati's two Triple-A affiliates. A fourth player, third baseman Willie Jones, was given his unconditional release, which had to leave hitting coach Dick Sisler feeling a little melancholy. He and Jones had been teammates on the Philadelphia Phillies "Whiz Kids" team that won the 1950 National League championship. Jones hit .267 with 25 home runs and 88 RBI for that team, but he was on the downside of his career by the time the Reds purchased his contract from Cleveland in 1959, and he was thirty-five when released by Cincinnati.

DeWitt wasn't finished with his tinkering. Before Cincinnati's game at Pittsburgh on May 13, the team announced that imposing right-hander Sherman Jones, a six-foot-four, 205-pound reliever known as "Roadblock," was the third player—the player to be named later—in the trade with San Francisco. Five days later, third baseman-turned-catcher Hal Bevan, who'd been sidelined with a fractured finger, was sent to Triple-A Jersey City and replaced on the roster by journeyman Pete Whisenant, a spirited outfielder who'd been released by Minnesota on May 16.

Whisenant, thirty-one, already had played for the Boston Braves, St. Louis Cardinals, and Chicago Cubs when the Reds first acquired him with Don Hoak and pitcher Warren Hacker for third baseman-outfielder Ray Jablonski and pitcher Elmer "Smoky" Singleton before the 1957 season. Whisenant spent three seasons in Cincinnati before his contract was sold to Cleveland on April 29, 1960. The Indians traded him less than a month later to the Washington Senators for infielder Ken Aspromonte, and Whisenant went with the Senators to Minnesota, where they became the Twins.

After yet another day off on May 11, Cincinnati's third in four days, the Reds traveled to Pittsburgh for their first visit of the season to cavernous Forbes Field, where Bill Mazeroski had shocked the New York Yankees the previous October with the ninth-inning leadoff home run that gave the Pirates the stunning 10–9 win—still history's only World Series Game Seven walkoff home run. Pittsburgh snapped Cincinnati's winning streak at nine games with an 8–5 win on May 12 and won again on Saturday before Robinson hit two home runs and Hunt and Brosnan teamed up to allow the Pirates just five hits and a Mazeroski home run in a 4–1 win on Sunday. Hunt wasn't exactly efficient, throwing 110 pitches in 6⅔ innings, and forty-six of them were curves or changeups.

"I've never seen a rookie pitcher cooler under fire than Hunt has been," Hutchinson said. "When you've got a good arm, you can do just about anything. The way we've been scoring, the poor kid hasn't had a minute's peace out there on the mound. Not once has he been in a position where he could say, 'Here's the ball, go ahead. Hit it.' I'll say one thing. It's making a better pitcher out of him, and he was darn good to start with."

Hunt believed he learned how to cope in 1960, when he helped Columbia win the South Atlantic League regular season championship.

"I don't think we had a .300 hitter on the team," he said. "I know we were way down in the club batting averages, and the fielding average wasn't too good, either."

That Sunday win also marked the return to Cincinnati's starting lineup of shortstop Eddie Kasko, who'd been hampered since being hit in the ankle by a Johnny Podres pitch on April 22. He'd started the next day and had played off the bench in four other games, but he hadn't started any of the games in Cincinnati's nine-game winning streak, even though he had one of the few hot hitters among the Reds in April, when he batted .356.

"Eddie is ready to play, but I'm not ready to break up a winning combination at this time," Hutchinson said while filling out the lineup for the May 12 series opener in Pittsburgh with Cardenas playing shortstop and batting eighth.

After losing again on Saturday, the winning combination obviously had run its course, and Kasko returned to the starting lineup and contributed a double to Cincinnati's win. After a day off and a trip to Philadelphia, an even more hopeful sign was delivered by Gene Freese, who had uncharacteristically delivered more with his glove at third base than with his bat in the first month of the season. Freese had hit just .238 with one home run and five RBI in April, and he'd produced just four RBI with no home runs in his first eleven May games, but he wiped out a 2–0 Phillies lead with a three-run home run off of right-hander Frank Sullivan. Robinson added a leadoff home run in the sixth and Jay finished his second complete-game win over Philadelphia in less than two weeks to improve his overall record to 3–3.

"That's three more victories than I had at this time last year," Jay said. "I'll be all right as long as they get me some runs."

Those runs would be more likely if Freese started to finally warm up—an eventuality about which the fun-loving New Orleans resident was supremely confident.

"Don't worry," he promised. "I'll get my twenty to twenty-five homers this year." He couldn't resist adding with a smile, "I don't want to hit forty, because the next year I'm liable to hit only thirty and have to take a cut."

"Our room will have more than a few homers and RBIs before the season is over," his road roommate, Coleman, chimed in—a prediction that would prove to be uncannily accurate.

Hutchinson was even happier about the desire shown by the Reds pitchers, who'd made a special trip to Connie Mack Stadium on May 15—a day off—to work out.

"That kind of spirit and enthusiasm can't help but make us a good club," he said. "We're going to cause a lot of eyebrow-raising before this season is over. I've seen every club at least three times so far this season, and I think we're as good as any of them."

The Reds finished the short road trip with another win at Philadelphia and headed home for the Kid Glove Game, an annual exhibition that generated funds used to buy equipment for the players involved in Greater Cincinnati's Knothole youth amateur baseball program, the area's version of Little League. The Reds had played a number of different opponents in this game through the years—sometimes one of their minor league teams, other times an American League club—and the Cleveland Indians made the trip in 1961 to Cincinnati with the Reds playing a return game in Cleveland later in the season.

The team also came home with a bit of unexpected bad news. Pitcher Jay Hook was suspected of having contracted, of all things, the mumps. The diagnosis was confirmed when the Reds got back to Cincinnati, forcing Hook to spend a week in bed and at least another week of inactivity. Players who'd never had the illness were scheduled to receive shots.

Cincinnati returned to the NL race the next night, with Milwaukee in for a four-game series, including the first scheduled Sunday doubleheader of the season. O'Toole and Burdette hooked up in a taut opener on Friday night, both of them turning in complete games. The Braves took a 2–0 lead that Freese wiped out with a two-run homer in the fourth, setting up Gus Bell's game-winning homer leading off the sixth, which gave the Reds thirteen wins in their last fifteen games—seven of them by one run. The complete game was O'Toole's fourth of the season, more than half the seven he'd logged in 1960.

"I'll say one thing—no runner on second base is ever going to get O'Toole's pitch from my signals," catcher Bob Schmidt said. "Half the time, I don't know which way the pitch is going to move myself."

Schmidt's comment echoed something former Reds catcher Ed Bailey had once said about the young left-hander: "If Jimmy O'Toole were as hard to hit as he is to catch, he'd be a thirty-game winner," Bailey said.

The Braves roughed up four Reds pitchers the next day, setting up the Sunday doubleheader that drew 25,809 to Crosley Field. Jay lurched through the opener, giving up ten hits and six runs, including three on two home runs that tied the score, 6–6, in the ninth. The Reds bounced right back against right-handed reliever Moe Drabowsky, who allowed a one-out single by Kasko and a pinch-hit, RBI double by the left-handed Bell—his second game-winning hit of the series.

Freese homered in the ninth inning of the second game to cut Milwaukee's lead to 3–2, capping a twin bill in which he went five for eight. Freese had enjoyed eleven hits in his last twenty-four at-bats with two doubles, three homers, and seven RBI over six games to improve his overall batting to .288. He also was a combined seven for fifteen against Milwaukee's two aces, Lew Burdette and Warren Spahn.

Pinson and Robinson followed with one-out singles to put runners on first and third, but right-handed reliever Claude

Raymond tried to pick Robinson off first base, prompting a rundown that led to Pinson being thrown out at home for the second out—first baseman Joe Adcock to rookie catcher Joe Torre. Robinson advanced to second, but was stranded when pinch-hitter Pete Whisenant lined out to Raymond.

The doubleheader split set up the first visit of the season by Los Angeles to Cincinnati. The Dodgers came into town for a two-game series with a 22–14 record and .611 winning percentage, fourteen percentage points behind San Francisco but still technically tied with the Giants for first place, one game ahead of Pittsburgh and one-and-one-half ahead of the Reds. Los Angeles was riding a four-game winning streak and had just finished sweeping the Giants in a three-game series at Candlestick Park.

Visits to Cincinnati were like homecomings for Dodgers manager Walter "Smokey" Alston, who grew up in Darrtown, Ohio, a sleepy little hamlet located about thirty miles north of the city, and he made his off-season home a few miles west of there in Oxford. Alston was a graduate of Oxford's Miami University, where he lettered in both baseball and basketball before launching a baseball career that included just one game in the majors—at first base for the St. Louis Cardinals in 1936. Alston struck out in his only at-bat and committed one error in two fielding chances, but his lack of major league experience didn't keep the Dodgers from bringing him up out of their farm system to manage Brooklyn in 1954. One year later, he led the famous "Boys of Summer" Dodgers to their only World Series championship in Brooklyn and another in their second season in Los Angeles in 1959.

A "crowd" of just 3,141 showed up for the series opener, won by Los Angeles, 2–1, in ten innings, the Dodgers' fourth win in four games against the Reds. The next night's game couldn't be considered as a must-win—it was way too early in the season for that—but a win over Los Angeles certainly would be nice.

Rookie Ken Hunt was matched against the equally imposing Don Drysdale, a six-foot-five sidearming right-hander who wasn't shy about plunking batters he believed were getting too comfortable at the plate. The Dodgers were still in Brooklyn when the Southern California native broke into the majors with them in 1956, and he'd put together a solid, though not spectacular, career, taking a 66–54 career record into the 1961 season and 3–2 mark into his first start of the season against the Reds.

Cincinnati pieced together a two-run sixth inning, which was all Hunt and reliever Bill Henry needed to combine on a five-hit shutout. They got help in the third inning from the

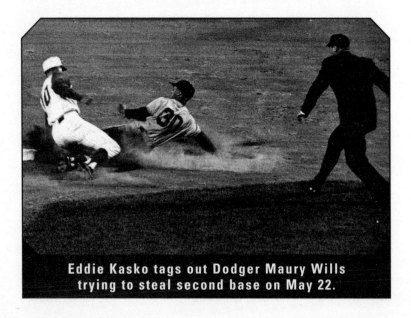

Eddie Kasko tags out Dodger Maury Wills trying to steal second base on May 22.

overly aggressive Dodgers. Shortstop Maury Wills reached on a bunt single and, one out later, took off for second base, only to put on the brakes and head back to first when Willie Davis lofted a fly ball to center field. Pinson got a glove on the ball, but he couldn't hold on. His throw to second was too late to get the sliding Davis, but it didn't matter—Davis already was out for passing Wills on the basepath.

The Giants followed the Dodgers into Crosley Field for the briefest of visits—one game—and the visitors made the most of it by capitalizing on four unearned runs during a 5–4 win. The Reds traveled to Indianapolis on May 25 for an exhibition game against their Triple-A farm team and got the next day off as rainy and unseasonably cold weather forced postponement of the series-opener against Philadelphia, a game that would be moved to August 2 as part of a twi-night doubleheader.

Cincinnati's 5–4 win on Saturday turned into a showcase for three players who were wrapping up tremendous months of May. Joey Jay improved his record for the month to 5–0 with eight innings of four-hit, two-run pitching before turning it over to Henry and Jim Brosnan. Pinson went three for four, with a double and an RBI, while Frank Robinson contributed a two-run single, and both players turned in run-saving catches. Robinson banged up his left elbow after running into the scoreboard while robbing Tony Gonzalez of two RBI with a running catch to end the sixth inning.

"You've got to be a real athlete to make that play," Phillies manager Gene Mauch said after the game. "I had already counted two runs for us when Robby made that play."

"It looked as if Robby had an ice cream cone in his hand when he got up," first baseman Gordy Coleman said. "The ball was lodged in the fingertips of his glove."

"Greatest catch I've seen in years," Philadelphia coach Peanuts Lowrey said. "Robby not only had to time his jump just right, but he risked serious injury to himself in making the catch. He's one of those rare birds who can beat you three ways—with his bat, glove, and speed."

Robinson also made a diving catch on pinch-hitter Clay Dalrymple's bid for a leadoff hit in the eighth, an inning that ended when Pinson reached over the right-center fence to rob Clarence Coleman of a home run.

"He actually reached over the fence for that ball," Mauch said. "They were the three best catches I've ever seen in one game."

The Reds wrapped up the homestand by improving to 8–0 against Philadelphia—all in May—with a 4–2 win on Sunday. Pinson hit two home runs, extending his hitting streak to seven games in which he went fifteen for twenty-seven with three doubles, three homers, and eleven RBI, and Bob Purkey turned in his fifth complete game of the season.

Cincinnati left right after the game for the second West Coast road trip of the season, starting with three games in San Francisco, including a Tuesday doubleheader scheduled to start at 10:30 a.m. on Memorial Day—always celebrated back then on May 30, regardless of the day of the week. Hunt continued his development in the first game of the series, turning in a complete game over the first-place Giants while stranding six runners on base and improving to 5–2. He'd logged two of his wins over San Francisco and one each over Los Angeles and Pittsburgh.

"The kid hasn't picked on any soft clubs in winning his five games," Hutchinson said. "He also beat some tough pitchers."

Gene Freese reported that even Willie Mays couldn't

help feeling frustrated after striking out on a sweeping sidearm curve in the eighth inning. Mays just dropped his bat at the plate and walked back to the dugout, mumbling to himself.

"Willie was cussin' himself even while he was finishing his swing," Freese said.

The Reds even were lucky enough to see Pinson escape with just a spike wound on his toe after colliding with right fielder Wally Post while catching pinch-hitter Jim Marshall's wind-blown fly ball in the fifth inning. Pinson returned the next day to go four for ten as the Reds swept the holiday twin bill, 7–6 and 6–4.

A sellout crowd of 41,692 showed up for the games, and it was estimated that another twenty thousand were turned away, but not before they indulged in a mini-riot that included throwing rocks at portable ticket booths and smashing windows, leading to several arrests. Cincinnati's team bus couldn't get through the crowd at the ballpark, prompting Hutchinson to lead the team on foot through the crowd the rest of the way.

Jim Maloney, starting near his native Fresno, California, celebrated with a third-inning home run, but he lasted only five innings, and the Reds had to watch the Giants score four ninth-inning runs, helped by Brosnan being charged with the first balk of his career after a gust of wind blew him off the mound.

"I took as long as I could trotting around the bases," Maloney said about his homer. "I figure that I might not ever get another chance to run out a homer."

Coleman committed two errors in the second game, but he also had three hits and drove in two runs. Bob Purkey, normally a starter, relieved Jim O'Toole in the ninth inning to seal the win that lifted the Reds into a tie with San Francisco and Los Angeles for first place.

The Reds headed south to Los Angeles, where they closed out the month with an 8–7 win despite Robinson being out of the lineup with a sore left elbow after he'd been hit by a pitch in the first game of the previous day's doubleheader. He left that game but returned to play the second game. Wally Post also was not available against the Dodgers after stiffening up following his collision with Pinson on Monday in San Francisco.

Freese helped make up for the absences with three hits, including two home runs, while Kasko, Pinson, Coleman, and Jerry Lynch had two hits each against Drysdale and three Dodger relief pitchers, but the Reds still needed a ninth-inning single by Lynch to drive in the go-ahead run and a leaping catch by Coleman of a line drive by Ron Fairly to escape with an 8–7 win, capping an impressive 20–6 month that had started with Cincinnati in seventh place and ended with the Reds tied for first.

Jay wasn't as impressive as he'd been in previous starts, but he still got the win to finish the month with a 6–0 record, 2.72 ERA, and three complete games. Pinson hit a sizzling .406 with six home runs and 21 RBI, while Robinson, despite sitting out the only game he would miss all season, hit .329 with eight home runs and 19 RBI. All three were candidates to be named the league's Player of the Month, which went to Jay on June 4. He became the first Reds player to win the award since it was instituted in 1958, but it wasn't his first. He'd also been named Player of the Month while with Milwaukee in July of that year.

SIX

What's Up with the Cubs?

With the imbalance in leagues created by the American League's expansion, the 1961 season was one for the books even before Jim O'Toole threw the first official pitch.

That didn't mean it couldn't get weirder—and it did, starting in Kansas City, where the Athletics' new owner, some insurance guy out of Chicago named Charles O. Finley, had the seats at Municipal Stadium painted yellow and blue-green and turned an area beyond the right-field fence into a pasture, complete with grazing sheep.

Finley, who liked to consider himself forward-thinking, also had installed a mechanical Bugs Bunny contraption under a trap door near the plate. "Bugs" would pop up out of the ground to deliver new baseballs to the umpire.

The wackiness wasn't limited to Kansas City. In San Francisco, at the first of that season's two All-Star Games, a gale-force gust of wind blew five-foot-eleven, 165-pound Giants relief pitcher Stu Miller off the mound, prompting the umpire to call a balk, much like what had happened to Cincinnati relief pitcher Jim Brosnan during a regular-season game in May.

Later that month, the season's second All-Star Game, played in Boston, became the first in history to end in a tie. The score was 1–1 when rain forced cancellation after nine innings.

That there were two All-Star Games was somewhat unusual. As a way of boosting the players' pension fund, the leagues played two from 1959 through 1962, before reverting to the one-game-per-season format.

Besides Brosnan's balk, the Reds were involved in their own share of bizarre incidents during the season. One occurred on July 21, when a Reds-Giants game at Crosley Field was postponed by a thunderstorm, during which a bolt of lightning struck and destroyed a flagpole on the roof. The pole was one of eight displaying the pennants of each National League team, in the order of that day's standings. The destroyed flagpole was the first-place team's, and it happened to be the one displaying Cincinnati's pennant.

Later that season, on September 4 against Philadelphia at Crosley, Frank Robinson was on second base when Gordy Coleman singled to right. Robinson rounded third and stopped, and Phillies catcher Clay Dalrymple yelled at pitcher Art Mahaffey to cut off the throw. Mahaffey caught the ball, but he bobbled it, and Robinson set sail for the plate. Mahaffey turned to throw him out, but there was no Dalrymple.

The catcher was on the ground, looking for his false teeth that had popped out when he yelled at Mahaffey.

Perhaps the most, um, interesting aspect of the 1961 season was the experiment conducted on Chicago's North Side. The Cubs, who hadn't finished above .500 or in the first division since 1946, scrapped the traditional one-team-one-manager approach for a new idea. They set up what was described as a "College of Coaches," a group of eight specialists who, for the purpose of signing the lineup card, would take turns acting as manager.

Eight minds proved to be no better than one for Chicago, which won four fewer games in 1961 than in 1960 while finishing seventh again, ahead of only the hapless Phillies, who would set what at the time was a major league record for consecutive losses in a season with twenty-three. When it came to the Reds, though, the Cubs knew what they were doing. They were the only team to finish the season with a winning record against Cincinnati, going 12–10 and positively pummeling Reds pitching in several games.

Cincinnati and the Cubs already had split four April games when they met on June 2 at Crosley Field for the first of a four-game series. The Cubs were slowly building what would become a contender by the last part of the decade. Ernie "Mr. Cub" Banks, who'd won back-to-back Most Valuable Player awards in 1958 and 1959, was in his prime and would remain a threat for the entire decade. Third baseman Ron Santo was in his first full season, and outfielder Billy Williams would reach the majors for good in 1961 and be named the league's Rookie of the Year.

But the Cubs still were struggling—against everybody except the Reds, who were in first place by a half-game when they returned from the West Coast and had seen the Las Vegas odds on them winning the National League championship drop from thirty-to-one to five-to-one. By the end of the weekend, they were tied with the Giants for second by a half-game. Chicago, winner of four straight going into the Cincinnati series, won three out of four, scoring a combined twenty-five runs in their three wins.

"They're a hot club," Reds manager Fred Hutchinson said. "They were hot when they came in here. No, we did not suffer a letdown after the early week success in California. The way we have been going, you know it's going to happen. The secret is you can't let down. If so, it's a different story. There's no sense panicking. These guys hate to lose. They take defeat hard. It's a good sign."

Frank Robinson was back in the lineup after missing the game in Los Angeles with a bruised left elbow that still was sore after he'd been hit with a pitch by Jim Duffalo in San Francisco during the Memorial Day doubleheader the previous Tuesday. X-rays revealed no damage.

Robinson's elbow wasn't Cincinnati's only health concern. Several players had been seen chatting with Los Angeles's Charlie Neal, who later had been diagnosed with chicken pox. Pitcher Jay Hook still was unavailable while getting over mumps, so the worry was understandable, but Neal was past the infectious stage when he encountered the Reds. Nobody became ill.

The Cubs capitalized on a pair of Reds errors—one mental by Hutchinson, one physical by Pete Whisenant—to score what proved to be the winning run in the top of the ninth. Whisenant batted for pitcher Marshall Bridges in the bottom of the eighth inning and stayed in the game to make his major league debut as a catcher in the ninth with Cincinnati trailing, 6–1. Don Zimmer reached base with a one-out single. He took off for second on a ball-three pitch to Santo and continued to third when Whisenant's throw sailed into center field past second base, which nobody bothered to cover because the pitch to Santo was ball four. Whisenant and Coleman also allowed Banks's popup to fall between them in foul territory, setting up Banks's sacrifice fly, which meant the Reds' five-run ninth inning left them one run short instead of tying the game.

"Pete shouldn't feel bad," Hutchinson said. "If anyone's to blame, it's me for putting him in there to catch."

The Cubs left after Santo and Banks each hit back-to-back, two-out solo home runs off of Jim O'Toole in the first inning of what would become an 8–2 Chicago win in the nightcap of the Sunday doubleheader. Milwaukee replaced the Cubs in Crosley's visiting team clubhouse for a four-game series, of which the Reds won three.

Robinson got them started with his first three-hit game of the season, including a two-run go-ahead homer in the eighth inning that Jerry Lynch followed with a solo shot in a 5–3 win.

"First time this season I've gotten that many hits in one game, and they couldn't have come at a better time," Robinson said.

Cincinnati's 7–3 win in the second game of the series still was tight in the eighth inning when Bob Purkey sprang off the mound, pounced on Johnny Logan's slow roller thirty feet up the third-base line and threw out Joe Torre trying to score what would have been the tying run.

The Reds wrapped up the series with a 10–8 win on June 8, but they had to hold off a record-setting display of Milwaukee power to do it. Cincinnati led 10–2 in the seventh when

Eddie Mathews hit a two-run homer with nobody out. Hank Aaron followed with another homer, prompting Hutchinson to replace Jim Maloney with Bridges, who gave up back-to-back homers by Joe Adcock and former Red Frank Thomas. No other game in major league history had featured four consecutive home runs.

After withstanding that barrage, the Reds left on their second eleven-game road trip of the season. They opened with three wins in four games at St. Louis, losing the opener and sweeping a Sunday doubleheader. Rookie righthander Ken Hunt turned in his second complete game in the 6–2 win in the opener, which featured second baseman Don Blasingame's first homer of the season and third baseman Gene Freese's twelfth, both in the first inning.

Blasingame had received much of the credit for the Reds performance since he was acquired from San Francisco in late April. That doubleheader sweep left Cincinnati with a 28–13 record since Blasingame joined the team. He had solidified an infield situation that was admittedly shaky coming out of spring training, and while his average wasn't overpowering—he hit .250 in May and .276 in June, usually while batting first or second—he had a knack for coming up with the big hit at the right time.

"Sure, we had an uncertain situation at second base, but we've remedied it, and Blasingame, since he's been with us, has done a great job," Hutchinson said. "He's given our offense a tremendous lift. When we traded for him, we knew we weren't getting the best fielding second baseman in baseball. He has good range and he's great going back on the grass for balls, but he does have some trouble making the double play and he doesn't have a great pair of hands. Even now, you'll have to agree that Blasingame has improved a lot in the field just in the short time he's been with us. I like players who give you that hundred-percent effort whenever they put on the uniform. Blasingame is that type of player."

"Blasingame is a much better player than he was last year," said his former manager with the Cardinals, Solly Hemus.

"You can't measure Blasingame's value by just his bat and glove," third base coach Reggie Otero said, pointing out that Blasingame went from first to second on a fly ball to center field in Pittsburgh. "You've got to include his aggressiveness. Players on the club see Blasingame do things like that and they become ashamed of themselves if they don't show the same hustle. Pride—appeal to a player's pride, reach him, and he'll do things he has never done before."

Blasingame had connections with the Cardinals and Reds even before joining both teams. His wife, Sarah, was the daughter of former Reds catcher Walker Cooper, who played on St. Louis teams that won the World Series in 1942 and 1944 before setting Cincinnati's single-game RBI record with ten against the Cubs on July 6, 1949. Sarah Blasingame was a former Miss Missouri who'd gone on to be a Miss America finalist.

The Reds' doubleheader sweep in St. Louis gave them seven wins in their last ten games, a stretch in which Blasingame had been on base twenty-three times—thirteen hits and ten walks—in forty-eight plate appearances and scored nine runs. Freese drove in seven runs in the doubleheader, and he also delivered after the games on Cincinnati's way to the airport. The team bus broke down, and Freese got off to join a family picnicking in a backyard adjacent to the road. He returned to the bus hauling a supply of beer in a bag.

In his book *Pennant Race*, Jim Brosnan writes that

Freese said, "They couldn't play horseshoes, but they had plenty of beer."

Cincinnati went into a day off at Pittsburgh having completed a little over one-third of the season. The Reds were twelve games over .500 at 33–21 and, after the Dodgers lost while Cincinnati was off, in first place all alone, one-half game ahead of Los Angeles. They didn't surprise Pittsburgh manager Danny Murtaugh, who knew a contending club when he saw one.

"They don't surprise me one bit," said Murtaugh, who'd guided the Pirates to the World Series championship the previous year. "I said during spring training this would be a six-club race, and they were one of the clubs I had in mind."

An anonymous source told one reporter that Cincinnati's performance stemmed from a meeting Hutchinson held in Columbia, South Carolina, on the team's way north from Florida.

"It was not one of those loud bawl-out sessions, though we needed one, because we looked terrible," the player said. "He told us about pride—in ourselves, our families, and baseball. He told us we were not playing for him, but for our families, ourselves, and the fans.

"Usually, in meetings like that, a certain few pay attention, but in this one, they were so attentive and the place so quiet that you could hear a mosquito buzz. He told us that if we play to our best and could look in the mirror and look our families in the eye and say honestly, 'I did my best,' he'd be satisfied. It was the finest talk to a group of athletes I've ever heard. Nobody, I'm sure, has forgotten it."

Gordy Coleman saw no reason the Reds couldn't keep it going.

"We've played fifty-four games, one-third of the season, and won better than sixty percent of them," he pointed out. "Even down south, in training, when things went wrong, we felt like we had a good club. We can win it now. The incentive, and everyone knows it, is that it means a lot of dollars for all of us."

Freese agreed and listed several reasons.

"We have spirit, speed, pitching, defense, (Frank) Robinson, (Vada) Pinson, Otis Douglas, and me," he said. "I don't want to sound boastful, but if we continue all these things and I hit thirty-five homers, we'll win it."

The impact of Douglas's conditioning efforts couldn't be ignored. When the Reds were at home, he worked in a small, well-equipped gymnasium just off the training room in the clubhouse, and he played a vital role in helping the players cope with the various bumps and bruises that can't be avoided during a grinding, 154-game season.

Of course, some observers still needed convincing. Milwaukee manager Chuck Dressen, perhaps still nursing the grudge of being fired by the Reds in September 1937, found some aspects of the team surprisingly impressive, but overall, he was less than intimidated.

"If you're lucky enough to get one of those Reds starters out of there, you have to look at either (Jim) Brosnan or (Bill) Henry," he told reporters. "Sure, (Joey) Jay's winning, but he doesn't finish many games. I never liked Don Blasingame. Gene Freese can't continue fielding like he has, and who knows what will happen to the Reds pitching before next October. The Reds have surprised even themselves with some of the best pitching in the league, but they haven't started feeling the pressure yet. That could make a big difference, and usually does."

**The bullpen tandem of Jim Brosnan (right)
and Bill Henry (left) played a key
role in the Reds' success in 1961.**

"I never could please Dressen, anyway," a bemused Jay responded. "If I won thirty games, he'd find something wrong."

The Reds opened the middle leg of their road trip with back-to-back one-run losses at Pittsburgh before salvaging the final game of the three-game series and moving on to Philadelphia, where they swept a four-game series against the Phillies, including both ends of their third consecutive Sunday doubleheader. Freese, who'd driven in seven runs in the previous Sunday's twin bill, went seven for eight with seven straight hits, including a triple and his thirteenth homer of the season, in the two games at Connie Mack Stadium.

"They made me mad Saturday when they stopped my hitting streak," said Freese, who flied out to left field in his last at bat to finish the road trip seventeen for forty-four, boosting his overall average to .297. "I've never before had a day like today, and I may never have another one like it. That last pitch I hit was the best one I had all day. I should have hit a homer."

Shortstop Eddie Kasko, a New Jersey native, went three for eight in the sweep before a group of friends who'd chartered a bus from his hometown.

"Twenty-nine of them made the trip, and they brought along seventeen cases of beer," Kasko said.

After a day off, the Reds faced their second doubleheader in three days, one of the games a makeup of the May 9 game that had been postponed. A standing-room-only crowd of 32,019, Cincinnati's largest since the 1959 season-opener, came out for the twi-night affair, which the teams split, the Reds winning the opener on Lynch's game-tying, pinch-hit single in the ninth and Blasingame's bases-loaded walk in the eleventh.

The second-game loss snapped two win streaks—Cincinnati's at six games and Joey Jay's at eight. The Reds bounced back to win the next three games, including a 5–4 win over Los Angeles in the first game of a three-game weekend series, of which the first and third were sold out before the first pitches.

Winning eight out of their last nine games had left the Reds even looser than normal. Kasko described a prank call he'd made to Freese from a "George Harris," supposedly a friend of Freese's from West Virginia. "George," at one point in the conversation, asks Freese for eight tickets to the game. Freese, of course, has none to give.

"None left," George exclaims. "What's the matter with you? Have you gone high hat, just because you're a star now? So that's it, huh? You don't know your old friends, anymore."

Even general manager Bill DeWitt was contemplating his own phone humor. DeWitt, living at the Netherland Hilton, kept getting calls for a hotel employee with the same name. The Reds' DeWitt smilingly described how he had to resist the urge to arrange a banquet on behalf of the hotel.

The high spirits carried over to the field, where Frank Robinson delivered a two-run homer to tie the game in the sixth inning, and Kasko came up with a line-drive single to left in the ninth for the walkoff win. Kasko displayed cool professionalism in his at-bat against right-handed reliever Larry Sherry, fouling off three two-strike pitches and taking two balls before getting the pitch he liked.

"I almost forgot to run out the hit," Kasko said. "Dick Sisler had to yell to me to touch the bag. That was a big one. We gained a game on each of the four clubs behind us. Fifteen more to go with them. I don't know whether I can hold up without getting ulcers."

"I was glad when Kasko worked Sherry into a fastball situation," Robinson said. "I knew he could handle a fastball."

Robinson's homer was his eighteenth of the season, tying San Francisco's Orlando Cepeda for the league lead.

"I've never had this many homers this early," said Robinson, who went into the game thirty-one of eighty-seven with five home runs and twenty-two RBI in the month. "I had eighteen at the All-Star break in 1956 and again in 1959."

Robinson, obviously, was blazing hot. He was hitting virtually uncatchable line drives, according to the Cardinals' Curt Flood, a Gold Glove-caliber center fielder.

"Trying to catch a liner off Frank's bat is like trying to catch a knuckleball," Flood said. "Without that spin, the ball does all sorts of tricks."

The large crowds during the homestand, which would reach 120,806 for the six dates, further exposed Crosley's traffic and parking problems, which were detailed in a *Cincinnati Enquirer* front-page story. Eight extra officers, including three on motorcycles, were assigned to the game.

"Last week, it was so crowded that people began to park in the prohibited areas," Cincinnati Police Sergeant L.W. Badgett told the newspaper before the first game of the Los Angeles series. "We were forced into towing them away. It's going to be packed again tonight."

Bill Henry, struggling with a viral infection that would keep him at home the next day, was roughed up for three runs in two innings in a 9–7 nationally televised loss on Saturday, but the Reds regrouped again behind Jay and Robinson for a 3–2 win in Sunday's finale. The Reds scored all three of their runs in the first inning, the third when Los Angeles starter Stan Williams was called for a balk, prompting Walter Alston to argue vehemently enough to be ejected. The Dodgers cut the lead to one with a two-run seventh, but Robinson threw out Junior Gilliam trying to score the tying run from first base on a Maury Wills double to preserve the lead.

The game was preceded by a home run-hitting contest— Robinson, Wally Post, Freese, Coleman, and Lynch for the Reds against Frank Howard, Willie Davis, Duke Snider, Wally Moon, and John Roseboro for the Dodgers. The winner received one hundred dollars, while second place earned seventy-five dollars and third fifty dollars. Of course, Robinson won, but he wasn't the only member of the organization feeling rewarded. After the game, the team announced a series of roster moves. Relief pitcher Sherman "Roadblock" Jones was called up from Triple-A Jersey City, replacing left-hander Marshall Bridges on the active roster and in the bullpen. Bridges was optioned to Jersey City on twenty-four-hour recall. At the same time, the team purchased the contract of catcher Johnny Edwards from Triple-A Indianapolis and sent catcher Bob Schmidt down to the Indians.

Jones, who was the player to be named later in the trade with San Francisco that had brought Blasingame and Schmidt to the Reds, pitched seven innings for Jersey City on Sunday and then drove all night to get to Cincinnati in time to join the Reds as they left on a seven-game road trip to Chicago and Milwaukee.

The new faces and Cincinnati's sustained presence in first place—the Reds had spent thirteen consecutive days on top of the league going into the June 27 start of the series in Chicago—did nothing to impress the Cubs. The Reds needed a five-run seventh—three scoring on Lynch's pinch-hit triple— to pull out a 10–8 slugfest win in the opener.

The win was a showcase for Cincinnati's deep bench. Besides Lynch's triple, Gordy Coleman delivered a pinch-hit double, and Edwards and Gus Bell both came up with singles off the bench. Reds pinch-hitters as a group were hitting .310 (twenty-seven for eighty-seven) after the game.

"I just kept trotting them in there," Hutchinson said. "They did the rest. I don't know of any bench that is stronger. I've said it before and I'll say it again. Lynch is the greatest pinch-hitter I've ever seen."

The Reds also survived another collision between Vada Pinson and Robinson while Robinson—by now the everyday right fielder—was catching Jerry Kindall's fly ball for the final out of the game.

"Did you see Frank showboating out there?" Pinson asked a writer with glee. "He caught the ball with one hand and used the other one to keep me from falling after we collided."

The teams returned to Wrigley the next day for a June 28 doubleheader, one game making up an April 25 postponement. Bob Purkey started the first game and was pounded for nine hits and eight runs in four innings. Jay Hook relieved him and was almost as ineffective, allowing eight hits and eight runs in four innings.

Jim O'Toole started the second game and lasted seven innings, but the Cubs capitalized on errors by Freese and catcher Jerry Zimmerman to score two unearned runs in the second inning on their way to a 7–2 win. Bob Purkey, valiantly trying to help out, pitched an inning of relief.

Chicago batters were teeing off on Reds pitchers with so much confidence that Cincinnati's players and managers became convinced that the Cubs were stealing signs. That didn't explain why the home team wasn't hitting every other team as well as it hit the Reds, nor did it explain the offensive eruption against Cincinnati pitching at Crosley Field earlier in June.

"It might be we're hanging too blank-blank many curve balls," Hutchinson said. "I never saw anything like it."

He would see more. The carnage continued the next day as the Cubs rolled to a 15–8 win, scoring six runs in three innings against Jim Maloney and eight in two innings against Jones. That gave Chicago forty-six runs in four games against the Reds, who had lost three straight games for the first time since their eight-game losing streak in April.

The problems hadn't cost the team its sense of humor—at least as far as the imperturbable Freese was concerned. The third baseman, who'd pulled a groin muscle in the series finale, had some fun while giving an interview to a national writer who'd been deployed to learn why the Reds were playing so well. The writer asked Freese about the team's unity.

"Unity?" Freese deadpanned. "Everyone on this club hates each other. You never saw so much dissension. That's why we're going so good. Everyone hates each other so much he tries his best to make the other guy look bad."

The writer asked about Otis Douglas's conditioning program.

"Nah, it hasn't helped," Freese replied. "All it has done is make everyone tired."

But didn't the conditioning have something to do with the limited number of injuries?

"The guys are too tired from doing those exercises to complain about injuries," Freese said.

This was the same Freese who'd left Cincinnati's 9–2 win over St. Louis on June 21 with a strained muscle in his right calf.

"I could feel it tightening up for the last three days," he said. He couldn't resist adding, "Guess it's because I've never been on base this much before."

Still, the Reds couldn't get out of Chicago fast enough, even though their next destination was Milwaukee to face a Braves team that had won four of its last five and eight of its last ten games. But just as the Cubs owned an inexplicable advantage over the Reds, so did the Reds enjoy an edge against the Braves—especially on their home field at County Stadium. Cincinnati went 15–7 against Milwaukee in 1961, including 9–2 in Wisconsin.

Former Brave Joey Jay ended June by scattering eleven hits over 8⅔ shutout innings and contributing a two-run, bases-loaded single off of Warren Spahn in a 4–0 Reds win, the first of three wins in the four-game series, including a sweep of a Sunday doubleheader that was anything but genteel. Jay's win extended what Milwaukee general manager John McHale called the pitcher's "vendetta" against the Braves.

"Just say that I take particular delight in beating them," Jay said. "I'd be lying if I said that I didn't. What the heck. I led the Milwaukee pitchers in earned run average in two of the five years I was with them. It wasn't my fault they didn't pitch me enough."

After losing on Saturday, the Reds fell behind 5–2 in the first game of Sunday's doubleheader when pitcher Jim O'Toole unwittingly lit a fire under the team. He was on first base with two outs in the fourth inning when Eddie Kasko doubled to left field. O'Toole rounded third, decided against trying to score and slipped on his way back to third. His only recourse was trying to dislodge the ball out of third baseman Eddie Mathews's glove, but Mathews felt that taking an elbow to the face was going too far. He jumped on O'Toole, and the two rolled around on the ground, sparking a bench-clearing brawl.

Fans were treated to the sight of Milwaukee shortstop Roy McMillan taking off his glasses and asking somebody to hold them while Hutchinson and Douglas started pulling bodies off of the pile and tossing them aside.

"I was only trying to get my guy out of there," Hutchinson said. "First, Spahn grabbed me, then (Lew) Burdette. I told them to let go, that I was just interested in pulling Mathews off O'Toole. I was saying, 'Eddie, what the hell do you think you're doing?' He said, 'But Hutch, he knocked the ball out of my hands.' I said, 'What's he supposed to do, give you a big kiss?' "

Pete Whisenant had the same mission.

"I was in there pulling and talking to Mathews," Whisenant

said. "I told Eddie not to hit O'Toole and kept trying to get him off our guy."

O'Toole, pitching on his first wedding anniversary, had more on his mind than just trying to stay alive on the basepaths. He'd given up three runs and four hits in the first inning, including a double and two homers, one to first baseman Joe Adcock.

"I couldn't understand it, because I was making those good pitches," he said. He figured it out when told by Joey Jay that Milwaukee relief pitcher Bob Buhl was stealing catcher Jerry Zimmerman's signs from the Braves bullpen. The two changed the signs, leading to Mathews taking three fastballs for called strikes in the third inning and O'Toole issuing a challenge after getting on base in the second inning.

"I told Adcock I was going to stick it in the next guy's ear if you guys ever steal our signs again," he said. Adcock denied any sign-stealing, but he also passed the message on to his teammates, including Mathews, who understandably thought O'Toole's baserunning aggressiveness was premeditated.

"I rolled him over, got him in a headlock, and ran him down," O'Toole said. "Both benches emptied, and we had a brawl. We ended up winning the doubleheader, and it seemed like we got a lot of juices into our feelings about what we could do and what we couldn't do."

The fight ended with Reds shortstop Leo Cardenas and Milwaukee outfielder Frank Thomas pulling Hutchinson out of the pile and Mathews being ejected, but the Reds weren't finished fighting. They tied the game and sent it into extra innings, which Hutchinson didn't see after being ejected in the ninth inning for arguing a call at first base. Sherman Jones and Jim Brosnan each pitched four innings of two-hit, shutout relief, setting up Coleman's thirteenth-inning, three-run homer off–who else?–Spahn in relief. Coleman's sixteenth homer of the season was his fifth hit in six at-bats in the game.

"It was a low fastball, the same pitch I hit for a homer off Spahn the last time," Coleman said, referring to Cincinnati's 5–4 win back on May 7.

The home run continued Coleman's inexplicable mastery of Spahn, which by the end of the season would add up to ten hits in fourteen at-bats with two home runs and five RBI.

"Hey, Coleman, how come you're always smiling on the nights Spahn's supposed to pitch?" one Braves player yelled at the Reds first baseman before the next day's game.

"Hey, Coleman, don't you have a toothache tonight?"

Gordie Coleman clubbed twenty-six homers in 1961.

Spahn asked good-naturedly before his next start against Cincinnati.

"Spahn can't figure Coleman out because Coleman can't figure Coleman, either," ex-umpire Larry Goetz said. "He falls down, he falls back, he sits down, but he hits the ball going away, and I have to like a fellow who does that."

Coleman added three more hits in the second game, improving to sixteen for twenty-seven while playing in seven of eight games on the road trip. Kasko led off the game with a homer in a three-run first inning, but the Reds still needed Frank Robinson's solo homer in the eighth for a 4–3 win that completed the doubleheader sweep.

"When you wake up a sleeping dog, somebody has got to get bit," Whisenant said. "Before that rumpus, we were a dead ballclub. Mathews gave us the spark we needed to get going."

The 29,487 fans at County Stadium weren't the only interested viewers. A front-page story in the next day's *Cincinnati Enquirer* described how WLWT lost $5,500 while devoting seven-and-one-half hours of continuous programming to the doubleheader. The broadcast was expected to finish around 7 p.m., with the station losing $2,500, but instead dragged on to 9:08 p.m., cutting into the lucrative prime time advertising revenue.

"With the Reds in first place and a rough series like Milwaukee coming up, we thought it was worthwhile to carry the extra game," program director Abe Cowan told the newspaper. "In fact, with the Reds in first place, I don't see how you can beat that programming."

The Reds didn't land at the airport until midnight, but several thousand fans were on hand to greet the front-running team, which would be in town for just two games against Pittsburgh before heading out on a six-game West Coast road swing leading up to the All-Star break. A capacity-straining crowd of just under thirty-two thousand showed up at Crosley Field the night before Independence Day to see Cincinnati squeeze out a 4–3 win behind what Jim Maloney described as his best outing of the season. He credited part of it to extra work under pitching coach Jim Turner.

"It's the best I've felt all year," Maloney told reporters. "I've been out of pitching rhythm. Jim Turner got a hold of me and had me pitch thirty minutes in Milwaukee until I got it back."

According to Brosnan, Maloney also got help from a pill—Dexedrine, an amphetamine. Aids of that nature were common in the major leagues of that era.

"This thing makes me feel like I had fifteen beers—only real strong," Brosnan quoted Maloney as saying.

The Reds moved twenty games over .500 at 49–29 the next day as Jay turned in a complete-game, three-hit shutout in a 2–0 win, sending them out west with a four-game winning streak. Their destination, San Francisco's Candlestick Park, also would be the site on July 11 of the first of the season's two All-Star Games—events in which the front-running Reds were significantly underrepresented, considering their performance up to that point.

Part of the fault might belong to the city and the team's fans, who notoriously stuffed the ballot box in voting for the starters of the 1957 game. At one point in the count, every one of the eight non-pitching positions was filled by a Red, prompting Commissioner Ford C. Frick to step in and drop three Reds in place of "also-rans" Stan Musial, Willie Mays, and Hank

Aaron. The blatant overzealousness shown by Reds fans led to the voting being turned over to the players in each league.

The 1961 balloting finished with no Reds players among the eight non-pitching starters—not even Frank Robinson, who was named as a substitute along with shortstop Eddie Kasko. Pitchers Joey Jay and Bob Purkey also were picked by NL manager Danny Murtaugh, which left relief pitcher Jim Brosnan bitterly disappointed. Brosnan, in *Pennant Race*, his diary of the season, describes spending most of the time before the flight to San Francisco and the flight itself in a drunken stupor.

Traveling secretary Avery Robbins had the job of breaking the bad news to Brosnan. Robbins had other issues as well. The Reds arrived in San Francisco to find the city in the middle of a strike by bus and taxi drivers, and he had to come up with a virtual fleet of rental cars to get the team to the hotel and ballpark.

Ken Hunt, the rookie right-hander who'd electrified the National League by going 8–4 to open his career, was scratched from starting the opener in cold, windy San Francisco due to soreness in his right shoulder. Sherman Jones got the start and responded by allowing just two runs and four hits against his former team in 8⅓ innings of a 3–2 Cincinnati win.

"Surprised?" the North Carolina native said when asked his reaction to learning about the start. "You bet, but awfully happy. How do I feel? As happy as a hound dog at a country hog killing. I guess it's the happiest I've ever been. No, it's the second happiest. I was happier the day I got married.

"Every ballplayer in the game takes pleasure in beating the club that traded him. I'm not bitter against the Giants. I just wanted to prove that they made a mistake, and I proved it."

Unfortunately, the Reds turned out to be not as completely

immune to pressure as believed. Of all people, the man who suffered the consequences was Dr. Richard Rohde, the team's trainer. He suffered what was described as a coronary occlusion, which led to a heart attack. Rohde left the team, traveling with fitness coach Otis Douglas to Chicago to meet Rohde's wife. Douglas then returned to the West Coast to add Rohde's duties to his own.

Rohde had served as Cincinnati's trainer from 1934 until developing tuberculosis after the 1946 season. He was out of baseball until returning to the Reds in 1960.

Cincinnati won the next day's game by the same 3–2 score behind O'Toole's first complete game since June 1 and Coleman's eighteenth homer of the season. The win extended Cincinnati's winning streak to six games, the last five decided as the final outs were recorded on 3-2 pitches with the tying run on base or at the plate. Vada Pinson made two more tremendous plays, a diving catch of Harvey Kuenn's sinking liner and a leaping one-handed snag of Orlando Cepeda's bid for extra bases to help set up yet another showdown with the Dodgers—this time, a four-game series at the Coliseum.

Los Angeles also rolled into the series with the momentum of six wins in seven games, the last win a 10–1 pummeling of the Cardinals that left the Dodgers three games behind the Reds. Both teams had played eighty games, more than half of the season.

The series started with a Friday twi-night doubleheader, with 68,742 fans working their way into the stadium to eventually form what would rank for a while as the largest crowd for a night game in National League history. The first game matched two of the league's brightest young pitching stars in Hunt and Los Angeles left-hander Sandy Koufax. Neither was on his game. Hunt gave up three runs in the first inning, throwing just one strike in his first fifteen pitches, but he got two back with a double in the second. Freese hit a two-run homer in the third to give the Reds the lead for good, and the Reds capitalized on a Frank Howard error to score four un-earned runs in the fourth—three on Vada Pinson's home run—and take an 8–3 lead on their way to an 11–7 win in a game that lasted three hours and thirty-one minutes.

The outcome might have been different if Pinson and catcher Jerry Zimmerman hadn't teamed up to throw out Wally Moon trying to score from third on a Norm Larker fly ball in the first inning.

"Give Jerry Zimmerman credit for that," said Hunt, who left with a blister on his finger after six innings. "He just stood there as if no play was going to be made. The next batter was yelling for Moon to slide, but he didn't hear him."

Purkey restored a semblance of sanity to the night by al-lowing eight hits and just one run in Cincinnati's 4–1 win in the nightcap, putting the Reds five games in front. The Dodg-ers cut a game off the lead with a 10–1 win on Saturday, but the Reds closed out the traditional first half of the season—the "half" before the All-Star Game break—with a stylish 14–3 rout. Cincinnati piled up fifteen hits against five Dodger pitch-ers, including Robinson's twenty-second and twenty-third home runs, part of his four-for-four, seven-RBI day.

"It's the best day I've ever had in the major leagues," said Robinson, who went into the break hitting .328 with seventy RBI. "It's the most homers I've ever had at this time of the year. In 1959, I had seventy-three RBIs at the All-Star break."

"Robby is taking over," Hutchinson said. "He's doing this year the things a great ballplayer should do. Don't ask me to enumerate them. A lot of the things are intangibles, which can't be described, but you can see the results."

The Dodgers didn't miss them. Don Drysdale, pitching in relief, threw at several Reds batters before finally finding Robinson's arm, earning an ejection from plate umpire Dusty Boggess, who'd warned the normally intimidating Los Angeles right-hander by yelling, "That's enough," after one pitch sent Robinson spinning.

"Boggess yelled, 'You're gone,' to Drysdale even before he stepped in front of the plate," Robinson said. "He threw one pitch behind Don Blasingame's head. He threw two inside pitches to Vada Pinson, and then he knocked me down with two pitches before he hit me. So, let's just say I don't think he's that wild."

"Drysdale isn't a major league pitcher, or he wouldn't do the things he does," Purkey said. "He's gutless. Bush—that's what he is."

"I don't know Drysdale, and I don't want to know him, but anytime he wants to meet me, he can name the place and I'll walk to it," Joey Jay said.

"I didn't throw intentionally to hit Robinson," Drysdale pleaded. "I told Boggess that would be a stupid thing to do with our team trailing 7–2. The first time Boggess came out, he told me I had better control than that. I told him the way Robinson hangs over the plate, any inside pitch could hit him."

Besides pitching a complete game, Jay contributed a two-run double.

"How about that?" he said happily. "Five RBIs for the season now. What the hell, I should be an even better hitter. I led the Little League in homers in 1948."

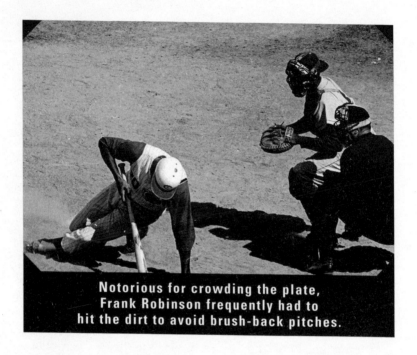

Notorious for crowding the plate, Frank Robinson frequently had to hit the dirt to avoid brush-back pitches.

Robbins and DeWitt might have been even happier than the players. Based on the twenty-seven-and-one-half cents per admission visiting teams received from each game, the Reds took home $35,395 as their take from the 128,712 series attendance. They probably weren't singing in the showers, though. They left that to the players.

"It's bad on the eardrums in there," pitching coach Jim Turner reported.

To Hutchinson, though, it was literally and figuratively music to his ears.

"It's a good sign, because when you're singing, you're winning," he said. "Too many times in the last couple of years, I've gone into the shower room and haven't heard a word."

SEVEN

Robby and Hutch

As if the Cubs didn't do enough damage to the Reds in the standings during the 1961 season, it looked for several minutes just four games into the proverbial second half of the season as if Chicago might cost Cincinnati any shot at getting into the World Series.

That's what Reds manager Fred Hutchinson was thinking while viewing the carnage in shallow right-center-field during the top of the eighth inning of what eventually would be a 4–2 loss to the Cubs. Right fielder Frank Robinson and center fielder Vada Pinson both were sprawled on the ground after colliding while chasing Sam Taylor's blooper. Robinson actually

**Vada Pinson and Frank Robinson
collide while chasing a fly ball.**

caught the ball, but he lost it after running into Pinson, who got the worst of the collision.

"We were both yelling, but with the noise the crowd was making, we couldn't hear each other," Pinson said, rubbing his right shoulder and chest. He also had a nick on his left ankle. "I got hit here. I don't know whether it's going to stiffen. Right now, I feel OK. I don't know what hit me in the head. I'm just glad neither one of us got hurt."

He wasn't the only one.

"It was the worst scare I've had this season," Hutchinson said. "I wouldn't have been so concerned if they had run together standing up, but they collided at angles and going full speed. Taylor had a full swing but got it on the handle. The swing is what fooled Robby. That's why he had a bad break on the ball."

Surviving that scare did nothing to shake the malaise that had plagued the Reds since the three-day All-Star break.

Aftermath of Pinson-Robinson collision.

Hutchinson had been concerned even before the break about its potential to rob the Reds of precious momentum.

"I know we're sitting pretty right now with a five-game lead and a good homestand coming up, but we've had to battle in every game, in every inning," he'd said. "In a race like this, everybody—all seven of them—can hurt you. It's too bad we have three days off right now when we've got momentum, but I'm sure the fellows, who have tremendous desire and hustle, will get it back."

The Reds won two of their first three games after the break, but that loss to the Cubs was the first of six straight defeats, a stretch interrupted only by a rainout against the Giants at Crosley Field on July 21. Rain had threatened many of the twelve games in the homestand—matching a September stretch for the longest of the season, though the second one covered a span of seventeen days—and the inclement weather prompted general manager Bill DeWitt to hire a helicopter, which hovered over the field trying to dry the grass before a game against Milwaukee earlier in the week.

"Tomorrow, we're going to have the helicopter fly upside down and cut the grass," joked Lewis Crosley of the ticket department.

Helicopters couldn't salvage the Friday series-opener against the Giants, which was expected to draw a sizable crowd but still was postponed two hours before the scheduled first pitch.

"We hated to call the game, but water was a foot deep in the area of the lower boxes," DeWitt said. "In a way, the postponement was welcomed. I think a day of rest will help us."

That sentiment was reflected by Charles Erskine in the next day's *San Francisco Examiner*.

"In a rank display of outright cowardice, unmatched in recent memory, the Cincinnati Reds called off tonight's game on the basis of a twenty-minute thunder shower that ended nearly two hours before game time," Erskine wrote. "The decision of the Reds to call off tonight's game might be termed a new yellow low in baseball behavior. But, an understandable low, for the Reds, losers of five in a row, have no business in first place anyway."

What Erskine didn't report was his failure to make the trip to Crosley Field and personally check out the conditions.

The Reds went into the losing streak with a six-game lead in the National League, their largest of the season. Two losses each to Milwaukee, Los Angeles, and San Francisco helped whittle the lead down to one game.

From at least one point of view, however, this was the time of the season during which Hutchinson peaked as manager. Two months later, Jackie Robinson was in Cincinnati on business for Chock Full o' Nuts coffee when he was asked about Hutchinson.

"He has done a fantastic job," said Robinson. "He has done what a manager should. He kept the club from falling apart. When the Reds slipped after the All-Star break and the Dodgers started coming hard, he didn't panic."

Nobody recognized the value of Hutchinson to the Reds more than DeWitt, whose appreciation of "The Bear's" contributions to Cincinnati's surge into first place was reflected in a curious incident during the All-Star break. DeWitt and Los Angeles general manager Buzzie Bavasi exchanged heated words in the hospitality room at the San Francisco Sheraton Palace stemming from a comment Bavasi made to a reporter.

"If Fred Hutchinson were available, any club which needed a manager would be a fool not to go after him," Bavasi said.

"What Buzzie said comes very close to tampering, and I may even go to the National League president with it," DeWitt said after talking with Bavasi. "I read the comment and sent Bavasi an air mail special delivery letter demanding a retraction of the statement."

Bavasi was taken aback by DeWitt's reaction.

"I honestly thought Bill was kidding me," Bavasi. "I think Hutch is doing a great job, and I said it. If DeWitt wants a retraction, OK, then quote me as saying that I don't think Hutchinson is a good manager."

"That's a fine thing for Bavasi to say," DeWitt responded, before being asked if he and Hutchinson had talked about extending the manager's contract. "No, I haven't talked to him about extending it, and I don't plan to right now. We're too busy trying to win a pennant."

"One of the reasons we think he is a great guy is he does not eat you out in front of the other players," one player said. "In fact, he still thinks like an active ballplayer, not like a manager. If you boot one or you pull a skuller, he talks it over with you, almost looking at it from the standpoint of, 'Well, if I were playing, I might have done the same thing.' When you leave him, you feel better. You feel that your manager is for you."

Much of Hutchinson's approach at this point in the season involved simply trusting his players to right themselves. Part of that process included a forty-minute team meeting they called themselves before their game against the Dodgers on July 20.

"We called the meeting ourselves," one player said. "The way we've been going, we just thought it would be a good idea to sit down and talk things over a little bit. If anyone had anything on his mind, he had a chance to speak his piece."

"Everybody seemed to get along pretty well," pitcher Jim O'Toole said. "We did have one meeting where guys kind of ripped each other, like about me getting pissed off when a guy made an error. I was sort of emulating (Joe) Nuxhall. Nuxhall had that temper. I was a little bit behind him. It was maturity. You learn not to display temper out on the field. I grew up that year."

Hutchinson's temperament wouldn't allow him to just sit around and watch his team's lead slip away. His frustration boiled over during a 12–9 loss to the Braves, to the point that he challenged plate umpire Tom Gorman to a post-game fight. Hutchinson was still at the ballpark, still in uniform, pacing up and down the Cincinnati clubhouse, when the time came for the fight. Gorman, of course, had left.

Like Hutchinson's post-game batting practice in Los Angeles in April, the clear-the-air meeting yielded no immediate results. Joey Jay gave up four home runs in five innings as the Dodgers completed their mini-sweep of the two-game series with a 10–1 win.

The next day's rainout also did nothing to help Cincinnati shake off its problems. Rookie Ken Hunt, who'd come almost out of nowhere to dominate the league through the first half of the season, recorded just one out while yielding five hits and five runs in the first inning of an 8–3 loss to the Giants on July 22.

The start was Hunt's second since he'd picked up his ninth win on July 7 at Los Angeles. He didn't know it at the time, but that win would be the last of his career. Prone to developing blisters on the fingers of his pitching hand, he altered his throwing motion in an effort to solve that problem and never was the same pitcher.

"I had reached that point where I had the confidence that I could beat anybody," Hunt said years later. After his outstanding rookie season, he had spent four years pitching in the minor leagues in an effort to find what he had lost. "I had a lot of confidence when I walked out on the mound. I knew that I had the stuff to beat people.

"I guess you could call it the Dizzy Dean Syndrome. All of a sudden, out of nowhere, I started throwing the ball a little differently. I got a callous on a different finger. I just—unconsciously, I guess—was making some adjustments there. All of a sudden, my right shoulder started hurting. I think I changed my grip then, and all of a sudden, the arm quit hurting, but I had lost something. I threw two one-hitters in the Sally League (in 1963) and struck out thirteen hitters in each game, and the manager said he was going to recommend that I come back to the Reds, but an old umpire that had been there in 1960 said, 'Ken, you pitched well, but your fastball is straight. It's not like it used to be.' I went to spring training the next year and got knocked around pretty good. It was over. There was no doubt about it. I was throwing hard, but there was nothing there. You pitch up there with those people and it doesn't do something, you're in trouble."

Hunt's case was the harbinger of a couple more one-year wonders that would haunt the Reds franchise over the next thirty years. Imposing twenty-one-year-old right-hander Wayne Simpson, a Bob Gibson clone down to wearing uniform number forty-five, roared to a 13–1 start in the first half of the 1970 season before overuse caught up with his shoulder, leaving it tattered enough that he never would pitch effectively again in the majors.

Twenty years later, in 1990, right-hander Jack Armstrong would go 11–3 through the first half of the season, earning the start for the National League in the All-Star Game, but he went 1–6 over the second half and never was the same pitcher.

The July 22 loss to the Giants represented sort of a changing of the guard on the Reds pitching staff. Right-hander Howie Nunn had been placed on the disabled list, and DeWitt–trying to shore up his suddenly bedraggled staff–acquired veteran right-hander Ken Johnson from the roster of minor-league Toronto in exchange for minor-league right-hander Orlando Pena and cash.

The twenty-eight-year-old Johnson was big enough at six-four, 210 pounds to be a hard-thrower, but his out pitch was a knuckleball. He'd spent the first three years of his career with the Kansas City Athletics, who were known in that era primarily for two things: losing and serving as a major-league-level farm team for the New York Yankees, who made a habit of parking prospects in Kansas City until they were needed in a pennant drive. Johnson never was one of those lucky players to get the call from New York. Instead, he was sold by the Athletics to Toronto in May of 1961 and was shagging balls in the Maple Leafs outfield when he learned that he'd been picked up by the Reds.

"I'd always wanted to pitch in games that were important—not just to me, but to the team," Johnson recalled. "In the minors and with Kansas City, we were nowhere near first place."

The Reds had been looking at the Florida native for several months. His name came up when the Reds traded Joe Nuxhall to the Athletics in January.

"His name was mentioned, but Kansas City, at that time, said we could have our choice of any pitcher on their staff with the exception of Ray Herbert, Dick Hall, and Bud Daley," DeWitt said. "We could have claimed Johnson earlier this season when Kansas City put him on the waiver list, but at that time, we didn't need a pitcher. It cost us a little more for waiting.

"Hutch knows him. He saw him when he pitched at Portland and says he's a real bear-down guy. He throws a lot of different pitches, including a knuckleball."

Johnson's move was the latest in what had been a rollercoaster kind of year.

"I picked up four defeats real quick, even though I pitched a total of only 8⅔ innings in relief," he said about why he was shipped out of Kansas City. He pitched as a reliever in Toronto before volunteering to start. He went two innings in his first start, won five straight games, then lost four in a row despite

Bob Purkey signs autographs for young Reds fans.

posting a 0.70 ERA. "Hutch knows I can start, though. He was managing at Seattle when I was at Portland. I pitched twenty complete games that year. I think I even shut out Seattle a couple of times."

When Hutchinson had to go to his bullpen after Hunt could get just one out against the Giants on July 22, the last pitcher he brought in was Johnson, who pitched the ninth inning.

Johnson didn't pitch the next day. None of the Reds relief pitchers were needed because Bob Purkey and Jim O'Toole both pitched complete games as Cincinnati snapped its losing streak by sweeping San Francisco in a Sunday afternoon doubleheader, 6–5 and 11–2–Cincinnati's seventh sweep of the season.

While Purkey and O'Toole were instrumental, the real story was the offense, led by Lynch and Robinson. Lynch had used his bat to insert himself into the left-field mix with Wally

Post and Gus Bell, and he made his start in the first game count with a home run to lead off Cincinnati's three-run seventh, which tied the score, and another to lead off the ninth for the walkoff win.

"When I saw the ball go out of the park, I was so happy I felt like sliding into third and home," said Lynch, whose shot capped Cincinnati's first game with at least four home runs since May 7.

"These are the Reds I used to know," said Purkey, the beneficiary of the pop.

The offensive onslaught continued in the second game. Wally Post won a four-hundred-dollar savings bond as the first player to hit the Sixty Second Shop sign on top of the scoreboard, ending up with a double in the fifth inning. Gene Freese, the very next batter, also bounced a double off the sign, earning a one-hundred-dollar bond.

The Reds already were leading 7–1 by the time Post hit his double, and the red-hot Robinson was the primary reason with a two-run homer in the first and an RBI double right before Post's shot. The right fielder, shaking off several aches and pains, went a combined four for nine in the doubleheader, with two home runs—one in each game—as well as that double and five RBI. He extended his hitting streak to eighteen games, during which he went thirty-three for sixty-eight with nine doubles, two triples, eight home runs, and twenty-three RBI. His five RBI in the twin bill gave him eighty-four, one more than he'd driven in the entire 1960 season.

Robinson would extend the hitting streak to nineteen games—the league's longest of the season—with a three-hit night, including a homer, a double, and three more RBI, as the Reds opened an eight-game road trip with a 9–3 win at Milwaukee. The right fielder would finish the month with a .409 batting average, thirteen home runs, thirty-four RBIs, twelve doubles, two triples, and six stolen bases without being thrown out. He walked twelve times with just eleven strikeouts.

"The most devastating hitter I've ever had on a ballclub I've managed," an admiring Hutchinson said. "He held up during our losing streak. If it hadn't been for him, we would have looked a lot worse than we did."

What made Robinson's month more remarkable was the pain with which he took the field on a daily basis. Besides the lingering effects of his collision with Pinson on July 15, Robinson was dealing with pain in his right side, the result of crashing into the fence trying to track down a double by Milwaukee's Lee Maye two days later.

"I don't think any ribs are broken, but if it hurts him, we'll have it X-rayed," said Otis Douglas, still acting as trainer while Doc Rohde recovered from his heart attack.

Robinson also had his ongoing arm problems—the chronic throwing-arm soreness that had plagued him since his minor league days and the left arm pain from getting hit by pitches.

"There are days when it's good and days when it's not so good, but as long as it doesn't hurt, it doesn't bother me," Robinson said of his throwing arm. "It's never been as strong as it was before I hurt it, and it never will be."

During a Cincinnati stop in Cleveland a couple of weeks later, former Reds and current Indians general manager Gabe Paul revealed that Robinson had narrowly avoided what could have turned into career-ending surgery shortly after sustaining his original injury.

"Every time I pick up a paper, I see where a Robinson hit has won another ballgame," Paul casually mentioned to reporters.

"If the advice of a couple of doctors had been taken about six years ago, Frank Robinson might not be playing ball today. It was after the winter season of 1954 that Robinson came up with the trouble in his right arm. He had been playing in Puerto Rico. We had the physician for the Oakland club of the Pacific Coast League look at Robby. He wanted to cut."

Another Bay Area physician agreed, Paul said.

"He wanted to cut, too, but at a different spot," he said. "We figured at least one of the doctors had to be wrong."

The team then turned to its own physician, Dr. George Ballou.

"Dr. Ballou didn't examine Robby, but he advised, 'Don't cut,'" Paul said. "Before assigning Robinson to Columbia, we sent him to Johns Hopkins Hospital in Baltimore for a thorough examination. The doctor told us that under no circumstances should an operation be performed on Robinson's arm. Who knows what might have happened if an operation had been performed? Robinson might never have played again, or the operation might have affected his swing."

Paul also chuckled as he recalled the Reds' efforts to acquire a third baseman named Danny O'Connell from Branch Rickey's Pittsburgh Pirates in 1954, while Robinson was playing at Ogden, Utah, in his first season in Cincinnati's farm system. Rickey, still the master at front office gamesmanship, said the Pirates would settle for that little-known outfielder out West named Robinson.

"Yep, Mr. Rickey knew so little about Robinson that he couldn't think of his first name," Paul recalled. "That is, if you wanted to believe him. I didn't.

"The best thing about Robinson is that he reacts favorably to pressure. A run down the stretch won't bother him."

Former *Dayton Daily News* sportswriter Jim Ferguson summed up the general sentiment about the Reds deceptively strong leader.

"Robinson obviously was a very combative person," Ferguson said. "I would rate him the toughest competitor I've ever been around, and I've been around a lot of really good ones. He's not so far ahead that there's nobody else in sight, but ...

"One of the stories at that period of time was (Los Angeles manager) Walter Alston had a standing rule for pitchers–'Do not ever knock Robinson down. He will get up and hurt you.' He hit a lot of home runs and doubles off the wall after getting knocked down. He was so strong from that standpoint."

Still, the Reds needed more than Robinson to maintain their edge in the standings. The night after Robinson's hitting streak was snapped in a 2–0 loss at Milwaukee, Johnson made his first start for Cincinnati and got the win with the help of two innings of relief from Jim Brosnan and Gus Bell's two hundredth career home run, a pinch-hit shot in the eighth that sparked a three-run rally. Johnson started the game by striking out Milwaukee leadoff batter Mack Jones with a knuckleball that rookie catcher Johnny Edwards couldn't handle cleanly, forcing him to complete the out with a throw to first base.

"It hit me on the finger of the right hand," Edwards said. "That's why I dropped the ball and had to throw to first. Boy, you should have seen that knuckler of his dance. He threw me one while he was warming up that I'll never be able to catch, even if I'm around twenty years."

The Reds made it five wins in their last six games the next night when, with Lynch at the plate in the ninth inning,

Vada Pinson was caught trying to steal home, but he ended up being ruled safe when catcher Sammy White lost the ball, earning an error that gave the Reds a 2–1 win.

Pinson had been injured the day before during batting practice, when a foul ball caromed off a steel support of the batting cage and hit him in the mouth, leaving him with a slight cut inside of his mouth and a broken upper dental plate. That didn't keep him from taking off for home the next night, risking a collision with the well-protected White. Pinson took advantage of pitcher Carlton Willey's deliberate windup.

"I noticed that he looked at me over his right arm in his long, slow windup," Pinson said. "I figured I had a pretty good chance."

"Vada kept getting bigger and bigger, and when he was almost as big as I am, I knew he wasn't bluffing–that he was coming home," Lynch said. "You can bet everyone in the stadium was surprised, but you know what they say in the Army–the good leader is the one with the surprise attack. Vada told me the way I've been swinging the bat the last two games, he had to try to steal home."

"Vada went on his own," Hutchinson said. "Did I hold my breath? I sure did when I saw the ball was ahead of him. White caught the ball moving forward and never did have real good possession of it. Pinson was running hard and he hit White hard."

Hutchinson was asked what his reaction would have been if Pinson had been out.

"If that had happened, I might have had to sleep on it before answering that question," he diplomatically replied. "Still, I'd rather have a player show some imagination than just sit back and not think at all. Vada thought he could make it, or he would never have tried. Willey was taking a windup and he hadn't paid any attention to Vada on the pitch before."

"That play reminded me of that Peanuts cartoon you see in the newspaper," Edwards said. "In one strip I saw, 'Peanuts' team is behind by one run in the top of the ninth and he tried to steal home. He didn't make it. The last cartoon in the strip showed Peanuts [Charlie Brown] still lying at home plate. The park was empty. It was night and the only light was from the moon. Vada probably would still be lying there at home plate tonight, too, if he hadn't made it."

Pinson's play helped drop fourth-place Milwaukee ten-and-one-half games behind the league-leading Reds, which didn't impress Hank Aaron.

"The Reds are lucky, and you can quote me," Aaron declared.

"That's what gets me," said Bob Purkey, who improved to 13–5 with the complete-game win. "Everyone says we don't belong where we are, that we're not that good. Yet the fellows saying it are on teams that are below us. So, what does that make them?"

The Reds made it six wins in seven games the next night in Chicago, but they couldn't shake the equally hot Dodgers. The teams became tied for first place the next day with a Cincinnati loss and Los Angeles win, and the Reds fell out of the top spot for the first time since June 15 when they split a Sunday double-header while the Dodgers were winning at Pittsburgh.

The season was interrupted on July 31 for the second All-Star Game, this one at Boston's Fenway Park. Purkey started for the NL and allowed a Rocky Colavito homer in the first inning. Eddie Kasko contributed an infield single to the NL's one-run sixth inning. As mentioned earlier, the game was called by rain after nine innings with the score still 1–1.

Robinson didn't play in the All-Star Game because of a pulled thigh muscle, but he was back in the lineup when Cincinnati's season resumed on August 2 at Crosley Field with an unscheduled doubleheader against Philadelphia, forced by the rainout of the May 26 game. The Reds swept a three-game series against the Phillies, improving Cincinnati's record against Philadelphia to 15–0.

Jim O'Toole got the win in the opener, the day before his wife gave birth to the couple's first child, a son they named James Jerome. His birthday coincided with Bill DeWitt's. The Reds general manager turned fifty-nine.

"The name's not official yet, and if it means a raise, I might be persuaded to name him William O. after you know who," O'Toole joked.

Another reason for the club to celebrate was the return to the trainer's room of Richard "Doc" Rohde, who'd been away for almost a month while recovering from his heart attack.

Following their sweep of the Phillies, the Reds split a four-game series with the Pirates, including a ten-inning 3–2 win on a Pinson walkoff homer in the second game of a doubleheader on August 6 that gave the Reds sixty-eight victories, one more than they'd logged the entire 1960 season.

Pinson credited Robinson with the game-winning homer.

"You made me so sick with that batting exhibition you put on that I didn't want to see you up there at the plate again," Pinson joked to his close friend.

Despite the Reds' 5–2 homestand, the Dodgers stayed right on their heels. Their persistence paid off as they took over first place on August 8 by beating Milwaukee while the Reds were losing at St. Louis.

If the Reds were ever going to collapse, this would be the time. Since matching their season-high by climbing twenty-five games over .500 while opening up a six-game lead, their widest of the season, on July 15, the Reds had gone 12–13 and fallen into second place by one game, a deficit that would grow to two-and-one-half by August 13 as Los Angeles stayed hot.

The two games at St. Louis were the first of a road trip that shaped up to be Cincinnati's most grueling of the season. After two games in Missouri, the Reds went east to Philadelphia for one game, then to Cleveland for an exhibition game, followed by three games in San Francisco, a day off and three more games in Los Angeles. That trip added up to ten games—nine of which actually counted in the standings—in eleven days in five cities, culminating in a matchup with the league's most heated rivals. None of the games on the trip were makeups of previously postponed dates. They all were on the original schedule.

"No one man could have worked out anything as horrible as this year's schedule," one unnamed NL executive told a reporter. "It would be impossible. It must have been three or four guys."

Cincinnati picked up its customary win over Philadelphia and headed west again to Cleveland, where Bell homered in the twelfth inning for an 8–7 win before a crowd of 34,549, the Indians' largest of the season at home. The team left Cleveland at 6:30 a.m. on August 11, arriving in San Francisco around midday before heading to Candlestick Park for a sleep-deprived 4–2 loss to the Giants. The 207 Barney Rapp Reds Rooters on hand for the game—fortified by their own five-piece band—probably were more awake than the players.

To further complicate the Reds' lives, the next day's game—on Hutchinson's forty-second birthday—was played in the afternoon. They suffered their fourth loss in five games to fall two-and-one-half games behind the Dodgers, a gap that remained unchanged even though Cincinnati salvaged the final game of the three-game series with an 8–1 win on Sunday in which Wally Post homered and drove in four runs.

The Reds moved on to Los Angeles, where they were joined by a new addition, catcher Darrell Johnson, whose contract had been purchased from the Phillies. The Reds were the thirty-two-year-old Johnson's third team of the season—though he'd been listed as a coach with the Cardinals to open the season—and sixth of his career. He'd broken into the major leagues in 1949 with DeWitt's St. Louis Browns, and he also was a third-string catcher on the New York Yankees teams that won the 1957 American League pennant and 1958 World Series.

The Reds, looking for stability in their young corps of catchers, had reportedly tried to get Johnson in July. They were trying to reach him after he was let go by the Cardinals, but couldn't make contact before he signed with the Phillies.

To make room on the roster for Johnson, who would manage the Boston Red Sox against the Reds in the 1975 World Series, utility player Pete Whisenant was taken off the active player roster and added to the coaching staff.

A 5–0 Los Angeles loss to St. Louis left the Reds trailing the Dodgers by two games going into the crucial three-game series—Cincinnati's last of the season in Southern California. Darrell Johnson got no time to get his feet wet, starting against Sandy Koufax in the series opener on Tuesday, August 15. The series would turn out to be one of the most significant the franchise had played in years—or would play in the decade of the 1960s.

Cincinnati starter Joey Jay gave up two runs before retiring a batter, but he got Frank Howard to ground into a double play in the first inning and, despite issuing eight walks, escaped two more bases-loaded situations later in the game to keep the Dodgers at two runs.

"You might say some of those walks were semi-intentional," said Jay, who finished the game. "I was being pretty careful."

"After that third inning, Joey was wonderful," Darrell Johnson said. "The first three innings, he couldn't throw a strike with his fastball. Then he came on like gangbusters."

Jay's dogged determination and some heads-up Cincinnati defense opened the door for the Reds to come from behind for a 5–2 win. Frank Robinson threw out Sandy Koufax as the Dodger left-hander loped up the first-base line on what he thought was going to be a single to right field.

"I can't remember the last time I saw that play pulled," Hutchinson said. "I know it had to be in the minor leagues when the fences are short and outfielders play shallow."

"If someone did that to me, I would want to sit down and cry," Cincinnati shortstop Eddie Kasko said.

Pinson followed up by throwing out Duke Snider as the Dodger center fielder tried to stretch a single to right-center field into a double leading off the eighth inning.

"It was beautiful," Hutchinson marveled. "I was standing in the dugout right in line with Vada's throw. It was a perfect strike. The ball was there waiting for Snider."

Robinson, who had five hits in his previous thirty-one at-bats and had gone eight games without an RBI, started the Reds' comeback with a two-run, bases-loaded double to left field in the fifth, lifting his RBI count to an even 100. Wally Post snapped the tie with a home run to lead off the sixth inning, and the Reds added an unearned run in that inning on Kasko's fourth consecutive hit before capping the scoring on Lynch's pinch-hit RBI double in the seventh.

The Reds were one game behind going into their second twi-night doubleheader of the season at the Coliseum. The National League record for attendance at a night game, which the two teams had set on July 7, was snapped as 72,140 fans turned out on a Wednesday night in hopes of seeing the Dodgers put away the Reds for good.

"I had personally never seen that many people in my life at a sporting event, and here they were, all around you," first baseman Gordy Coleman said. "That was a real tough ballpark to play in, because it was built for other sports."

Among the fans were the 200 Red Rooters who'd followed the Reds down the coast, and Whisenant, who was serving a league-mandated five-day waiting period before joining the coaching staff. Whisenant started watching the games from the press box.

"I can't stand this," he said. "I've got to get out in the bleachers where I can yell."

The Reds gave him plenty to yell about as they turned in an historic performance. Bob Purkey and Jim O'Toole produced back-to-back complete-game shutouts as Cincinnati rolled over Los Angeles, 6–0 and 8–0, to leapfrog over the Dodgers into first place–for good. The Reds would lead the league for the rest of the season.

The twin-bill shutout was the first suffered by the Dodgers since July 28, 1935, and the first time they were shut out in consecutive games since 1949.

The Reds wasted no time setting the tone for the evening. Eddie Kasko led off the first game against right-hander Larry Sherry with a single to left and scored on Don Blasingame's triple to right. Vada Pinson drove in Blasingame with a single to right and, after Robinson was hit by a pitch, moved to third on Gordy Coleman's fly ball to right fielder Duke Snider.

Robinson stole second base, and Pinson took off for home, scoring when Roseboro couldn't handle the return throw. Robinson alertly advanced to third on Gus Bell's groundout to Sherry, and scored on a wild pitch to give the Reds a 4–0 lead.

That was all Purkey needed. The right-hander went into the game concerned about soreness in his arm and asked Rohde to rub Capsolin, a hot salve derived from chili peppers grown in China, on it throughout the game. Whatever the reason, Purkey throttled the Dodgers, retiring them in order in six of his nine innings and allowing just one runner to reach third base and another to get to second.

"My changeup tonight was the best I've had," said Purkey, who had seven strikeouts and didn't walk a single batter. "It was real slow, and I had good motion. I must have thrown about ten or fifteen—and about thirty knucklers."

Pinson led off the third inning with a double, and Sherry violated Alston's standing order by knocking down Robinson with a pitch. Robinson hit the next pitch for a two-run homer.

"I don't know whether Sherry's pitch was intentional or not, but I know it made Frank mad," Hutchinson said. "They don't scare him."

O'Toole still wonders why the Dodgers never learned their lesson.

"Inevitably, if we had a rally going, the first thing they'd do if Robinson was coming up and we had men on base was to knock him down," the pitcher recalled. "They never learned their lesson, because every time they'd knock him down, he'd get up and hit the next pitch out of the park. He hated the Dodgers."

"I remember he used to stand on the top step of the dugout and call the Dodgers' pitchers every name in the book," Coleman once recalled with glee. "Then he'd turn around, point to his name and number, and say, 'Yeah, that was me who said that.'"

Notoriously feisty Los Angeles coach Leo Durocher, who liked antagonizing opponents, tried to play mind games with Robinson, Reds coach Dick Sisler said.

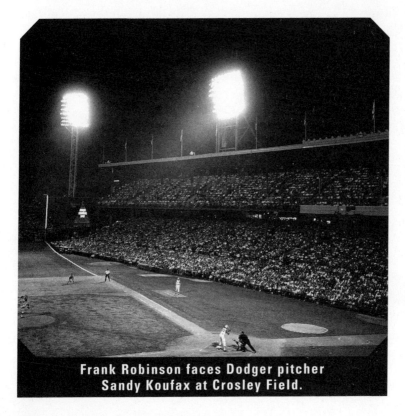

Frank Robinson faces Dodger pitcher Sandy Koufax at Crosley Field.

"Durocher got all over Robby when he was on first base Wednesday," Sisler said. "He called him gutless, said he couldn't have played twenty years ago. It was something awful. I had to calm Robby down, because I didn't want him to get into a fight. I'm sure that's what Durocher wanted to happen. He was hoping to get Robby thrown out of the game. All Durocher succeeded in doing was getting Robby mad, and the Dodgers should know by now that getting him mad isn't the smart thing to do.

"It proves again that Robby is at his best when the pressure is greatest, and it should convince the Dodgers once and for all that he doesn't scare at the plate."

Imposing Dodger right-hander Stan Williams hit Pinson in the head with a curveball with two outs in the seventh inning, prompting a trip to the hospital. He was back before the first game ended, lying on a table in the clubhouse.

"I saw the ball leave his hand, but then I lost it in all those white shirts in center field," Pinson said.

"The ball that hit him was a high curve," Hutchinson said. "Williams wasn't throwing at him. You don't throw curves when you're trying to hit somebody."

Robinson started the second game in Pinson's place in center field, with Gus Bell playing right and batting in Pinson's customary third spot in the lineup. The game started out tighter than the opener, but O'Toole was up to the task, facing one batter over the minimum through the first three innings. Gene Freese rewarded the left-hander with a one-out, solo homer in the fourth that barely cleared the screen down the short left-field line.

"I think it touched the back of the screen on the way down," Freese joked about his second homer of the month and first in ten days.

"When I left St. Louis as manager, I told Bavasi that he should get Freese," Hutchinson said. " 'He will wear out that screen at the Coliseum, the way he pulls a ball,' I told Buzzie. I'm glad now that Buzzie didn't get him."

The Dodgers got runners on first and second in the fourth, the closest they would come to scoring on O'Toole. He walked Jim Gilliam to lead off the sixth, but Tommy Davis lined out to Kasko, who caught Gilliam off first base to complete a double play. Gilliam also led off the ninth with a walk, but Davis grounded into another double play.

By then, the Reds had piled up an 8–0 lead to virtually clinch their sweep. Darrell Johnson hit a solo homer in the seventh, the second and last of his two career home runs. He hit his first on June 15, 1957, at Kansas City off of Virgil Trucks.

Cincinnati broke open the game in the last two innings. Freese hit a three-run homer in the eighth, following an intentional walk to Robinson, and the Reds added three with two outs in the ninth on a single by Pinson—who entered the game as a defensive replacement in the eighth—and a two-run single by Robinson.

The double plays allowed O'Toole to face the minimum three batters in six innings, and he set the side down in order in four of them while allowing just one runner to reach second base. He extended to twenty-six the Dodgers' streak of consecutive scoreless innings against the Reds.

"Somebody told me my complete game was the only complete game by a left-hander at the Coliseum that year," he recalled. "I was in such a groove when I pitched against them that day that I had complete confidence. Darrell Johnson, wherever he put his glove, I was hitting it. I was throwing everything—backdoor sliders, up and in, down and away, slow curveballs for strikes. When that happens, it's Katy bar the door for the other team.

"When I think of 72,000 people at a game, that doesn't happen. That's the biggest crowd ever assembled for a night game. You're thinking (he pauses and whistles), 'Important game, man.' I don't even know how I got there. When you get them out one-two-three, you block out the crowd. I was ahead of every hitter. I just went right at them, popping them up or striking them out. Those runs they got me in the late innings made me feel awfully good. I had been bearing down all the way, and the big lead gave me a chance to relax a little–not worry so much about walking a batter.

"I threw only four curves, and both of their hits came off two of them. The rest of the pitches were sliders and fastballs."

"O'Toole had good stuff all the way," Hutchinson said. "Sure, he got a break when Kasko caught a liner by Tommy Davis in the sixth and doubled Gilliam off first base, but Kasko should catch a few liners. A few that he hit were caught on him."

Making the sweep even better was the Reds beat Johnny Podres in the second game. The left-hander had been 3–0 previously against Cincinnati. The Reds headed home at noon the next day, having survived the road trip with a 5–4 record and increasing their income just in the eleven games played at the Coliseum to $105,000. The team plane landed at the airport about 6 p.m., one-and-a-half hours late, but the several hundred fans on hand to greet the league leaders didn't seem to mind the wait. The photos in the next day's newspapers included one of O'Toole getting a congratulatory smooch from his wife.

The bandwagon was starting to fill.

EIGHT

Blowing the Lid Off

Dave Parker knew something big was
going on at Crosley Field during the 1961 baseball season, but
the future Reds outfielder was too busy being ten years old
and trying to scare up spending money to know how big–that
is, until he opened a taxi door and the Rifleman stepped out.

Chuck Connors was the actor who portrayed Lucas
McCain, the lead character in a popular television Western
called *The Rifleman*. Before turning to acting, the six-foot, five-
inch Connors had played professional basketball and baseball
and remained an avid fan, especially of baseball and the Dodgers, the team he grew up watching when the franchise was

located in Brooklyn and one of the two teams he played for in the majors. Connors and the Reds crossed paths several times that season as Cincinnati and Los Angeles battled for first place in the National League, including a doubleheader against the Los Angeles Dodgers on August 27 at Crosley Field.

"I remember that year opening the door for Mickey Rooney and Chuck Connors at the same time," Parker recalled. "They were in the same cab. I'm like, 'Hey, you look like Mickey Rooney,' and then I saw Chuck Connors, and I'm like, 'Hey, Rifleman.' They gave me a nice little tip for opening the cab door."

Connors's interest in the unfolding pennant race wasn't anywhere near the frenzy that was starting to build in championship-starved Cincinnati as the Reds maintained their presence at the top of the standings. One area in which the fervor was reflected was in attendance. Of that season's total home attendance of 1,107,603–the franchise's third seven-figure season and first since 1957–431,510 showed up for the final twenty-one home dates after the historic doubleheader sweep at Los Angeles.

That means that 39 percent of the attendance was crammed into the final 30 percent of the sixty-nine home dates.

Reds officials, ever mindful of aging Crosley's cramped conditions, hoped to parlay the team's improved performance and rising attendance into upgrades of the aging ballpark. General manager Bill DeWitt talked about possible expansion plans that could include moving the plate back twenty feet, replacing the right field Sun Deck with a covered grandstand and adding three thousand bleacher seats in left field. A newspaper photo showed two Reds officials, Mike Dolan and Lewis Crosley, standing in the middle of York Street, just outside the left field fence, and discussing adding seats with three city officials: city engineer A.D. Bird, assistant city manager Bill Wickman, and administrative engineer C.C. Patten.

Another city official, Stadium Development Committee secretary Ben Stoner, created headlines with his proposal for a forty-thousand-seat stadium to be built on the Ohio River bank near the since-demolished Central Bridge—virtually the same location of the Reds' current home, Great American Ball Park. Stoner's plan included moving sidewalks between the stadium and Fountain Square, and he estimated the project would cost between seven-and-a-half million and ten million dollars.

"It is possible to cover such a stadium to make it useable all year, but this runs into considerable additional money," Stoner told the *Cincinnati Post and Times-Star*.

In the second half of the summer of 1961, though, Crosley Field was the place to be, and the Reds were the favorite topic of conversation. The local newspapers couldn't get enough about the team. Game results were reported regularly on the front page, often with banner headlines stripped across the very tops of the front pages with the score and its impact on the pennant race.

The Reds weren't just on the front and sports pages, either. When the DeWitt family moved from the Netherland Hilton into a house in August, the *Cincinnati Enquirer* was on hand to gush about the white stucco structure on three-quarters of an acre at the corner of Grandin Road and Ambleside Place in East Walnut Hills, including the eleven "open, spacious" rooms.

During the last week of the regular season, a fashion spread in the *Post and Times-Star* featured models displaying the latest outfits in various photos shot at Crosley. In one shot, several women were shown at a ticket window "buying tickets" from long-time groundskeeper Matty Schwab. Also modeling clothes at Crosley was Dave Grote, the National League public relations director who'd previously filled the same job for the Reds.

The Reds also were edging into the arts. Scores were announced during breaks in Summer Opera productions, which at the time were staged at the Cincinnati Zoo and Botanical Gardens—lions' roars mixing with arias.

The team's performance even inspired local songwriters. Larry Vincent, a piano-playing singer in the Celebrity Room at the Beverly Hills nightclub in Southgate, Kentucky, just across the Ohio River from Cincinnati, composed "The Whole Town's Batty About Cincinnati." The catchy tune had Reds fans singing, "What a team, what a team, what a team."

A more popular local entertainer, television star Ruth Lyons, came up with a piece entitled "Rally 'Round the Reds" that she performed regularly on her live, daily talk-variety television show, WLWT's *Fifty-Fifty Club*. It went like this:

> *Rally 'round the Reds,*
> *Oh, let's rally 'round the Reds.*
> *Give us a season to remember.*
> *Rally 'round the Reds,*
> *Oh, let's rally 'round the Reds.*
> *We want a pennant in September.*

Lyons had the clout and charisma to spur regional support for the team. Her show was seen daily on WLWT sister stations in Indianapolis, Indiana, and Columbus and Dayton, Ohio, which meant advertisers got a huge audience for their money. Her show was a must-visit for everybody who had something to promote, from prominent authors to entertainers of the caliber of comedian Bob Hope, so if she was behind the Reds, then it became even more of the "in" thing in Cincinnati.

Members of the team were regular *Fifty-Fifty Club* guests.

"Somebody said, 'Go on the Ruth Lyons show,'" pitcher Jim Maloney recalled. "They said, 'Ruth Lyons didn't know much about baseball, but she's a power lady.'"

Maloney knew that fan interest was intense, because the young right-hander, who would be married shortly after the season, lived for most of the summer with a fan. Like several players, Maloney started the season living at the Netherland Hilton Hotel during home stands, sharing a room with teammate Harry Anderson and checking out when the team left on road trips. Many of those players frequented a cocktail lounge called The Rendezvous, which was located below street level across Vine Street from the Netherland-Carew Tower complex. Upstairs from The Rendezvous was a diner called George's, though it was owned at the time by Joe Lask. Many of the players would stop and get something to eat before heading to the ballpark.

Lew Silverman also was a regular at George's, usually stopping in at lunchtime for a corned beef sandwich with potato salad or cole slaw. Silverman had been an all-around athlete at Walnut Hills High School, good enough at golf to earn a scholarship to Ohio State. He attended the famous 1950 Ohio State-Michigan football game, which was played in a blizzard, and lived across the hall for a while from 1950 Heisman Trophy-winner Vic Janowicz.

Silverman also was an avid baseball fan whose family had box seats at Crosley Field, so he wasn't going to pass up a chance to meet a Red.

"I was sitting in George's diner when some guy came over and said, 'This guy wants to meet you,'" Maloney recalled.

"He was blind. I went over and sat down, and we started talking. Everybody else in the restaurant knew him."

Maloney learned that Silverman, a diabetic, had lost his eyesight at Ohio State when he slipped into a diabetic coma.

"We had nothing to do that day, so we went to River Downs," said Silverman, who turned twenty-nine in September of that year. "I got to be friends with him. I would consider him to be my best friend. I said to him, 'How'd you like to move out with me?' He liked the idea. We went and packed his bags on a Saturday night. From that point on, he lived with me until he got married at the end of the '61 season. We became dear friends."

The Silverman family had moved the previous November into a house in the Cincinnati suburb of Amberley Village.

"It was great for me," Maloney said. "That was my first full year in the major leagues."

"We would go to almost every game," Silverman said. "Jimmy would drive my car down there, and I'd wait and leave with him."

Silverman ended up meeting many of the Reds.

"I knew Ken Johnson real well," he recalled. "They were all congenial and friendly to each other. It was just enjoyable to be around them. Jimmy would always take me wherever they went. When they won the pennant, he took me to the party."

In mid-August, the prospect of a pennant-clinching party remained in doubt. The Reds had returned in triumph from Los Angeles on August 16, fresh off of their doubleheader shutout of the Dodgers, but their hold on first place was tenuous enough that they couldn't afford to relax. Johnson and Joey Jay turned in back-to-back complete games in wins over St. Louis—extending to five Cincinnati's streak of consecutive complete games—that

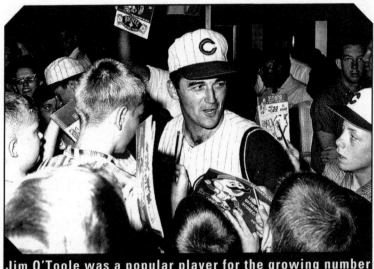

Jim O'Toole was a popular player for the growing number of Reds fans during the pennant race.

helped the Reds open up a three-game lead over the Dodgers, who were in the middle of a ten-game losing streak. A loss in the Sunday series finale was the first of four straight and six out of seven, costing the Reds half of that lead.

"The way they are playing now, they should win, but they can't afford to relax—not even for one game," Cardinals coach Harry "The Hat" Walker said.

Shortstop Eddie Kasko had hit two line drives for outs in that August 20 loss to the Cardinals, snapping his hitting streak at eleven games. He still was twenty-two of fifty-four over his last twelve games. Frank Robinson was able to extend his hitting streak to six games despite playing with a spike wound and strained ligaments in his left knee, sustained during a rundown in the previous day's game, during which he also went three-for-four with a double and two RBI.

The burden of carrying the Reds for much of the season,

combined with the accumulating bumps and bruises, was starting to catch up with him. He would hit just five home runs and drive in just thirty-one runs after July, a month in which he hit thirteen homers and drove in thirty-four runs.

As if to prove "The Hat" right, Cincinnati went on to lose the next three games, all to San Francisco. The Giants arrived at Crosley Field in third place, seven games behind the Reds, and harboring faint hopes of a miracle comeback. They fueled those dreams by sweeping a doubleheader, one of the games the makeup of the July 21 postponement, and adding a record-setting 14–0 win on August 23 in which they scored twelve runs in the ninth inning—the National League season high for runs in one inning—while tying a major league record for home runs in one inning with five. The record had been set by the Giants when they still were in New York during a game against the Reds in Cincinnati's pennant-winning 1939 season.

The Reds got an inkling that something unusual was about to happen with the first batter of the game. Catcher Darrell Johnson, thinking strike three had been called on what actually was strike two to Joe Amalfitano, threw the ball to third base.

"He'll probably hit one out now," reliever Bill Henry observed in the bullpen. Amalfitano, in fact, did homer off the left-field netting.

That was just a harbinger of what would occur in the ninth, which included Jim Davenport's inside-the-park homer and nine unearned runs on three Cincinnati errors, prompting Hutchinson to close the clubhouse to reporters and call a brief meeting.

"Go get drunk or something," he told the players, according to Jim Brosnan in his book *Pennant Race*. "Try to do something right. You look awful."

"You've got to get mad, when a team plays as lousy as we did," Hutchinson told reporters the next day.

Hutchinson's outburst paid brief dividends, though he also shook up the team by replacing Kasko with Leo Cardenas and starting Dick Gernert at first base ahead of slumping Gordy Coleman on the annual "Family Night" promotion, which gave the players the opportunity to show off their families on the field. Cardenas contributed three hits, three runs, and three RBI and Gernert two hits and an RBI to an 8–5 win in the series finale, setting up the final series of the season between the Reds and Los Angeles.

The Dodgers were coming off their tenth consecutive loss and arrived in Cincinnati three and one-half games behind the Reds, a margin that dwindled by a game with a 7–2 Los Angeles win in the opener.

The Reds got a grand slam from Vada Pinson and a solo shot from Robinson in the second game, but they weren't enough to overcome the poor performance by Jay Hook, who was making his first start since June 20. Hook was rocked for six hits and four runs in less than two innings in what would be his final start of the season. Maloney also gave up six and four in two innings of relief, giving the Dodgers hope of returning to first place with a sweep of the August 27 doubleheader–Cincinnati's second twin bill in a span of six days and the second between the two teams in less than two weeks.

Chuck Connors reportedly watched the games through the back window of the press box, standing on a soft drink case.

Hutchinson, always looking for a way to snap his team to attention, put slugging third baseman Gene Freese in the leadoff spot for the first game. The move seemed fruitless as Los Angeles took a 5–1 lead into the bottom of the seventh inning, which became 5–4 when Freese launched a three-run homer with two outs in the bottom of the inning. The Reds capitalized on an error by second baseman Charlie Neal to add two runs in the eighth on Cardenas's triple off the scoreboard and Wally Post's pinch-hit double for a 6–5 lead that was preserved by, of all people, left-hander Jim O'Toole, a starting pitcher who turned in an inning of perfect relief.

The second game wasn't nearly as dramatic. Vada Pinson hit a two-run homer in the first off of Don Drysdale, and pitcher Ken Johnson capped a three-run seventh with a two-run double as the Reds cruised to an 8–3 win that solidified their hold on first place.

Freese's home run was the last of a whopping nine he hit against the Dodgers that season—and, perhaps, the most crucial.

"That was the one that turned it around," he recalled. "We were in kind of a slump, and they were hot. They were coming after us pretty good. Stan Williams was pitching a pretty good ballgame. I hit it on the fists, right down the line, and we won the ballgame and came back to win the second game, and from then on, we were unbeatable. I think we beat Drysdale in the second game, and we never beat Drysdale at home."

That year, though, Drysdale finished 0–2 with a 6.39 ERA in six games, including four starts, against the Reds. He suffered both of those losses in Cincinnati.

A day off the next day gave DeWitt a chance to take care of some unfinished business. Despite earlier comments that any talk about extending Hutchinson's contract would wait until after the season, DeWitt offered the manager a two-year extension—after the Saturday loss to the Dodgers. Hutchinson agreed, and the Monday off day was the perfect opportunity to build on the Sunday doubleheader sweep and keep the Reds in the newspapers.

"You see, this proves we're not signing as front runners," DeWitt said. "We didn't do this just because we won that big doubleheader Sunday."

"I'm very happy with everything, and particularly with the way things have gone this season," Hutchinson said. "I'd like a little wider gap in the standings if we could get it, but it looks as though it ain't going to be one of the seasons in which it can be done."

"It couldn't have happened to a nicer guy," Frank Robinson said. "He's the top manager in baseball in my book. He has the respect of all of his players and the ability to have them go into a big series perfectly relaxed."

The news didn't exactly galvanize the team. Cincinnati alternated wins and losses during an eight-game road trip that ended with an 11–5 loss at St. Louis on September 6 in which reliever Jim Brosnan allowed six hits and five earned runs—the first earned runs he'd allowed since July 20. The Reds' lead dropped to one game over the Dodgers, who won seven out of nine after being swept at Cincinnati.

This time, the tonic for the Reds came from simply returning home. Brosnan, getting right back up on the horse, pitched two innings of two-hit, shutout relief and Kasko drove in Elio Chacon with a tenth-inning walkoff single that lifted Brosnan's record to 9–3 and sparked a six-game winning streak—over nine days—that left the Reds four-and-one-half games ahead of the Dodgers.

Robinson won the September 9 game with a twelfth-inning single, and Bob Purkey kept the momentum rolling with a complete-game two-hitter in the series finale. Three days later–on September 13, the day after a one-game "series" against the Cubs–Joey Jay pitched a complete-game four-hitter for a 1–0 win over his old team, Milwaukee, to become the first Cincinnati pitcher with twenty wins since side-arming Ewell "The Whip" Blackwell in 1947.

That win left the Reds with a lead of five-and-one-half games and eleven to play and the town ready to party. Dixieland bands were regular features in the stands at Crosley Field. They were supplemented on September 10 by a pre-game sideshow featuring acrobats and a line of chorus girls during a party sponsored on the field by the team for the fifteen hundred Reds Rooters, who also indulged in a buffet dinner.

The beauties congregating around the team didn't stop with chorus girls. A photo on the front page of the September 13 edition of the *Post and Times-Star* showed coach Pete Whisenant instructing actress and January 1960 *Playboy* magazine centerfold model Stella Stevens on the proper way to hold a bat.

Stevens wasn't the only celebrity to find the way to Crosley Field. Actor Forrest Tucker, starring in a production of Meredith Willson's *The Music Man* at downtown Cincinnati's Taft Auditorium, was spotted at a game and admitted that he'd like to see the Reds win the pennant.

"It'll be a wonderful thing for baseball," said Tucker, a long-time film and stage actor who would become most famous for portraying Sgt. Morgan O'Rourke on the ABC television situation comedy *F Troop*, about a frontier United States Army fort. "It's what keeps the game alive. I'm a Dodger fan in the National League, and I root for the White Sox in the American League, but it's a wonderful thing when teams like Pittsburgh and Cincinnati win. I don't like monopolies on pennants or trophies of any kind. That's one reason I'm anti-Yankee."

DeWitt, business manager John Murdough, publicity director Hank Zureick, and ticket manager Roger Noble left town on September 14 to meet in Chicago with Commissioner Ford Frick about World Series arrangements. The rest of the city already was preparing. The football game scheduled on October 7 between crosstown rivals Xavier University and the University of Cincinnati was moved from the afternoon to the evening. The annual Catholic Holy Name Parade, traditionally held on the second Sunday of October, was pushed back a week to October 15.

Two of Cincinnati's major hotels, the Sheraton-Gibson and Netherland Hilton, both issued dire warnings of room shortages during the Series. The Netherland had three hundred rooms committed to a convention, while the Sheraton had three conventions scheduled simultaneously with the Series. Just a few days later, the *Post and Times-Star* published a photo of a Sheraton sign announcing, "Sorry World Series Rooms Sold Out!"

While local hotels might be missing out on the World Series bonanza, other local citizens were exercising their entrepreneurial muscles. Thirty boys who lived near Crosley Field were cited on August 27 for demanding money to "watch" cars parked on the streets by fans. They were scheduled to appear before long-time Juvenile Court Judge Benjamin Schwartz. Fifteen failed to appear for their court date, while seven denied the charge. The remaining eight were sentenced to working on the Juvenile Court grounds—that era's version of community service.

Slugger Wally Post cools off Bob Purkey in the clubhouse.

"This is just a mild form of extortion," Schwartz commented during the proceedings.

Another front-page story reminded readers that city ordinances required that folks hoping to sell tickets above face value needed licenses that included a one-thousand-dollar fee for each. A deputy city treasurer mentioned that two men had asked in August about licensing.

"They said they'd be back after they see how many tickets they can get," the city official said. "Presumably, they were talking about World Series tickets."

They had their work cut out for them. The Reds planned to charge ten dollars and twenty-five cents for box seats, seven dollars and twenty cents for grandstands seats, four dollars and ten cents for standing-room, and two dollars and a nickel for the bleachers.

Money, though, was no object. Reds switchboard

operators Lydia Mack and Rose Bode were handling three hundred calls per hour as the team closed in on clinching. Front-page newspaper photos showed lines of fans at windows purchasing money orders–the preferred way to pay for tickets–while one paper included a story on fake Series tickets and both offered detailed instructions on the ordering procedure.

One newspaper photo summed up the pressure on "insiders"–players and franchise and National League employees–who were hearing from the most distant of acquaintances. Dave Grote was shown with his fingers in his ears and wearing a sign saying, "I Have No World Series Tickets."

The team received 87,600 ticket orders by mail, stuffed into seventy-three mailbags, on the first day and capped orders at 146,000. The Reds could make only ten thousand per game available to the general public after satisfying the needs

Jim O'Toole celebrates a victory over the Cubs with Darrell Johnson on September 12.

of Major League Baseball and the team's season ticket holders, but Noble still had to hire fifty-five women and transfer
thirty-five ushers to temporary duty handling orders.

Pat Harmon, the *Post and Times-Star* sports editor, wrote
a column that highlighted some of the more unusual requests.
One applicant sent five dollars for two tickets. Some sent personal checks instead of certified checks, some sent cash, some
included no money at all. One wanted to be billed.

One woman, Harmon reported, included this information: "I have some Girl Scouts who have never seen a major
league baseball game. Reserve twenty-one seats for us at the
World Series."

Another request offered this deal: "Send me four box-seat
tickets. I won't pay you now, but if we like the game, we will
send you the money."

A third was bluntly realistic: "Roses are red, Violets are
blue, I know durn well, I'll get no tickets from you."

Presumably, all three were among those who received
this letter from the Reds:

> *Dear World Series applicant:*
> *Thank you very much for your order, but WE'RE*
> *SORRY. All of our World Series tickets were gone*
> *before we could fill your order. Our limited seating*
> *capacity has made it impossible for us to take care*
> *of all of our friends who have supported us so loy-*
> *ally these many years. We genuinely appreciate your*
> *patronage and regret our inability to fill your order.*
> *As you know, all games will be televised locally*
> *over WLW stations.*
> *Sincerely,*
> *The Cincinnati Baseball Club.*

A Reds clerk holds World Series tickets.

A long-time fan from Kentucky, Newport resident William Thompson, said he was going to dust off the plan that got him into Cincinnati's last World Series, back in 1940. The Hudepohl Brewery employee had spent two days and nights camped out at the ticket windows to get bleacher seats back then.

"I'm going to put in my order for grandstand seats," said Thompson, a regular at Cincinnati weekend home games. "If I don't get them, I'll be in line for the bleachers again, and I'm taking my vacation so I can see the games in New York, too."

Fervor of that level might've been admired by some. Other, supposedly more sophisticated observers, found it—and Cincinnati—a bit too, um, homey for their tastes. One was Jim Murray, the sharp-witted columnist for the *Los Angeles Times*.

Murray, who died in 1998, was an outstanding writer, talented enough to win the 1990 Pulitzer Prize for commentary and be enshrined in the writers' wing of the Baseball Hall of Fame in 1988 as winner of the 1987 J.G. Taylor Spink Award.

He was well known for his inventive, and often acerbic, turns of phrase. For example, he punctuated his distaste for auto racing by suggesting that races should start with, "Gentlemen, start your coffins." He also pointed out that Hall of Fame leadoff hitter Rickey Henderson had a strike zone "the size of Hitler's heart."

Subjects of his columns often bristled at being the target of his caustic wit. Sportswriter and former Reds public relations director Jim Ferguson remembers Reds second baseman Tommy Helms once observing, "That Jim Murray guy is pretty funny—when he's not writing about you." The citizens of Cincinnati knew what Helms was talking about after Murray reported his observations while visiting Cincinnati with the Dodgers in August.

"You come into a city like Cincinnati at 3 o'clock in the morning," he wrote. "Now, if you have any sense, you don't want to be in Cincinnati at all. Even in daylight, it doesn't look like a city. It looks like it's in the midst of a condemnation proceeding. If it was human, they'd bury it.

"You have to think that when Daniel Boone was fighting the Indians for this territory, he didn't have Cincinnati in mind for it. I wouldn't arm-wrestle Frank Finch for it. To give you an idea, the guys were kidding on the bus coming in here and they decided that if war came, the Russians would bypass Cincinnati because they'd think it had already been bombed and taken.

"I was glad to get out of Cincinnati. It wasn't only what the Reds did, it was what the weather did. I mean, the next time I take a steam bath, I want to be dressed for it.

"To give you an idea, the humidity in Cincinnati is so thick you don't walk to work, you breaststroke. If you can't swim, you can't live there in the summer. Without water wings, anyway. It's the only town I know of which seems to be under water even when the river is low.

"A couple of days in Cincinnati and my clothes look like I'd been standing in the rain overnight. Mahatma Gandhi would be overdressed on a hot day there. A diaper and monacle is about all the apparel you can handle. The best part about it is it gets hotter at night. For kicks, you can just sit there on your porch and listen to the tar in the streets bubble.

"There really isn't much to do in Cincinnati, unless you count sweating. And I must say the people there are extremely healthy, because I was having my usual breakfast–a well-done Alka-Seltzer–one morning when the people next to me ordered hot fudge sundaes. I thought it was just to get their picture taken for a Sealtest ad, but they actually began to eat them. I think that's when I began to feel the Reds were in. You can't beat that kind of fortitude."

Planning also gained momentum on more crucial levels. Western Union announced that it would be bringing in sixty teletype operators to handle the overflow of newspaper copy that would be generated by the teams of writers sent to cover the Series.

Meanwhile, Hutchinson, pitching coach Jim Turner, and third-base coach Reggie Otero took advantage of two days off between series in Pittsburgh and Philadelphia to check out the top two American League teams, the Yankees and Tigers, who were playing at Yankee Stadium. New York went into September leading Detroit–a team partially built by Bill De-Witt–by one-and-a-half games.

"Having no game of my own, I decided to have a look at the American League contenders," said Hutchinson, knowing full well that farm director Phil Seghi and scout Chuck Ward had been following the Yankees, who had scouts Johnny Neun and Bill Skiff studying the Reds.

The Reds split a Saturday-Sunday series against Philadelphia, going over one million in attendance with a second-game crowd of 14,671 on September 17. After another day off, Cincinnati swept Pittsburgh in another two-game series, giving the Reds eight wins in the first nine games of the home-stand and a five-game lead with eight to play. Third baseman Gene Freese, who'd tied his single-season career-high with his twenty-third home run in the first game of the August 27 doubleheader sweep of Los Angeles, hit his last two of the season in Cincinnati's 10–1 win on September 19. His three-run shot highlighted the Reds' seven-run fourth inning, the team's single biggest inning of the season. Left-hander Jim O'Toole turned in a complete-game seven-hitter for his sixth consecutive win and eleventh in his last thirteen decisions. He also improved, as pointed out by a teammate, to 17–13 as a husband and 6–1 as a father after going 11–15 as a bachelor.

"By the time you have five children, you should just about be the winningest pitcher in baseball," was the joke.

"I'll have to be just to support them," O'Toole responded.

Freese missed the next couple of games with a jammed left ankle. Of course, he joked about it.

"Actually, I've been playing on a broken ankle for a month," he deadpanned. "Haven't you noticed I haven't been stealing many bases? Actually, it started a few weeks ago when I got hit on the ankle with a foul tip. Then I aggravated it Tuesday night when (Pittsburgh shortstop Dick) Groat slid into me."

Freese returned for the three-game weekend series against San Francisco, Cincinnati's last home series of the regular season. The Reds lost two–including the Sunday afternoon finale before a robust crowd of 29,272, which appreciated Frank Robinson's first home run since August 26–but they still owned a four-game lead with just four games to play. The Dodgers had six games left on their schedule as they headed for Pittsburgh while the Reds took off for a game at Chicago.

WKRC-AM, the flagship station of the Reds' radio network, planned to air the Dodgers-Pirates game from Pittsburgh's Forbes Field on September 25, with Jack Moran scheduled to provide play-by-play, but the game had to be postponed because a malfunction in the equipment designed to mechanically retrieve the tarp left it partially deployed on the field. A photo on the front page of the *Post and Times-Star* showed players in Pittsburgh gazing forlornly at the tarp on the field. The game, which most likely would have been played if the tarp had been handled by hand, was rescheduled as a doubleheader on September 26.

Clinching now was a daily possibility. Cincinnati police added forty officers (to the normal traffic contingent of fourteen), forty-eight detectives, and nine supervisors for the night the pennant was clinched. Police Lieutenant Guy York said traffic would be blocked from Fourth to Sixth streets and Main to Race streets.

That was just fine with regulars at the Bay Horse Café on East Fifth Street, where a sign announced: "The day or night we clinch it, we'll celebrate from the last out of the ball game until the last one put out of here."

The Reds managed a come-from-behind win at Wrigley Field with two familiar faces leading the way. After rookie catcher Johnny Edwards broke up the shutout with a home run to lead off the sixth inning, Robinson followed Gordy Coleman's walk with a two-run homer in the seventh inning to tie the score, 3–3. One inning later, Vada Pinson singled with two outs and Jerry Lynch hit a 2–2 pitch over the right field seats for a 5–3 lead.

Lynch had electrified Reds fans all season, starting with his exploits as perhaps the best pinch-hitter in the game. He finished the season with nineteen pinch hits, leading the league and matching the club record he'd set in 1960, and a club-record five pinch-hit home runs. He drove in twenty-five runs as a pinch-hitter. "Lynch in a pinch" quickly became a popular Cincinnati slogan.

By mid-season, he'd used his bat to pry his way into Hutchinson's outfield rotation. The left-handed hitter went into September with thirty-eight runs batted in on thirty-eight hits and finished the season hitting .315 with thirteen homers and fifty RBI in ninety-six games. Few meant more than that homer against the Cubs.

"I would say that would have to be one of the highlights of my career," Lynch said. "I finished everywhere from last place to first, so I know what it all feels like. First place feels the best."

Twenty-five years later, Coleman still remembered Lynch's galvanizing impact on the 1961 Reds.

"There used to be some great one-on-ones," Coleman recalled. "When a pitcher would challenge him with a fastball, oh, he'd just leave the ground to get at him. He was a fun hitter to watch. He never got cheated in his life.

"He, from the time he got in the dugout prior to the game, had a bat in his hands all the time. He walked around the entire ballgame, up and down the dugout, with a bat in his hands. He couldn't wait for his time. He knew that, sometime in the ballgame, he was going to get a chance to swing. He was always ready. He had the feel of the bat in his hands.

"He took so much pride in it. He would get so mad when he didn't get a hit. I remember one day in Chicago, going up the tunnel after he made an out on a pitch he thought he should've hit, he completely ripped his uniform up and jerked that sucker off. It was a personal thing with him. If you got him out, you made him mad. That was the kind of hitter he was.

"He was colorful. Jerry was a character. He walked up and down the dugout with that bat in his hands, and if things got a little quiet and people weren't hollering and cheering, he'd beat on the wall. We used to have this big steel pole in the middle of the dugout at Crosley, and he'd beat on that.

"He left the dugout swinging. He always said he felt like that was one of the reasons he had so much success, because he was so aggressive with the bat. He used to swing at bad pitches, and he said he would do that just to get loose. That was one of his things. You could never take a pitch. I'm sure he did, but I don't remember him ever taking a strike. He just didn't do it."

"I've always been able to hit bad pitches," Lynch said. "The pitcher might think I'll swing at the first pitch, so he'll throw me a curve in the dirt or a curve at my noggin and I might just hit it to left field. However, that isn't the main thing. The good pinch-hitter is the guy who can relax enough to get the pitch he can hit. Old-timers will tell you that every hitter gets one pitch to hit, so you have to have patience to wait, and then you've got to be able to handle the pitch when you get it.

"I just stood there and watched it," he added about his September 26 homer at Wrigley. "It wasn't the distance I hit it, but the time, the place, and the game. I would have been just as happy if it had dropped into the front row of the bleachers. I had to hit that homer. All I brought on this trip was a shaving kit in my big bag. I didn't plan to go on to Pittsburgh."

Robinson doubled to lead off the ninth and scored on a single by, of all people, relief pitcher Jim Brosnan, who got the win with three innings of one-hit, shutout relief and the game ball. The Reds, who'd originally planned to fly to Pittsburgh from Chicago, instead returned to Cincinnati after giving each other shampoos of beer and soft drinks. Gordy Coleman serenaded the team with harmonica music on the bus from Wrigley to the airport in Chicago. The party that was a possibility when they left Chicago was almost a reality by the time they arrived at the airport, where Lynch was greeted with a kiss from an unidentified girl and the rest of the players were met with hugs and kisses from family members.

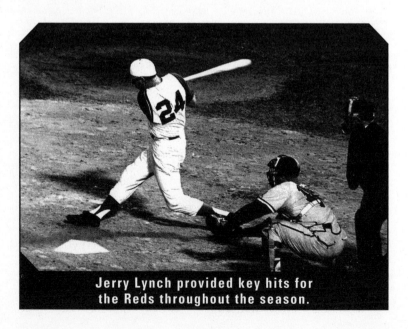

Jerry Lynch provided key hits for the Reds throughout the season.

"When we got down to Fountain Square, we couldn't move," Maloney recalled. "It was getting a little shaky. We didn't think we'd be able to get off the bus. Somehow, we did."

After the final out of the Dodgers' 8–0 loss at Pittsburgh was broadcast, officially clinching Cincinnati's championship, the fans erupted. Two of Cincinnati's three television stations covered the celebration live, preempting network feeds. *Post and Times-Star* television columnist Mary Wood later cleared up the mystery of who murdered a character on an NBC show preempted by WLWT's coverage of the party.

WKRC, which didn't own a mobile unit, couldn't join its competitors in the coverage of the event, which required twenty highway and property maintenance employees for cleanup the next day and cost the city $4,682.88 in overtime.

The party produced nine truckloads of debris and five disorderly conduct arrests for throwing beer bottles. Each perpetrator was fined fourteen dollars. Five more fans were arrested for swimming in the Tyler Davidson fountain and another for climbing to the top of the "Queen of Waters" statue. Someone poured bubble bath into the fountain, turning the water pink.

Another fan was fined fifty-four dollars for ripping a telephone from a wall.

At the next day's meeting of Cincinnati City Council, all of the council members wore Reds caps.

While the fans painted the town red, so to speak, the Reds adjourned to their own, private, well-deserved party at the Netherland Hilton.

"Hutch bought all the drinks," Maloney said.

At one point, Freese stuck a baseball to his ear and loudly proclaimed to anybody who would listen that, "I just faced Don Drysdale."

Barney Rapp's band provided music, supplemented by relief pitcher Howie Nunn, who sang well enough for teammates to call him Perry Como, and Hutchinson, who sang "My Blue Heaven" and "I Understand," among other pieces.

Also on hand, of course, was Chuck Connors, who happened to be in town as part of an eight-city tour asking people what they like or don't like about his series and television in general. Connors was available because his show wasn't filming while co-star Johnny Crawford, who portrayed his son, recovered from a lung infection.

"We're all thinking, 'What a frontrunner this guy is,'" Maloney recalled. "When we go out to L.A., he's always pulling for the Dodgers, and here he is, at our victory party."

NINE

Bronx Bombed

One of the many humorous stories spawned by the laughably inept 1962 New York Mets–who still hold the single-season (since 1900) record for losses with 120–involves Elio Chacon. After playing a valuable role for the Reds in 1961, the Venezuelan middle infielder had been picked by the Mets in the expansion draft and was the regular shortstop in their inaugural season, but his problems with the English language created a dangerous situation with center fielder Richie Ashburn. As the story goes, the two were constantly colliding while chasing bloopers in short center field because Chacon didn't understand when Ashburn called "I got it."

Fans were "batty" about the pennant-winning Reds.

Left fielder Frank Thomas, another former Red, suggested that Ashburn yell "*Yo la tengo,*" which is Spanish for "I have it." Thomas also mentioned the plan to Chacon, and when Ashburn repeated the magic words to Chacon before the next day's game and Chacon nodded in agreement while saying, "*Si, si,*" the situation seemed to be solved.

Sure enough, there was a blooper. Ashburn came charging in, yelling, "*Yo la tengo, yo la tengo.*" Chacon backed off, Ashburn prepared to make the catch—and was run over by Frank Thomas.

While the story helps characterize the lovably hapless Mets, it also serves as a painful reminder of what might've been the play that turned the 1961 World Series in favor of the New York Yankees and against the Cincinnati Reds.

The Yankees didn't expect to need much help from their opponents going into the Series. They were, after all, perhaps the most power-laden of all of the Bronx Bomber teams that had ravaged the American League since Babe Ruth traded pitching for slugging. In the first year of the expanded AL—ten teams, each playing 162 games, two more teams and eight more games than the National League—New York had set a single-season team record by cranking out 240 home runs. They included, of course, the sixty-one by right fielder Roger Maris, breaking Babe Ruth's single-season record of sixty set in 1927. Maris didn't hit his sixty-first until the last game of the season, prompting Commissioner Ford Frick to rule that there would be two records—one for the 154-game season played by Ruth, the other for the longer season.

That wasn't the only controversy surrounding the chase. Maris and local favorite Mickey Mantle were neck-and-neck for much of the season, until Mantle developed an abscess on his hip that forced him to miss several September games and most of the World Series. If Ruth was going to be knocked out of the record books, many Yankee fans preferred to see Mantle do it.

That's one reason a mere 23,154 fans were on hand at 67,000-seat Yankee Stadium on Sunday, October 1, for the last game of the regular season when Maris took his last shot at number sixty-one. Among them were Reds left-hander Jim O'Toole, sent ahead of the team by manager Fred Hutchinson to get used to the surroundings. Also on hand were O'Toole's wife, Betty, right-hander Joey Jay, and catcher Darrell Johnson, who'd pulled a muscle swinging at a pitch during O'Toole's last start.

"We were sitting right behind home plate," O'Toole said.

O'Toole had gone five innings in Cincinnati's 8–1 win at Pittsburgh the previous Friday to get tuned up for his start in Game One of the World Series. One reason for Hutchinson's decision was he hoped that O'Toole could thwart the left-handed power of players such as Maris, Yogi Berra, Johnny Blanchard, Tony Kubek, and, of course, the switch-hitting Mantle. Their production was further bolstered by the stadium's famous "short porch" in right field, a mere 296 feet down the line.

O'Toole also had earned the right to start the opener after going 13–2 over the last three months of the season, including a sparkling 5–0 with a 2.53 ERA in September and October. He won his last eight decisions.

"Hutch said he wanted me to start the first game," O'Toole said. "I was hot. I was the best pitcher on the staff at the time. I had the best ERA in the league for a while. I got beaten out by (Warren) Spahn."

The rest of the Reds didn't exactly roll into the Series. They lost the last two games of the regular season in Pittsburgh to finish 93–61, four games ahead of Los Angeles. Team leader Frank Robinson, worn down by the rigors of the season and dealing with pain in his elbow and knee, hit .253 with two home runs and ten runs batted in over the last month of the season. Robinson took enough batting practice to raise blisters on his hands, but he couldn't get back on track.

Experience also favored the Yankees—by a wide margin. Maris had played in just one World Series, but players such as Mantle, Berra, and crafty left-hander Whitey Ford had spent most of the 1950s playing in—and winning—World Series. The 1961 Series would be Berra's twelfth, and he'd already played on eight winning teams. Ford and Mantle both had appeared in eight World Series, while the double-play combination of shortstop Tony Kubek and second baseman Bobby Richardson had three World Series under their belts.

Richardson, in fact, had been named Most Valuable Player of the 1960 World Series, even though it was the other team's second baseman, Pittsburgh's Bill Mazeroski, who'd led off the ninth inning of Game Seven at Forbes Field with a tie-breaking home run. Richardson hit .367 and led both teams with an eye-popping twelve runs batted in during that Series.

On the other hand, no player on the Cincinnati roster had ever appeared in a World Series game. Pitcher Joey Jay appeared in one regular-season game for the 1957 Milwaukee Braves team that went on to beat the New York Yankees in that season's World Series. He saw more extensive action for the Braves as they repeated in 1958, but he again was left off of Milwaukee's postseason roster.

Catcher Darrell Johnson played in a combined twenty-six games for the 1957 and 1958 Yankees, and he was on New York's World Series roster both years, but he didn't get into a game.

Cincinnati had to turn to the coaching staff to find the team's only Series experience. Hutchinson pitched for Detroit against the Reds in the 1940 World Series. Pitching coach Jim Turner pitched for Cincinnati in that Series and for the Yankees in the 1942 Fall Classic before serving as New York's pitching coach in nine World Series over the span of ten years from 1949 through 1958. Coach Dick Sisler also had World Series experience, playing for the St. Louis Cardinals in 1946 and for the Philadelphia Phillies in 1950.

Even with Robinson struggling and the experience gap, many believed the Reds could mount a challenge to the Yankees. Among them was Pittsburgh manager Danny Murtaugh, who knew a little something about that very topic, since he'd led the Pirates to that stunning seven-game win over New York the previous season.

"Yes, sir, they'll beat the Yanks," Murtaugh said. "I wish them the best of luck. I think our whole club will be pulling for them. Last year, we won those close games, and they did the same thing this year—scoring just what they needed."

Former major league umpire Larry Goetz also liked Cincinnati's chances.

"The Reds have the pitchers who could bother the Yankees in the Series," Goetz observed. "These pitchers aren't like Bob Friend of the Pirates, who tried to throw the ball past the Yankees last year. Joey Jay throws the breaking ball. So does Jim O'Toole, and Bob Purkey mixes them up."

Lethal pinch-hitter Jerry Lynch predicted the Reds would win in five games.

"I say five because I've given out tickets for five games," Lynch explained. "I don't want any complications."

Robinson would take that outcome.

"I want to win it in five games," the outfielder said. "I don't want to come back here. I don't like it. Tension? I think we'll be looser than we were during the season—if that's possible."

The general consensus was a prolonged absence by Mantle would hurt the Yankees and help the Reds, but Hutchin-

Vada Pinson and Frank Robinson take aim at a world championship.

son, in fact, was hoping the slugging switch-hitter would play. "We want to beat their best," he said.

The Reds went directly from Pittsburgh to New York, where the Series was scheduled to start on Wednesday, October 4. They were joined by members of the front office, including general manager Bill DeWitt and farm director Phil Seghi, who flew on the first regularly scheduled American Airline Fan-Type Astrojet from Greater Cincinnati Airport.

The team stayed in Manhattan at the Roosevelt Hotel, known as the "Grand Dame of Madison Avenue." Guy Lombardo and his orchestra, most famous for their annual New Year's Eve renditions of "Auld Lang Syne," performed their first show at the Roosevelt Grill in October 1929 and were regulars there for the next thirty years.

The players weren't the only members of Cincinnati's traveling party enjoying the opulent Roosevelt. The team paid the expenses for the wives of the players and coaches, and general manager Bill DeWitt even arranged for batboy Billy Ferguson to take a break from his classes at Xavier University and make the trip to New York. Pitching coach Jim Turner was impressed.

"This is wonderful," Turner said. "I've been on nine other championship teams, and the club never did this for the players."

Joey Jay jokingly lamented that the team's largesse only freed up more spending money for the wives.

"If I'm lucky, this World Series may wind up costing me only three thousand dollars," he said with a mock grimace. "My wife didn't get in until this morning. I might save a little since she's getting a late start."

First-year traveling secretary Avery Robbins caught a

huge break. The team's last regular-season stop was in Pittsburgh, giving him the chance to bend the ear of Pirates' traveling secretary Bob Rice, who'd been through the same experience in 1960.

"That was very fortunate," Robbins said. "He and I were
good buddies from way back."

Back in Cincinnati, the town geared up for the Series with
a two-hour rally on Fountain Square the night before Game
One. Guests included three misses—Miss Teen-Age Cincinnati, Holly Shick, Miss Cincinnati, Laurie Hallett, and Miss
Ohio, Darlene T. DiPasquale—whose appearances were part
of the nationwide broadcast by ABC.

Two radio stations, WLW-AM and WKRC-AM, planned
to carry the NBC Network broadcasts of the games. Long-
time Reds play-by-play announcer Waite Hoyt would be behind the microphone with Bob Wolff of the Minnesota Twins
on the coast-to-coast radio broadcasts, which were expected
to be carried by 350 stations in the United States, another fifty
in Canada, and on the Armed Forces Radio Network. The
television broadcasts—sponsored by Chrysler and Gillette,
produced by Perry Smith and directed by Harry Coyle, who'd
practically invented covering baseball on television, with
Yankees broadcaster Mel Allen and Cardinals announcer Joe
Garagiola handling announcing chores—were expected to be
carried by 205 television stations in the United States and another fifty-five in Canada.

Fans in Cincinnati could watch the Series in color at the
Cincinnati Gas and Electric Company recreation center in
Hartwell. Watchers could indulge in free peanuts and pop-
corn, and scorecards also were available.

Occasional color announcer Jack Moran also was doing

a ten-minute show daily with third baseman Gene Freese on what was advertised as "WCPO Color Radio 1230."

They had plenty to talk about, even before the Series started. In one of the more bizarre byproducts of the Cold War between the United States and the Soviet Union, Pennsylvania Supreme Court Justice Michael A. Musmanno, a former judge at the Nuremberg trials, sent Hutchinson a letter urging that the Reds change their name to Redlegs to avoid panic-inducing headlines such as "Reds Murder Yanks" or "Reds Bomb Yanks." Hutchinson and DeWitt politely declined.

"I hope we have some scares like that," DeWitt observed.

Workouts scheduled for October 3 were canceled due to a chilly rain, but many of the Reds headed to the Bronx to get, for many of them, their first look at Yankee Stadium.

"I had never been to Yankee Stadium," recalled Jim Maloney, who'd reached the World Series in his first full season in the majors. "I was like a kid in a candy store. I remembered watching the games in school—the World Series. That was something. I remember there was a picture of two or three of us. It was raining lightly. You can't believe you're there."

"I had never been to Yankee Stadium," Robbins said, echoing Maloney. "I can still remember walking out through the tunnel and staring up at Yankee Stadium. When you run into and become aware of Mel Allen and Red Smith and Mantle and Maris ... you had come to know them a little bit, then there you are, cast into a celebrity environment and the bigness of it."

Shortstop Leo Cardenas remembers the weather more than the hoopla.

"We had no chance to come back to Cincinnati," he said.

"We had to leave from Pittsburgh. The World Series was going to start up in a couple of days. It was cold—forty-five degrees."

The weather cleared up for Game One, scheduled to start at noon on Wednesday, October 4, though the skies were overcast enough to force the lights to be turned on in the second inning. O'Toole, whose sleep was disturbed by two long-distance telephone calls from what he described as "some drunk guy in Dayton," was the last player on the bus from the Roosevelt to the ballpark, earning a round of applause from his amused teammates.

O'Toole was matched up with his self-described pitching idol, Whitey Ford. The Yankees' ace, at the age of thirty-three, already had fourteen World Series starts and seven wins under his belt, including back-to-back shutouts of the Pirates in 1960 that left him with a streak of eighteen consecutive scoreless innings in World Series play. He hadn't allowed a run in the World Series since October 8, 1958, when he gave up an RBI single to Warren Spahn with one out in the second inning of Game Six at Milwaukee's County Stadium.

"When I was going to the University of Wisconsin, I'd rush home from school so I could see the Yankees on television in the World Series," O'Toole said before Game One. "I never missed a game Ford was supposed to pitch. When I was practicing at Wisconsin, I would pretend that I was Ford. I'd try to figure out what I would throw to certain hitters. All of a sudden, here I am, pitching against him. I never thought it would happen, so it's a dream that's going to come true."

Another dream come true was Mantle's absence from New York's lineup. Maris, whose defensive skills were overshadowed by his power hitting, moved over from right field to handle the responsibility of covering the vast expanse of

Yankee Stadium's center field, which extended to 461 feet at its deepest point.

Shortstop Eddie Kasko blooped a one-out single to left field in the first inning, but Maris ran down Vada Pinson's line drive to deep center field and Robinson struck out to end the inning. The Reds got a sense of how the game was going to go in the second inning when Gene Freese hit a sharp one-hopper that third baseman Cletis Boyer grabbed with a backhand stab. His throw to first baseman Bill "Moose" Skowron got Freese by two steps.

New York catcher Elston Howard led off the fourth inning and made the right field "short porch" pay off, going with a high, outside fastball to smash an opposite-field home run that just cleared the glove of right fielder Wally Post, who was playing there while normal right fielder Frank Robinson started in left field—the stadium's sun field.

"I missed it by about eighteen inches," Post said. "When I saw it lying there in the front row, I was tempted to reach over the fence and pick it up, but someone grabbed it first. Sure, I could have caught it if I was there—another two feet. The ball just got in there."

Howard led off the sixth with a fly out to deep center field. Pinson flagged it down, but Skowron hit O'Toole's next pitch four hundred feet into the lower left field stands for a 2–0 New York lead.

"I made two mistakes," O'Toole told reporters after the game. "I wanted Howard's pitch outside, but not that high. I was trying to pinpoint each pitch. The mound here is a little higher than ours at home, and I was throwing against my body, pushing me off stride. I had gotten Skowron out the time before on a curve. I thought I'd give him another one just tempting enough to make him swing. It was too tempting."

That was all Ford needed—that and Boyer, who turned in another sparkling play in the seventh. Boyer, one of three Missouri brothers to reach the majors, dove to his left to glove pinch-hitter Dick Gernert's hard-hit two-hopper and threw Gernert out by two steps from his knees to end the inning.

"It was the best play I ever made," said Boyer, who was making plays similar to those that Baltimore's Brooks Robinson would make during the Orioles' five-game Series win over Cincinnati nine years later. "I didn't believe it myself. Actually, I had more trouble on the first one. I lost the ball for a second in those flags that drape behind home plate, but I found it in time."

"When someone told me Cletis was a better fielder than his brother Ken, I said, 'That I have to see,'" Hutchinson told reporters. "Well, Cletis showed me today."

"You can call him whatever you want," Freese groused. "I got other names for him."

After the game, O'Toole was approached in the visitors' clubhouse by *New York Times* columnist Arthur Daley, who wondered about the pitcher's post-game plans.

"I told him, 'Well, my wife and I would like to see *The Sound of Music*," O'Toole said. "He goes, 'I can get you tickets. You're all set.' I thought, 'This is great.'"

A larger crowd showed up for Game Two, but it still was four thousand short of capacity. Former Yankees catcher Darrell Johnson remained sidelined with the pulled muscle in his side, and second baseman Don Blasingame wasn't available after jamming the fourth finger on his right hand while fielding a grounder in Game One. The Yankees lineup still was minus Mickey Mantle.

The Reds' streak of consecutive scoreless Series innings reached twelve before they finally broke through in the fourth. After collecting just two hits against Ford in the opener, they managed one and a walk against right-hander Ralph Terry in the first three innings of Game Two. They got an opening in the fourth when Boyer committed an error on Frank Robinson's bouncer, and Gordy Coleman capitalized with a two-run homer into the right-center-field bleachers for Cincinnati's first lead of the series.

"I didn't think it would reach," Coleman said. "It's a deep part of the park. I thought it would be up against the wall for extra bases."

The Yankees quickly tied it up against Joey Jay, on Maris's walk and Berra's two-run homer into the lower right-field stands with nobody out in the bottom of the fourth, but the opportunistic Chacon gave the Reds the lead for good with some heads-up baserunning in the fifth. Batting in the leadoff spot, Chacon reached on a bloop single to center field with two outs and hustled to third on Kasko's single to center.

Terry uncorked a pitch to Vada Pinson that got away from catcher Elston Howard and rolled no more than twelve feet away from him to his right. That was all the room Chacon needed to sprint home and just beat the tag of a lunging Howard with a leaping, feet-first slide. Howard was charged with a passed ball.

"I see the ball all the way," Chacon said. "I go because I think I got a chance."

"The little guy's got good baserunning instincts," Freese said. "I don't think there's another player on the club who could have made it."

"He's a funny little guy—doesn't seem to get nervous at all," Kasko said. "He just wants to play, and he's quick as a cat."

Boyer, playing with a headache and puffy lip that resulted from being run down by Wally Post while making a tag in the fifth inning of Game One, came up with another brilliant play to rob Robinson leading off the sixth. Robinson slapped a one-hopper up the line, but Boyer made a diving backhand stop, got to his feet, and threw the batter out by one-and-a-half steps. An out later, Post banged a double off the wall in the left-field corner, and after Terry walked Freese intentionally, rookie catcher Johnny Edwards drove in Post with a single to right field for a 4–2 lead.

The Reds took advantage of shaky New York defense to break open the game in the eighth inning against left-hander Luis Arroyo, who pitched in ten games for Cincinnati in 1959. Robinson drew a leadoff walk and scored all the way from first base when Arroyo threw Coleman's bleeder between the mound and the third-base line past Skowron at first base for an error. Coleman was thrown out trying to get to third, but the inning continued when Post's single to left field skipped past Berra for a two-base error. Freese again was walked to get to Edwards, who promptly blooped an RBI double to left field.

New York's problems even reached the plate, where Howard was called out for hitting the ball twice with his bat, a very rare occurrence. That helped Jay finish his four-hitter, which included six walks and six strikeouts, and the Reds come away with a 6–2 win that sent the tied-up, best-of-seven Series to Crosley Field.

The Yankees traveled to Cincinnati by train, while the Reds filled two planes, which were greeted by an estimated fifteen hundred fans at the airport. They returned to a city overdosing on baseball. Newspaper photos showed workhouse prisoners watching the games from New York on television, a female hospital patient listening on a radio, and strippers at the Gayety burlesque theater sharing the stage with a television tuned to the games. Former Reds pitching great Eppa Rixey was among the fans watching the games on television at the CG&E recreation center in Hartwell. A potential juror was excused from duty because he claimed he would have trouble concentrating on the case because of the World Series.

Crosley Field was, of course, at the center of the fervor. The walls were cleaned for the first time since the park was built in 1912, and the place received a seven-hundred-gallon coat of paint. Platforms for photographers were built on the roof, eighty feet down the first-base side and sixty feet down the third-base line. Additional darkrooms were added, and the runways from the clubhouses to the field were refloored with a slip-proof compound painted "Socko Red."

Game Two hero Elio Chacon proudly holds a newspaper as the Reds head back to Cincinnati.

Additional room was needed for the media, which came up with five hundred applications for credentials. Western Union installed ninety-four wires at Crosley and another twenty-four at the press room adjacent to the Pavilion Caprice at the Netherland Hilton, which was designated as the Series headquarters. Western Union also brought in seventy teletype operators to handle the load of copy generated by the writers.

"In those days, all of the Series games were day games, so everybody went back to the Netherland Hilton press headquarters and wrote their stories," recalled Jim Ferguson, who covered the Series for the *Dayton Daily News* with sports editor Si Burick. "Si and I had rooms there. They had a press party every night, and food and drinks were always available."

"We got better cooperation from everyone concerned here—the city, the ballclub, the city police, special police, and ushers—than we've ever had in a World Series before," reported Frank Slocum, Commissioner Ford Frick's assistant. "We had no trouble with anything. If any little thing developed, it was handled right now by the police and ushers, who were really outstanding here.

"Not only was the commissioner's office extremely happy, but the president of the Baseball Writers Association came to me and expressed the appreciation of the writers for their fine treatment here."

Some folks had a difficult time containing their excitement. One newspaper devoted a full page to photos of scenes from around the area, including a shot of a mental hospital outpatient who somehow climbed to the top of the Crosley Field elevator shaft, took off his clothes, and stood there until coaxed down.

Demand for access to Crosley Field, where the seating capacity was less than half of Yankee Stadium, was impossible to meet. Major League Baseball claimed four thousand seats for its use, and six hundred more were set aside to handle the media overflow. Nine thousand seats were saved for Reds season ticket holders.

"They are the fans," ticket manager Roger Noble said. "They are the ones that we know have put their money up all season in a lump."

That left about 12,500 seats for mail orders and three thousand for bleacher seats. A crowd estimated at three thousand camped out at the team's Union Central Annex to buy those bleacher seats. Three Miami University students were first in line.

How difficult was it to acquire tickets? Also camped out was Virginia DiPasqualie, the mother of Miss Ohio, and she had to be treated for a cut on her head after being hit by a carelessly discarded beer bottle.

Some fans who'd been unable to come up with tickets resorted to catching what glimpses of the action they could from the Interstate 75 construction site beyond the Sun Deck in right field. The stretch of dirt prompted acerbic *Los Angeles Times* sports columnist Jim Murray to observe that, ""They still haven't finished the freeway outside the ballpark. It's Kentucky's turn to use the bulldozer."

Other celebrities were more fortunate than Mrs. DiPasqualie. Among those in the crowd of 32,589 for Game Three—the first of three consecutive games with that exact attendance figure—were Mary Pickford, the silent film star known as "America's Sweetheart," and her husband, musician Buddy Rogers, who lent his name to a chain of music stores.

The Reds return from New York

Jim Maloney and his fiancee, Lyn.

Leo Cardenas, Jim O'Toole, and their families.

for Game Three in Cincinnati.

Bob Purkey and Joey Jay.

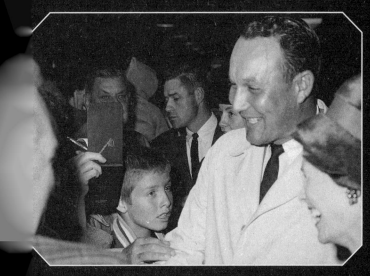

Wally Post and fans.

Also on hand was the Democratic ticket for the 1952 presidential election, Tennessee Senator Estes Kefauver and Alabama Senator John Parkman, along with former Reds Johnny Vander Meer and Dummy Hoy, who threw the ceremonial first pitch for Game Three.

Bill McKechnie, who managed Cincinnati's last championship teams in 1939 and 1940 and was a close friend and Bradenton, Florida, neighbor of Reds manager Fred Hutchinson, was spotted in the crowd, as was the ubiquitous Chuck Connors, shown in a newspaper photo eating roast duck out of aluminum foil.

Actor Broderick Crawford, the star of the syndicated *Highway Patrol* television series, was in town. So was comedian Jerry Lewis, staying at the Terrace Hilton, where Ford Frick and Yankee co-owners Dan Topping and Del Webb also were guests. The Honorable W.D. Black, deputy minister of British Colombia, was staying at the Alms Hotel, while reservations had been made at the Sinton for Frank Blair and Rick Ballard of NBC's *Today* show. Former Reds general manager Gabe Paul and dancer Eleanor Powell were housed at the Sheraton-Gibson, while three team owners—Philadelphia's Bob Carpenter, the Angels' Gene Autry, and St. Louis's August Busch—had scored rooms at the Netherland Hilton.

Perhaps the biggest name to make his first Series appearance was Mantle, who started in center field and batted cleanup for the Yankees after missing the first two games. He would go hitless in four at-bats.

Right-hander Bob Purkey started for the Reds against Bill Stafford, also a right-hander, and Cincinnati was able to cash in on another pitcher's throwing error to take a 1–0 lead. Chacon led off the third inning with a bunt single and went to second on Stafford's wild throw. Two outs later, Robinson lined an RBI double that one-hopped the left-field wall.

Purkey faced one batter over the minimum while allowing one hit through the first six innings before Yankees shortstop Tony Kubek led off the seventh with a single and, one out later, was on second after a passed ball. Purkey struck out Mantle to close within an out of escaping unscathed, but Berra fought off a pitch and launched a blooper into short right-center field.

Chacon raced back to his right and was poised to make a backhand catch. He had the ball in his glove for a split-second before a charging Robinson, trying to make a lunging grab, ran into Chacon's outstretched arm and knocked the ball free. Pinson retrieved the ball, but not before Kubek raced across the plate with the tying run.

"I came straight in on a dead run and, actually, I didn't see Chacon until the last second," Robinson recalled. "I had a shot at catching the ball, but I would have had to dive for it, and I might have caught it and I might not have, but Chacon seemed to have the best shot at it, and I think he did have the ball in his glove just a second before I hit him."

The Reds shook off the play and responded in the bottom of the seventh with a one-out double by Edwards into the right-field corner and Eddie Kasko's two-out single to left, but the lead was only one run instead of two, allowing Johnny Blanchard to tie the game with a two-out, pinch-hit homer into the Sun Deck in the eighth inning.

That set up Roger Maris's game-winning homer leading off the ninth inning. Maris, hitless in ten at bats going into the ninth, caught hold of a Purkey slider and drove it into the Sun Deck for a 3–2 Yankee lead.

Fans watch the World Series from rooftops near Crosley Field.

A local newspaper salesman named Dave Doeker was sitting right behind former and future Reds pitcher Joe Nuxhall, and Doeker recalls Nuxhall covering his face with his hands as soon as Purkey threw the pitch. Nuxhall had thrown enough home run pitches to recognize one when he saw it.

"I'll never forget it," Doeker said. "As soon as that ball left Purkey's hand, Nuxhall covered up."

"You think Nuxhall covered up?" Purkey said. "I threw that pitch. I knew what was going to happen. The problem was I didn't get the pitch where I wanted it. It should've been low and away, but instead, it was slightly in and over the plate. That pitch wasn't too bad. I'd gotten him out all day with my slop slider away. That was the first hard slider I threw him all day. Maybe I should've tried to get into him like they said— maybe, that is."

Pinch-hitter Leo Cardenas banged a one-out double off the scoreboard in the bottom of the ninth, but Arroyo stranded him with two groundball outs to give the Series lead back to the Yankees. To many observers, Maris's homer seemed to suck the life out of the Reds.

"It's a game I'll never forget until my dying day," Purkey said years later. "I think that game will stand out for the rest of my life. I felt that game was the turning point of the Series."

"That was the most damaging blow of the Series," Hutchinson said when the Series was over. "That loss hurt us. Bob Purkey had pitched a fine game, and after Maris ruined it with that homer, we didn't bounce back."

There's no way to say that the game would have progressed in the same manner if Chacon had been able to hold on to the ball, but if he had and it had, Maris's home run would have merely tied the score instead of giving New York the lead. The Reds had pulled off so many late-inning wins during the season that another was not out of the question, and a win would have given Cincinnati the 2–1 Series lead with two more games on their home field.

At the same time, it might have planted seeds of doubt in the minds of the Yankees, many of whom had bitter, still-fresh memories of their stunning loss to Pittsburgh the previous season. That Series had cost Casey Stengel his job as New York's manager, and Ralph Houk–who had never managed anywhere else–now was in charge. Could he have handled the pressure?

To strengthen the similarity between the 1960 and 1961 Series, the National League teams shared uniform styles. Both wore vest-type jerseys, and they were the only teams in the majors wearing them at the time.

"The third ballgame was really ours to have," Edwards

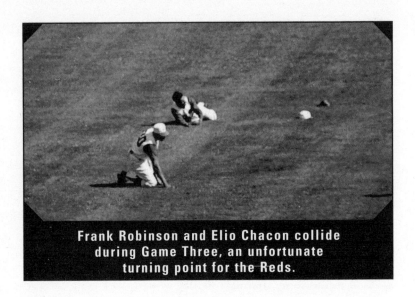

Frank Robinson and Elio Chacon collide during Game Three, an unfortunate turning point for the Reds.

said. "If that ball is caught, we go into the ninth leading in Cincinnati. I think it would've made a big difference if we could've won that third game."

"If Chacon had held on to that ball, I'm convinced we would have gone on to win that game and possibly the Series," Robinson said.

Instead, the Yankees were sitting in what popular baseball broadcaster Red Barber—who worked during his career for both the Reds and the Yankees—liked to call the "catbird seat." They were leading in the Series with their ace scheduled to pitch Game Four. Whitey Ford turned in five more shutout innings, extending his streak of consecutive scoreless Series frames to thirty-two and breaking the record of twenty-nine and two-thirds set by Babe Ruth.

"I pinch-hit for O'Toole, and I had to face Whitey Ford," Leo Cardenas said. "He had about thirty different pitches, I think. I think I fouled it once, and then I struck out.

Jim O'Toole, Ford's Game One opponent, also started Game Four. After McKechnie threw out the ceremonial first pitch, O'Toole threw three shutout innings before Maris scored on a double-play in the fourth, and in the fifth Ford himself walked with two outs and eventually came around to score on Kubek's single.

The Yankees tacked on two runs in the sixth and three in the seventh against normally reliable reliever Jim Brosnan, while Cincinnati generated nothing in four innings against Yankees relief pitcher Jim Coates. The Reds' 7–0 loss was their second shutout loss of the Series after they'd suffered just six during the regular season.

"The Yankee pitching has been good, but not that good," Hutchinson said. "Too many of our guys are feeling for the ball instead of swinging the bats."

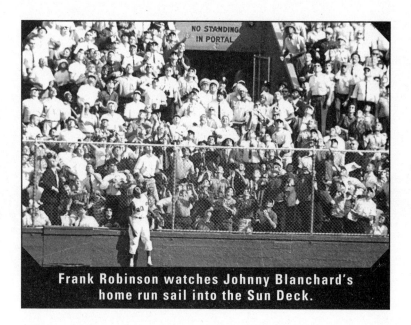

Frank Robinson watches Johnny Blanchard's home run sail into the Sun Deck.

**Game Two hero Joey Jay struggles
in the first inning of Game Five.**

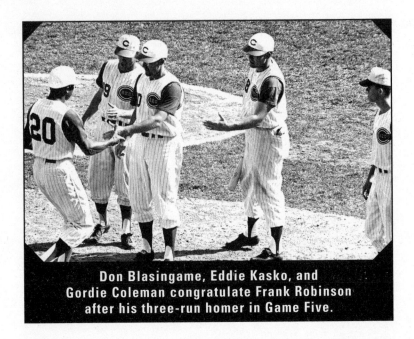

Don Blasingame, Eddie Kasko, and
Gordie Coleman congratulate Frank Robinson
after his three-run homer in Game Five.

The Reds started Joey Jay, who'd led the team in wins during the regular season and got the decision in their only Series victory, in Game Five, but New York now was rolling. Blanchard's homer gave the Yankees the first two of five runs they would score with two outs in the first inning of Game Five, effectively burying the Reds. Jay didn't get out of the first, and Hutchinson eventually would set a Series record by using eight pitchers in what became a 13–5 New York Series-clinching win.

Maloney was the first reliever, but he gave up four hits and two runs while getting only two outs.

"I was so nervous, I couldn't even see straight," he recalled. "Every time I threw the ball up there, they were hitting it somewhere. It was a long day, but it was really a thrill. Here I was in my second year, and I could say I got into a World Series."

Robinson hit a three-run home run over the right-center-field fence in the third inning to briefly cut New York's lead to three runs, and Wally Post added a two-run homer to left field in the fifth for Cincinnati's last runs of the season. By then, the Yankees had piled up eleven runs.

Robinson would finish the Series with three hits in fifteen at bats, a .200 average, but he also led the team in runs batted in with four. Post hit .333 while playing in all five games, while Kasko finished at .318 with a team-leading seven hits in five games.

"I was hitting in a good spot," said Kasko, the number-two batter in all five games. "When you're hitting in front of guys like Vada Pinson and Robby, they look at you and say, 'Don't walk him,' so I got a lot of good pitches, especially in Yankee Stadium. They knew I wasn't going to hit a ball out."

Also enjoying a breakout World Series was rookie catcher Johnny Edwards, who hit .364 in three games, but it was far from enough to stem the Yankee tide. The Yankees hit .255 as a team, led by Richardson's nine hits, six more by Skowron, seven RBI by Hector Lopez, and two home runs by Blanchard, New York's version of Jerry Lynch with four pinch-hit home runs during the regular season.

Led by Ford, New York pitchers compiled a sparkling 1.60 cumulative ERA against the Reds, holding Cincinnati to a .206 team batting average. Going into the 2010 World Series, New York's eight-run margin of victory in Game Five was the third-widest for a clinching game in history. Three teams—the 1911 Philadelphia Athletics, 1934 St. Louis Cardinals, and 1985 Kansas City Royals—clinched their titles with eleven-run wins, while the 1956 Yankees clinched their championship with a nine-run win. The 1908 Pittsburgh

Hutch faces the media at his desk following the Reds' Series defeat.

Pirates matched the '61 Yankees with an eight-run win in the finale.

"We were overwhelmed, but they're a fine team, and they can do that to you," Hutchinson lamented.

A full share of the profits for the winners was $7,389.13. A full share for the Reds was $5,356.37.

TEN

Moving On

New York's convincing win over the Reds in
the World Series no doubt left some so-called baseball experts
nodding their heads in satisfaction. Their assessment had been
confirmed. The Cincinnati team really wasn't that good.

That still didn't explain, for them, how the Reds had been
able to hold off the supposedly more-talented Dodgers and
Giants and Braves and win the National League championship. It didn't make sense, yet Los Angeles and San Francisco
and Milwaukee were sitting at home, watching World Series
games being played at Crosley Field.

"The Cincinnati team is one of the freaks of nature,"

Dodgers vice president Fresco Thompson said late in the season. "They are leading the league with a club consisting mostly of castoffs and nondescripts. This whole Cincy team defies form, but you have to give the guys credit. They have banded together, many in a last-ditch stand, and they are trying to show their former employers that unloading them was a mistake."

"It was great—a really fun season," William O. DeWitt Jr., the son of general manager Bill DeWitt, said with a hint of wistfulness. "Of course, they weren't picked to win anything. It was quite a summer, and the town really got behind the team. There was a good feeling. I don't think anybody thought it was a fluke. I think there was real talent on the club. You get on a winning habit and you keep it up, because if you're good enough, you've got the incentive to keep it going. They were winning and excited. They had a lot of players who'd never really won—first-timers. There were a lot of kids—a lot of players who'd never been in that situation."

Motivation certainly was a factor in the Reds' performance, but there was so much more involved that it's almost impossible to chronicle. One of the dominating traits of that ballclub was its demeanor—the way the players approached the game, which was best described by Sandy Grady of the *Philadelphia Bulletin* in an essay detailing his reasons to root for the Reds.

"The Cincinnati Reds in the clubhouse wear the beefy amiability of a good semi-pro team, perhaps a club of farmers intent on winning the Corn Valley Championship," Grady wrote. "They are sweaty and beefy and congenial, shunning the big-city arrogance some teams adopt. Any minute, you expect somebody to blow *You Are My Sunshine* on a two-bit harmonica.

"Maybe that's a reason, too. I hope they win the pennant."

The Reds also were, quite simply, a good team. They didn't dominate the league in any one category, but they certainly posted the best overall numbers. Their .270 team batting average was third in the league, behind top-ranked Pittsburgh and number-two St. Louis. Their 3.78 team earned-run average also was third-best in the league, behind the number-one Cardinals and second-ranked San Francisco. So, why didn't the Cardinals finish better than fifth? Because their .972 team fielding percentage ranked seventh in the eight-team league. Cincinnati's .977 figure tied San Francisco for second-best, behind Milwaukee.

The Reds, by many accounts, had two other major attributes going for them. One, they didn't beat themselves. Sure, they made physical errors, but they did what they were supposed to do with the balls they caught. They played solid, smart, fundamental baseball—throwing to the right base on defense while laying down sacrifice bunts and hitting behind the runners on offense—all of the little things that get lost among the shutouts and home runs.

Similarly, while they avoided giving opponents extra opportunities to do damage, the Reds themselves were adept at capitalizing on opportunities presented by opponents. If the other team made a physical or mental error, the Reds were more than happy to take advantage.

"We're more of a team this year instead of a bunch of fellows wearing Cincinnati uniforms," said outfielder Gus Bell, who hit .255 in his ninth season with the Reds while splitting time in left field with Wally Post and Jerry Lynch. "Another thing. We're taking advantage of the breaks. Guess you might call it an opportunity ballclub. We've won a lot of games that way, beating the other team rather than beating ourselves."

"I think that team, overall, was fundamentally sound," Maloney said.

How much of that had to do with the manager Fred Hutchinson's spring training night classes? Certainly some, but there also was the impression that the players had too much respect for their manager and the game to play it incorrectly.

"Hutch was a great baseball man," DeWitt Jr. said. "What made him a good manager was he could manage the players. He had sort of a tough exterior, but he was a really good person inside and a warm person, but he also knew how to be tough with the players when they needed it and kept them disciplined and kept them in line and got them to play."

That approach and the strength of Cincinnati's bench were reflected in the team's records in close games–those that go extra innings or are decided by one run or both. The Reds finished 1961 with an impressive 34–14 record in one-run decisions, including 8–1 against the frustrated Braves and 6–1 against the hapless Philadelphia Phillies. That computes to a .708 winning percentage. In extra-inning games, Cincinnati finished 6–3, including 3–0 against St. Louis, 2–0 against the Braves, and 0–2 against the Chicago Cubs.

By comparison, the 1975 Reds were 32–20 in one-run games–a .615 winning percentage–and 11–4 (.733) on their way to setting a club record for wins in a season with 108. The 1976 team, which gained some measure of revenge for 1961 by sweeping the Yankees in the World Series, went 31–24 (.564) in one-run games and 10–4 (.714) in extra-inning games.

The 1990 "wire-to-wire" Reds, featuring the much-ballyhooed "Nasty Boys" bullpen, finished one game over .500 at 20–19 in one-run games and below .500 at 6–8 in extra-inning games.

The 1940 Reds, which was the last Cincinnati team to win a National League championship before 1961 and went on to beat Detroit in a seven-game World Series, were another title-winning team that finished below .500 in extra-inning games at 8–9, but they also set the franchise record for one-run wins, going 41–16 (.719).

Jerry Lynch, with his nineteen pinch hits that stood as the club record until 2005 and five pinch-hit home runs that still stood as a franchise record fifty years later, was the undisputed leader of the Cincinnati bench corps, but he was by no means the only late-inning bullet Hutchinson had in his arsenal. Platooning former everyday starters Gus Bell and Wally Post kept both of those players fresh enough to be productive pinch-hitters. The left-handed hitting Bell, a proud man who chafed at playing a part-time role, was Cincinnati's second-busiest pinch-hitter with thirty-five at bats and second most productive with ten hits.

"It's really hard for me to recollect anything outstanding for me from that year," Bell said a quarter-century later, sitting in the green seats at Riverfront Stadium and watching his oldest son, Buddy, play third base for the Reds. "Maybe I didn't notice it because I was platooning and I wasn't real happy about that. Of course, you can't knock winning.

"Managers have their own way of doing things, I guess. Hutch was very successful managing over here. He got real good pitching out of the staff he had. I guess I was about thirty-three (actually thirty-two) and, in those days, when you were thirty years old, they would start calling you 'graybeard.'

Long-time Reds star Gus Bell signs autographs.

We had a writer in this town, (the *Enquirer*'s) Lou Smith, who I think liked to see new faces every week for somebody new to write about.

"It's a crazy game. You just don't know. It just seems like it's your time to win the pennant. It was just a fantastic year. Everything went right–just all-around. Guys were doing things they'd never done before, and that's what it takes. It was like a one-year club."

Post, the right-handed-hitting part of the duo, finished the season with eight pinch-hit RBI–a distant second to Lynch's twenty-five–while going seven-for-twenty-five for a .280 average.

"That was one of those summers where the reason we had so much success was, every day, we had a different star," first baseman Gordy Coleman said. "We had twenty-five bodies on that team, and I'd say twenty-three of them saw action on a regular basis."

The flip side of that late-inning prowess was the bullpen, anchored by veterans Jim Brosnan and Bill Henry. They couldn't have been more different. Brosnan was right-handed, a sophisticated jazz-loving writer who was born in Cincinnati, lived in Chicago, and already had his diary of one season published as *The Long Season*, a chronicle of 1959. He wore glasses and was nicknamed "The Professor." Brosnan was an imposing six-foot-four and 211 pounds, but he depended mostly on his off-speed pitches.

Henry was a rail-thin (six-foot-two, 180) Texan who was so quiet that everybody called him, of course, "Gabby." Despite his lean frame, Henry depended on his surprising fastball.

"The fastball was my best pitch—my out pitch," Henry said. He couldn't say how fast. "Back in those days, they didn't test that much. I'd bet it was in the low nineties (miles per hour). I had a real live fastball. Of course, I also had the curveball, slider, and changeup, but when it came down to the nitty-gritty, well, it was the fastball."

Brosnan had put together a solid-but-undistinguished career before joining the Reds midway through the 1959 season. He was 23–25 in his career before the trade but posted a 15–5 record in his first season-and-a-half with the Reds, including 7–2 with a sparkling 2.36 earned-run average in 1960.

Henry seemed to go the other way after joining the Reds prior to the 1960 season. He went 1–5 for the Reds that year after bringing a career record of 29–36 to the team, but his career 3.34 ERA suggested that he'd been more effective than indicated by his record.

Brosnan and Henry became the anchors of the Cincinnati bullpen. Brosnan appeared in a career- and team-high fifty-three games in 1961, and though all of them were in relief, he finished fourth on the team with ten wins and led the team with a .714 winning percentage on a 10–4 record. Henry, a workhorse who'd led the National League with sixty-five appearances for the Cubs in 1959, worked in forty-seven for the Reds in 1961, going 2–1 with a 2.19 ERA that was the best of his career to that date.

Although saves were not yet an official statistic–that wouldn't happen until 1969–official scorers already had the authority to award them in 1961. Brosnan and Henry both were credited with sixteen.

Saves wasn't the only statistic in which the Reds displayed remarkable uniformity. Amazingly, the new regulars at the corner infield spots–first baseman Gordy Coleman and third baseman Gene Freese–each hit exactly twenty-six home runs and twenty-seven doubles and drove in eighty-seven runs. Coleman hit .287 while playing in 150 games. Freese hit .277 in 152 games.

Freese's home run breakdown, in fact, indicates consistency that borders on astonishing. Of his twenty-six home runs, thirteen were hit at home and thirteen on the road; thirteen were hit in night games and thirteen during the day.

"I was surprised that we won," the outgoing West Virginia native reminisced years later. "We had a good ballclub. It was hard to win with that club, for the simple reason that you're supposed to be real good up the middle to win. We had five different catchers that year. We didn't have the best double-play combination either, with (second baseman Don) Blasingame and (shortstop Eddie) Kasko. And Coleman and me at first and third, we weren't the best out there, either."

Coleman, though, did lead NL first basemen with 121 assists.

Of course, the '61 Reds would've easily lived down to the preseason projections if their heavyweights hadn't come through. Robinson finished the season with a .323 batting average and team-high thirty-seven home runs, which ranked third in the league behind Orlando Cepeda's league-leading forty-six and Willie Mays's forty. Robinson also drove in 124 runs, second in the NL to Cepeda's 142.

Robinson led the league with a .611 slugging percentage, as well as ten sacrifice flies and, in a measure of the respect with which he was viewed by opposing teams, twenty-three intentional walks. His close friend and roommate, center fielder Vada Pinson, led the league with 208 hits while finishing as the only player on the team to appear in each of Cincinnati's 154 games. Pinson also led the team and finished second in the league with a .343 batting average, eight percentage points behind Pittsburgh's Roberto Clemente, and thirty-four doubles, five behind Milwaukee's Hank Aaron, and he finished one ahead of Robinson for the team lead in triples with eight.

Pinson, who turned just twenty-three years old in August, also was the only Reds player to win a Gold Glove, the only one he would receive in his career. The speedy Pinson, who seemingly could cover acres, led all NL outfielders with 420 chances and 391 putouts.

That level of defense helped the pitchers. Right-hander Joey Jay tied former Milwaukee teammate Warren Spahn for the league lead with twenty-one wins and four shutouts. Left-hander Jim O'Toole finished right behind them with nineteen wins and led the team with a career-high 178 strikeouts, and his 3.10 ERA was second in the league to Spahn's 3.02.

Despite their achievements, neither Spahn nor Jay received the coveted Cy Young Award, which at the time was awarded by the Baseball Writers Association of America to just one pitcher from both leagues, instead of one from each league. New York left-hander Whitey Ford, who finished the regular season with a glowing 25–4 record, won the award.

That was part of a disappointing trend for the Reds. Jay was the right-handed pitcher on the *The Sporting News* National League all-star team, where he was joined by Frank Robinson. That was the first year *TSN*, known for decades as the "Bible of Baseball," picked one team from each league. Previously, the weekly newspaper had chosen one overall team.

Right-handed pitcher Ken Hunt, who piled up nine wins before the All-Star Game and never won another game in the major leagues, still was named by *TSN* as the NL Rookie Pitcher of the Year, but the newspaper's Manager of the Year award—which was limited to one for both leagues—went to Yankees' rookie skipper Ralph Houk. Fred Hutchinson, who did such a masterful job of alternately guiding and prodding the Reds to the pennant, had to settle for being named the Associated Press National League Manager of the Year.

"I've been close to baseball for more than a half-century, and this is one of the greatest managing jobs," former Reds manager Bill McKechnie told Harry Grayson of the Newspaper Enterprise Association. As manager of the 1939 and 1940 Reds pennant-winning teams, McKechnie explained, "I had a much better club. Hutch has no catcher remotely resembling Ernie Lombardi, either behind the plate or at bat. Hutch's pitching has been excellent, but he hasn't any two to compare with Paul Derringer and Bucky Walters. We had a solid infield, where Hutch has had to do a lot of juggling at the vital positions on either side of second base in order to keep enough hitting in the lineup."

Hutchinson tried to divert the credit to the confidence his players built in themselves early in the season.

"Ballplayers are funny, you know?" he said. "You take a team that's been in the second division for several years, and it's natural for them to wonder what it would be like to be with a pennant contender. Well, after the nine-game winning streak, which moved us near the top, they felt they belonged up there."

In perhaps an even bigger injustice than Hutchinson's, *The Sporting News* named New York co-owner Dan Topping its major league Executive of the Year over DeWitt, who'd done such a masterful job in transforming the Reds into a winning team. Besides his off-season acquisitions of Jay and Freese, DeWitt pulled the trigger on the late-April trade of popular catcher Ed Bailey to San Francisco for second baseman Don Blasingame, which helped stabilize the infield and batting order. He also came up with the mid-season acquisition of veteran right-hander Ken Johnson, who filled the hole left in Cincinnati's starting rotation when Hunt faltered. Johnson stepped in and went 6–2 down the stretch.

Certainly, the Reds were denied some post-season honors they rightfully deserved, but the franchise did collect perhaps the most prestigious available award in November when Robinson was named by the Baseball Writers Association of America as the National League's Most Valuable Player. Winning the award capped his personal journey from the low point of being arrested back in early February.

"I was speechless," he wrote in his book, *My Life Is Baseball*." "It really took me by surprise. I really didn't think I could win it. I had figured myself about third because Orlando Cepeda had had a tremendous year with the Giants, leading the National League in home runs and runs batted in, and Vada also had that great year. I honestly thought the two of them had the best shot at it.

"Winning the MVP was a tremendous thrill. It's a tremendous thrill to be the best of anything in the major leagues, but this was something special. My team had also been the best in the league. You always want to have a good year, but you also take a lot of pride in what your team does. If you have a good year and your team doesn't do anything, that takes away something from your performance. In 1961, the greatest year of my life to date, my team was the best in the league, and I was named the best player in the league. You can't do much better than that."

Basically, the Reds had just enough of everything—including, to be sure, good luck—to pull off the improbable.

"I remember one thing from that year," Lynch said years later. "We had a hell of a ballclub, and all of the writers around the league and around the world thought we were ragamuffins. I thought we had a great ballclub. I'd like to manage that ballclub today. We'd have won it the next year, too, if we hadn't had a couple of injuries."

Cincinnati barely had time to bask in the glow of its championship before starting to think about 1962. Even before the awards were handed out—in fact, almost before the Yankees got back to New York after finishing their collective clubbing of the Reds—the NL champions were thinking about how to stay on top.

The 1962 season would be the one in which both leagues got back on an even footing. The Mets in New York and the Colt 45s in Houston were due to start playing in 1962, when the schedule was set to grow to 162 games. To stock the new teams, they were allowed to pluck players from the rosters of the other teams after each holdover franchise protected a number of its players. The Reds lost outfielder Gus Bell, infielder Elio Chacon, and pitchers Jay Hook and Sherman "Roadblock" Jones to New York and pitcher Ken Johnson and first baseman Dick Gernert to Houston.

That left the Reds with the key members of their championship team, and they were confident going into the season. DeWitt had formed a corporation that purchased controlling interest in the franchise from the Crosley Foundation, so the entire franchise was in the hands of an astute, lifelong baseball man.

Even losing Freese for five months after he fractured his ankle and tore ligaments sliding into second base during a spring training intra-squad game did little to harm the team's demeanor. Eddie Kasko moved from shortstop to third base, where he'd been named the team's Most Valuable Player in 1960, and with Leo Cardenas playing shortstop full time and the rest of the team virtually intact, the Reds actually enjoyed a better season in 1962 than they did in 1961. Cincinnati finished 98–64, a .605 winning percentage that was slightly better than 1961's .604. Robinson batted .342 with thirty-nine home runs and a career-high 136 RBI, and he avoided the previous season's second-half meltdown, setting what at the time was a club record for home runs in a month with fourteen in August. Gordy Coleman hit twenty-eight home runs, and Don Blasingame hit a solid .281, while Bob Purkey won twenty-three games and Joey Jay won twenty-one for the second consecutive season.

Unfortunately for the Reds, Los Angeles and San Francisco both enjoyed super seasons. The longer season wasn't long enough to settle the pennant race, as the Dodgers and Giants finished the schedule tied for first place, forcing a best-of-three playoff won by the Giants, who went on to lose to the Yankees in a seven-game Series.

The changing of the cast accelerated in 1963 as Hutchinson made the gutsy decision to replace the popular Blasingame at second base with an untested hometown kid named Pete Rose, who went on to be named Rookie of the Year. Those Reds finished ten games over .500 but mired in fifth place, thirteen games behind Los Angeles.

Deron Johnson took over at first base in 1964, helping the Reds stage a stirring run that had them in first place with five games to play before stumbling down the stretch and finishing tied with Philadelphia for second, a game behind St. Louis.

By then, coach Dick Sisler was serving as interim manager. Hutchinson had left the team on August 13, the day after his birthday was celebrated in a pre-game party on the field at Crosley Field, to be treated for lung cancer, which claimed his life on November 12. The Reds immediately retired his uniform number 1–the first number to be retired in franchise history.

DeWitt knew the truth, even before Hutchinson left the team. As the crowd serenaded the shockingly frail Hutchinson with "Happy Birthday" on August 12 and Hutchinson thanked them, DeWitt had tears in his eyes.

Earlier that year, on April 23, former Reds pitcher Ken Johnson pitched a no-hitter against the Reds in Houston–and lost, 1–0, on two ninth-inning errors, one of them his own. Joe Nuxhall was the winning pitcher.

The 1965 Reds, led by Sisler as manager and paced by Deron Johnson's league-leading 130 RBI and twenty-win seasons from right-handers Jim Maloney and Sammy Ellis, finished 89–73 and fourth in the NL. DeWitt again displayed his astute eye for talent, giving final approval in the first-ever amateur draft to selecting outfielder Bernie Carbo with the team's top pick and catcher Johnny Bench in the second round. The next year, the Reds made right-handed pitcher Gary Nolan their number-one pick.

But, in that same year, DeWitt's pragmatic style of roster management clashed with his eye and produced a deal considered to be the worst in franchise history. Frank Robinson hit a solid .296 with thirty-three home runs and 113 RBI in 1965, but knowing the toll ten years of leading the Reds had

Young Leo Cardenas blossomed in 1961 and took over as the Reds starting shortstop the next season.

taken on Robinson's body and firmly believing in the Branch Rickey theory that it's better to trade a player a year too early than a year too late, DeWitt dealt the franchise centerpiece to Baltimore for pitchers Milt Pappas and Jack Baldschun and outfielder Dick Simpson.

DeWitt explained the trade by saying Robinson was an "old thirty," a quote that would forever tarnish all of the accomplishments he'd compiled in his first five years in Cincinnati. It didn't help when Robinson won the American League Triple Crown and led the Orioles to a World Series championship.

DeWitt had made a decision almost equally as regrettable a few weeks earlier. He fired Sisler as manager and replaced him with Don "Jeep" Heffner, who played for the St. Louis Browns teams operated by DeWitt in the 1940s. Heffner had never managed in the major leagues and it showed. The Reds could manage only a 37–46 record under Heffner before he was replaced by coach Dave Bristol.

The suddenly embattled Reds owner also was having problems on another front–the riverfront, so to speak. City leaders, mindful that major league baseball was outgrowing quaint facilities such as Crosley Field and hungry for a professional football franchise, were hoping to join the trend toward multi-purpose stadiums by building one on the riverfront to serve as the new home for both sports. DeWitt, who believed sports in general and baseball in particular were better off following population shifts from the cities to the suburbs, was hoping for a baseball-only facility fifteen or twenty miles north or northeast of the downtown area.

Cities that didn't have major league teams, aware of De-Witt's concerns about getting the ballpark and location he wanted in Cincinnati, were trying to convince him to move the franchise. He wanted to keep his options open, especially since he had serious misgivings about the viability of a multi-purpose stadium hemmed in by the Ohio River on one side and downtown Cincinnati on the other, while the city wanted whomever ran the Reds to agree to a forty-year lease with no option to leave.

When National League president and former Reds general manager Warren Giles said he would block any move of the franchise, DeWitt had no other option but to sell to a group of local businessmen.

His departure left very few faces with the Reds from the magical 1961 team—in and out of uniform. DeWitt's top assistant, Phil Seghi, left in 1967, the same year popular first baseman Gordy Coleman moved into the front office and took a job that boiled down to traveling around the Midwest selling Reds baseball. That left center fielder Vada Pinson, shortstop Leo Cardenas, catcher Johnny Edwards, and pitcher Jim Maloney as the remaining holdovers. Edwards was dealt away after the 1967 season, while Pinson and Cardenas lasted one more year before also being traded.

Maloney had lived up to the potential the Reds had seen when they gave him a large bonus to sign in April 1959. He turned in two twenty-win seasons, won no-hitters of ten and nine innings and lost another one in the eleventh inning after reeling off ten hitless frames. He'd become the franchise's career strikeout leader in 1967, and he still was only twenty-nine years old going into the 1970 season.

Unfortunately, Maloney ruptured an Achilles tendon running out a grounder on April 16 at Crosley Field. He returned in September to make four relief appearances for a Reds team rolling to its first National League championship since 1961.

He made his last career start in Cincinnati red on September 20, but he was left off the Reds' World Series roster before being traded in December to the California Angels, for whom he pitched in thirteen games before retiring.

He was the only player to bridge the transition from the Ragamuffin Reds to the Big Red Machine.

Acknowledgments

Going back almost a half-century to recreate a magical baseball season requires help, especially when one's personal memories are limited by virtue of being only five years old at the time.

You could say this book took twenty-five years to write. It started in 1986, when I wrote a series of stories about the 1961 Ragamuffin Reds for a newspaper called *RedsVue*, which no longer exists. Twelve of the players from that team graciously agreed to be interviewed for that series, which celebrated the Silver Anniversary of the season. They were, alphabetically, Gus Bell, Leo Cardenas, Gordy Coleman, Gene Freese, Bill Henry, Ken Hunt, Ken Johnson, Eddie Kasko, Jerry Lynch, Jim O'Toole, Vada Pinson, and Bob Purkey.

Joe Nuxhall, who wasn't on that team but still was close to it, also shared his memories of that season for that series.

After deciding in 2009 that the Golden Anniversary of that season merited a book, I drew upon those interviews and added to them with help from other members of the team and interested non-uniformed participants and observers. Jim O'Toole and Jerry Lynch added to the experiences they'd already related, and Jim Maloney added some new insights from a player's point of view.

Avery Robbins contributed his memories as the team's first-year traveling secretary, and Bill DeWitt Jr., son of the 1961 team's general manager and a successful baseball executive in his own right, added his recollections, along with a copy of the team's yearbook, which became well-thumbed.

Jim Ferguson, who covered the Reds for the *Dayton Daily News* before becoming the team's publicity director in 1973, had some unique observations.

Former Reds outfielder Dave Parker didn't play for the 1961 team, but he grew up with Crosley Field as practically his backyard, and his memories of the neighborhood in that era were priceless. Bruce Johnston also followed the Reds while growing up, including that season as his family lived in Fairview Heights, which loomed over Crosley's center-field fence. His descriptions of traveling by bus with his older brother to doubleheaders recalled simpler times.

Cincinnati Reds Hall of Fame Operations Manager and Chief Curator Chris Eckes helped accumulate the photos in this book, the vast majority of them contributed by Reds historian Greg A. Rhodes from his collection of shots snapped by long-time *Cincinnati Post and Times-Star* photographer Jack Klumpe.

The staff in the periodicals section of the Main Branch of the Public Library of Cincinnati and Hamilton County were uniformly helpful, polite, and friendly, to the point where they would try to guess which newspaper and month I would be asking for when I reached the top of the spiral staircase leading to their second-floor perch.

Heather Kasner Nienaber was helpful with a key translation, while Ruth Lyons biographer Michael A. Banks diligently tried to locate the lyrics of the song she wrote about the Reds and Gary Schatz sang the song from memory while sitting in the media dining room at Great American Ball Park.

Having never written a book before, many of the associated tasks and differences in style from what I was used to caught me by surprise and, I'm sure, tested the patience of my editor, Jack Heffron. If he ever lost patience, he never showed it. Instead, he was consistently supportive and enthusiastic.

Many, many thanks to all of you, but especially to my wife, Sharon, and daughter, Kalli, whose enthusiasm for the project match their love of the game. All of you made it really seem like no work at all.

Bibliography

Angell, Roger, *Five Seasons*, 1978

Brosnan, Jim, *Pennant Race*, 1962

Cohen, Richard M., and Neft, David S., *The World Series*, 1986

Kahn, Roger, *The Boys of Summer*, 1972

Lawson, Earl, *Cincinnati Seasons, My 34 Years with the Reds*, 1987

McClure, Rusty, with Stern, David, and Banks, Michael A., *Crosley: Two Brothers and a Business Empire That Transformed A Nation*, 2006

O'Toole, Andrew, *Paul Brown, The Rise and Fall and Rise Again of Football's Most Innovative Coach*, 2008

Reidenbaugh, Lowell, *Take Me Out to the Ballpark*, 1983

Rhodes, Greg, and Snyder, John, *Redlegs Journal*, 2000

Rhodes, Greg, and Erardi, John, *Cincinnati's Crosley Field*, 1995

Rhodes, Greg, and Erardi, John, *Big Red Dynasty*, 1997

Robinson, Frank, *My Life Is Baseball*, 1968

Also:

Cincinnati Reds 2010 Media Guide

Xavier University 2009-2010 Men's Basketball Media Guide

MAGAZINE: *Sports Illustrated.*

NEWSPAPERS: *Cincinnati Enquirer, Cincinnati Post, RedsVue.*

INTERNET:

retrosheet.org

baseball-reference.com

baseball-almanac.com

cincinnati-transit.net

crosley-field.com

Baseballchronology.com.

About the Author

Except for twenty-two months from 1989 into 1991, Mark Schmetzer has lived his entire life in Greater Cincinnati and spent most of that time following, rooting for, and writing about the Cincinnati Reds. In 2010, he co-authored *The Comeback Kids* (Clerisy Press) with Joe Jacobs. That season was the twenty-fifth out of the last twenty-seven in which the La Salle High School and University of Cincinnati graduate covered the Reds on a daily basis. He started in 1984, the Reds' first season without an active Johnny Bench, writing for *RedsVue*, a paper that later became *Reds Report*. The 1961 Reds clinched the National League pennant on his sixth birthday. He lives in Forest Park, Ohio, with his wife, Sharon.

Mark is standing next to a replica stadium of old Crosley.